WILD swimming
Hidden Beaches

Contents

Swims by Region

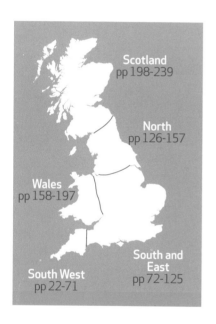

Scotland pp 198-239

North pp 126-157

Wales pp 158-197

South and East pp 72-125

South West pp 22-71

South West

South and East

North

Wales

Scotland

Introduction

That first summer the sun beat down every day. The scent of gorse and heather filled the air, the whiteness of the sand was almost blinding and the ocean shimmered like a pool.

I had just moved to the far west of Cornwall and was meant to be studying, but the heat was so stifling I ended up going swimming every day, looking for secret swimming coves and interesting places to snorkel. Poring over my map in the evenings, I was amazed at the places waiting to be discovered with just a bit of scrambling and exploring off the beaten track: a little beach that no one knew about, a natural rock pool large enough to swim in or a deep inlet for jumping.

That amazing summer was the beginning of an aquatic odyssey as I embarked on a journey around Britain, searching for its most wild and wonderful coves, caves, beaches and islands. Ten years on and I have travelled thousands of miles on foot, by bike, kayak and camper van. I have twisted ankles, drowned camera bags and suffered from hypothermia and heatstroke. But I found solace, too, in the wonders of our foreshores – a secret slice of beach, an archway to swim through or a sea cave encrusted with pink coralline.

Our island race has long been enchanted by the sea, and tales of Cornish mermaids and Scottish selkies are symptoms of our fascination with its watery underworlds. But our fondness for swimming and bathing for health and leisure is a relatively recent affair. Not until the end of the sixteenth century did the fashion for 'taking the waters' begin to develop. Much of this popularity was spurred on by the attendant health benefits. When Dr Richard Russell wrote about the restorative qualities of bathing at the tiny Sussex fishing village of Brighthelmstone in 1783, the Prince Regent was quick to visit and rented a small farmhouse there. The Prince enjoyed it so much that he bought

the building and converted it to the flamboyant Brighton Pavilion we know today.

The more austere Royal Sea Bathing Infirmary in Margate was constructed at about the same time and opened its doors around 1791, offering treatment for complaints such as tuberculosis, skin conditions or jaundice. Patients were not only instructed to immerse themselves in the sea but, sometimes, to drink it too. Professional 'dippers' were employed to thrust patients under the waves, though if you were wealthy you would enter the sea from the privacy of a bathing machine: the ritual immersions were always performed naked.

Today we have a better understanding of the health benefits of sea bathing – and nakedness is definitely optional. Swimming is not only an excellent all-round activity for building fitness and strength, but cold-water dipping also has restorative effects. A plunge dilates the blood vessels and expels toxins from the body while at the same time releasing endorphins that elevate mood, creating an urge to dive straight back in. Regular dipping across a season leads to 'cold adaptation', which can strengthen the immune and cardiovascular systems, as well as increasing libido and improving our spirits.

The combination of a watery pick-me-up and some risqué excitement meant the sea-bathing craze was set to spread. Soon the Victorians were coming to the beach resorts simply to have fun and watch the bathing spectacles. A spate of new

Sea-based activities – kayaking, surfing and coasteering – are some of the fastest growing sports in Britain. With new access laws opening up large swathes of coast, and water quality better than at any time in living memory, there has never been a better time to swim and explore the natural wonders of our coastline.

railways – plus the introduction of public holidays – accelerated the growth of the seaside resorts familiar to many of us. The seaside was leading a revolution in leisure, social progress and outdoor enjoyment.

The coast has long been central to our literary heritage as well. Daphne du Maurier's *Rebecca* and *Frenchman's Creek* were based on her childhood haunts around Fowey and Helford; Virginia Woolf's *To the Lighthouse* was inspired by holidays at Godrevy; and the wild undercliffs and remote beaches of the Jurassic Coast were beloved by Jane Austen. Arthur Ransome set his *Secret Water* tales of the Swallows and Amazons at locations on the Essex shore and Scotland was home to the real Robinson Crusoe, its uninhabited islands firing the imagination of Robert Louis Stevenson, author of *Treasure Island*.

Our coastline has many ancient associations. Tintagel is the home of Arthurian legend, while from many small islands holy men spread the Christian message: communities and monasteries, churches and abbeys were established at Bardsey Island in Wales, Iona in Scotland, Holy Island on the Northumberland coast and St Peter-on-the-Wall in Essex. Today these places continue to offer a spiritual retreat, a place to swim and immerse oneself in nature and reflect on our fascinating history.

Many parts of our coast reveal clues to our industrial past, too. There are old quarries breached by the sea, such as the Blue Lagoon in Wales. In Portland and the Purbecks you can enjoy the perfect lagoons and inlets that were left behind after quarrying for the great stones of St Paul's Cathedral. On a hot day with calm seas, at locations such as Dancing Ledge or Durdle Door, you could be on Crete or any other Greek island as you watch people skin-dive into the perfect blue waters, leap from ledges and sunbathe on the golden rocks.

Whether you are exploring the sea caves of the Witches' Cauldron near Cardigan or playing with seals in the Isles of Scilly; collecting oysters and samphire in East Anglia or basking in the ethereal blue glow of the Outer Hebrides' shallow lagoons, wild swimming offers a spectacular introduction to our island's natural history. Britain is as rich in wilderness and secret places as ever and, if you can pick a sunny day, the swimming is out of this world!

Our 8,000 mile foreshore with its remote inter-tidal zone is perhaps Britain's greatest wilderness area today.

Getting Started

10 ways to be wild and safe

1 Never swim alone. Keep a constant watch on weak swimmers

2 Never use inflatables at sea – they can drift on currents and wind

3 In surf and swell avoid swimming where rip currents ⚠ can form: along the edge of coves, on wide beaches and at river mouths

4 If caught in an offshore rip ⚠ don't swim against it. Swim parallel, then return to the beach on the surf

5 In high swell avoid steeply shelving beaches as the waves can 'dump' you and the undertow around your legs ⚠ can be strong

6 Never enter sea caves or swim near rocks in high swell ▼

7 Never jump or dive into water unless you have checked it for depth and obstructions ⛟

8 Swim within the shelter of coves and bays unless you understand the ⚠ tidal streams that operate at headlands and in the open sea

9 Wear a wetsuit if you know you'll be in the water for more than 15–20 minutes. Cold water limits swimming ability and hypothermia can kill ♨

10 Do not approach seals or pups

See safety annex (pp252-253) for more information and refer to symbols in each swim box.

Britain's coastline is one of the most beautiful in the world and offers some exceptional wild swimming. Here's how to get going.

Staying warm It takes a few minutes to get used to British sea temperatures, so persevere and you'll be amazed how warm it can feel. Regular dipping makes you less sensitive to cold and has health benefits. Unless you are an experienced swimmer, however, 20 minutes is enough for most people; never allow yourself to start shivering. Come out for a rest, put on lots of layers and exercise to warm up. The sea is at its warmest in September and when the tide has come in over large expanses of warm sand or mud. Swimming in the late afternoon, a few hours before high tide, is often the best time.

Footwear and kit Few of the swims in this book require kit but footwear is always useful. Jellies, surf shoes and beach footwear are cheap and available at seaside stores or in supermarkets. These will protect you from sharp rocks as well as weeverfish that bury themselves in the wet sand at low water (if stung, immerse your foot in hot water for 20 minutes to relieve the pain). Goggles are great fun and good for navigating while swimming among rocks. Wetsuits will help you stay in longer and, should you get into difficulties, they will protect you from hypothermia. For the intrepid, a 'dry' bag (sold in kayak and sailing shops) is a good option – for sandwiches and dry clothes too.

Tides and currents You need to understand the tides, so buy yourself a small tide timetable at any local seaside shop or download one from www.bbc.co.uk/weather/coast/tides. The tide repeats itself twice a day, advancing 30 minutes day-on-day. 'Spring' (does not refer to the season) tides repeat every two weeks and occur at every full and new moon throughout the year. These tides are much stronger and higher than regular tides. In between, at half-moons, are 'neap' tides, which are much weaker. Tides create slow currents in the open sea, but you need only worry about these if you are outside the protection of a cove or a bay. Rip currents are completely separate from tides and are created in surf conditions where there are breaking waves. They are localised and possible to avoid and escape from. Read the annex to find out more and refer to the hazard symbols key on the back flap.

Finding the beaches and using this book

Co-ordinates: Each of the 400 locations are provided with a latitude and longitude in decimal degrees (WGS84 standard). This format is universally accepted by all online and mobile mapping services and most car satnavs. For those using paper maps the National Grid references are at the back of the book, together with a conversion formula if you need minutes and seconds. Postcodes are not accurate enough to locate most coastal locations but have been provided in the directions where they are helpful in getting you close to an area where you might be able to park.

Ordnance Survey maps: Landranger maps at 1:50,000 (Purple Cover) and Explorer maps at 1:25,000 (Orange Cover) are still the best maps for exploring the countryside as they provide reliable footpath information. You can access these online at *bing.com, streetmap.co.uk* or *getamap.ordnancesurveyleisure. co.uk*. Make sure you 'screengrab' the map to your phone or print it out before you leave home, or why not load one of many apps which turn your phone into a GPS (e.g. ViewRanger, MemoryMap or EveryTrail). You can also buy this book as an app with links to all these resources built in.

Using the directions: The new map annex provides composite maps based on OS and Open Street Map data. These will support the written directions but you will need a road atlas to get you to the overall area first. The foreshore and any land below high water are common ground.

Abbreviations: N, NE, E, SE, S, SW, W, NW refer to the points of the compass. Left (L) and right (R), when used in relation to the shore, are based on looking out to sea. Swims are numbered consecutively around the coast.

Best for Beach Camping

Paddle in the sunset, pitch your tent, wake up with a splash

Best for Friendly Inns

A pub within reach, for après-swim warmth and refreshment

Best for Sunset Views

West-facing coves; perfect for watching the sun go down

Best for Food

From curry to crab sandwiches, cream teas to big breakfasts

Best for Secret Islands

Uninhabited islets and lagoons: be Robinson Crusoe for a day

Best for Skinny-dipping

Beautiful naturist beaches and remote locations

* semi-official naturist beach

Best for Caves and Arches

Temples of the ocean. Swim through arches and explore sea caves

Easily Accessible

Off the beaten track, but less than ten minutes from the car

Best for Plunge Pools

Deluxe rock pools, warmed by the sun and big enough to swim in

Best for Jumps

Traditional places to jump and dive. Always check the depth

Take the Train

Swims and beaches an hour or so walk from a train station

Literature and Legend

Atmospheric haunts of artists, writers and adventurers

South West

Along Devon and Cornwall's dramatic coastline, sandy coves and smugglers' inlets are set amid rugged scenery. The south coast is gentle with several meandering estuaries while the north is wilder and bears the full brunt of south-westerly swells. The region, which has inspired writers and artists from Daphne du Maurier to Barbara Hepworth, has become very popular, but there are plenty of secret places if you want to escape the crowds.

Highlights
South West England

Our favourites include:

7 A delightful walk beside a wooded stream leads to Heddon Mouth shingle beach where German U-Boats once docked.

19 The Hartland peninsula is one of Devon's forgotten corners, dominated by dramatic folded cliffs. Speke's Mill Mouth is its jewel, with a giant waterfall plunging down into pools on the beach below.

27-28 King Arthur's castle towers above Tintagel Haven with access to Merlin's caves below. Or continue on to find the Rocky Valley waterfall plunge pools and dramatic Bossiney Haven beach.

39 Treyarnon is a wonderful pool set in the rocks by the cove.

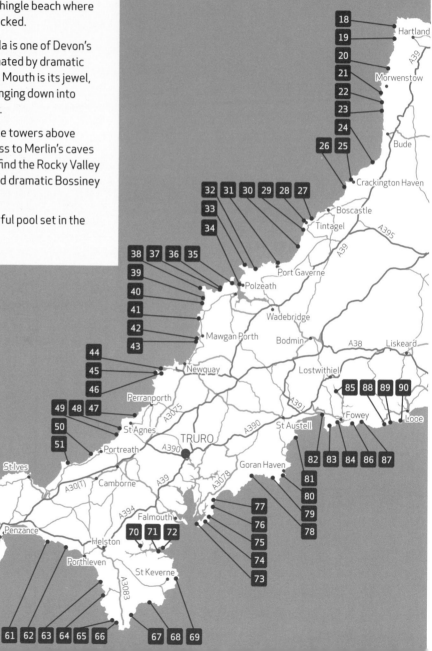

41 The great rock stacks at Bedruthan Steps are legendary, but take this approach to the beach and avoid the crowds.

48 The adventurous can explore the base of Chapel Porth cliffs at low tide and even enter the old sea caves beneath the famous Wheal Coates engine house.

52-45 The Isles of Scilly are Britain's own tropical archipelago with the clearest waters and miles upon miles of dazzling white sandy beaches.

60 Pedn Vounder Sands is one of the most spectacular tidal beaches in Britain with shallow sandy lagoons, Logan Rock and a cliff-top theatre nearby.

65-66 Serpentine cliffs and extraordinary rock formations dominate the west side of the Lizard, from spectacular Kynance to Mullion Cove.

103-104 The coves around Prawle Point are some of the most remote and beautiful in the whole of this region.

9 Broad Sands

The Exmoor Coast

The steep cliffs are cloaked in woodland and waterfalls tumble from moorland down to the sea. As you explore the Exmoor coast it's difficult to imagine an easy way to access the remote and dramatic foreshore lying far below, often invisible from the land.

The same thoughts were probably in the minds of German sailors over 60 years ago. It's now known that this coast was favoured as a place for U-boat landings during the Second World War. According to one German veteran's account, his U-boat moored at Heddon Mouth one night to refill with much-needed fresh water. He rowed ashore with some of the crew, carrying pipes to collect water from the stream. After months cramped in the tiny living quarters it felt wonderful to be free in the night air for a few hours. They took a swim to get washed and played football on the shingle beach with a ball fashioned from rolled-up overalls. The scenery was so spectacular in the moonlight that the German sailor promised to return one day in peacetime.

Today, on the beautiful walk from the Hunter's Inn down to the stony beach, it feels that little has changed since the U-boat visits. Bilberries, gorse and heather grow on the hillside and sessile oak, rowan, holly and hazel flourish along the pretty stream. After a two-mile walk to the east, Woody Bay opens up dramatically beneath the trees. High moors give way to dizzying drops of 800 feet or more, and the cliffs are studded with deep, dark ravines. Far below, the boulder-strewn beach is almost unvisited, save for gulls and guillemots, but a few visitors do make the long descent. Look carefully and you'll see the remains of the old pier. There were plans for a Victorian resort and cliff railway but these remained the unfulfilled

7

3

5

fantasy of entrepreneur solicitor Benjamin Lake who ended up bankrupt and imprisoned for embezzlement. Predating this an ancient cobbled track winds down past a limekiln. This is a very rocky beach but a waterfall and a semi-natural rock pool are hidden on the far side, offering a welcome opportunity to bathe if the sea is too rough to swim. Float in the pool here, stare up into the steep wooded cliffs and you may hear the sounds of the woodpeckers, warblers or pied flycatchers that inhabit these wild shores.

To the west, at Combe Martin, Wild Pear Beach has long been used by naturists, but Broad Sands is the best-kept secret. It's a deep double cove set far beneath wooded cliffs with many caves, and a refuge from the busy campsites at Watermouth harbour. Development of this area as a tourist destination began in the 1820s with the decline in fishing and eventual arrival of the railway. Indeed, the only obstacle to Ilfracombe becoming a leading seaside resort was its lack of sand, so the 'Tunnels' were drilled by a local entrepreneur to provide access to a cove on the other side of the cliffs. Two separate tidal bathing pools were also built, one for men and one for women. Naked bathing was common in the early 19th century – its health benefits were deemed excellent – and guards were employed to ensure no peeping Toms caused trouble. Today the complex has been renovated and re-opened, and provides a fascinating insight to the history of sea bathing.

Heading in the other direction from Heddon's Mouth you pass a second Lee Bay (not to be confused with swim 34 near Ilfracombe) and the dramatic formations of the Valley of the Rocks, evidence that Devon was once glaciated. Nearby Lynton was also developing as a fashionable resort and proved popular with writers Coleridge and Wordsworth; Coleridge wrote his unfinished poem, *Kubla Khan*, at an isolated house between Lynton and Porlock. Lynton's wild beach is Sillery Sands while Porlock has Selworth Sands; both are steep walks to north-facing sand and shingle beaches. Despite being the only two significant stretches of sand along the entire coastline, you're likely to have them much to yourself, even on the hottest days of summer.

The Exmoor Coast

1 SELWORTHY SANDS & HURLSTONE
Low-tide only sands beneath Bossington Hill. Sunsets from Hurlstone Pt lookout.
→ As for Porlock (below) but climb up around Hurlstone Point, past the ruined coastguard lookout. After 300m find path: a steep scramble down scree, with rope.
30 mins, 51.2328, -3.5667 🏖🏕

2 EAST PORLOCK BAY, BOSSINGTON
Huge, wild pebble beach. Good jumps and dives from Hurlstone Point at high tide.
→ Pretty walk along stream from car park in Bossington (TA24 8HF). 🏕 Pool Bridge, Horner Wood (TA24 8JS, 01643 862521)
15 mins, 51.2303, -3.5795 🚶🍴🏕

3 SILLERY SANDS, LYNMOUTH
Shingle and sand beach with a backdrop of steep cliffs. Part-naturist.
→ Leave Lynmouth on steep A39 coast road, dir. Minehead. After ¾ mile park in small lay-by on R and climb down to coast path below. Follow lower path E (R) for 500m, dropping down steep and difficult zig-zag path to beach.
20 mins, 51.2332, -3.8065 🏖🏝

4 WRINGCLIFF BAY, LYNTON
Steep zig zag descent to tiny LT sand bay.
→ From Valley of Rocks roundabout find descent 300m to W.
10 mins, 51.2312, -3.8601 🏖🏝

5 CROOK POINT SANDS, LEE BAY
Perhaps the most secret sand beach on this wild coastline. Hedge tunnel & ropes!
→ From Lee Bay (EX35 6JN, facilities) follow coast path W to open paddock at Crock Point (500m). 100m beyond the apex there is gap in the hedge / fence on R. Steep path leads down through thicket. With cables descend down steep slabs.
15 mins, 51.2267, -3.8833 🏝🏖

6 WOODY BAY, MARTINHOE
Wild, rocky cove with tidal pool, waterfall, and old lime kiln. Rocky at HT.
Continue along narrow coast road W. 1 mile from Lee Bay find parking layby on L. Descend down 'no access / dead end' tarmac road 1½ miles, to cove by limekiln. Tidal pool is hidden on far side, beyond waterfall.
25 mins, 51.2248, -3.8949 🏚🏝

7 HEDDON'S MOUTH, MARTINHOE
Stony beach at the end of stream valley.
→ W via Martinhoe, or signed Trentishoe / Hunter's Inn off A39, between Combe Martin and Parracombe. Park 🅿 Hunter's Inn (EX31 4PY, 01598 763230) and follow stream down, crossing bridge halfway.
20 mins, 51.2304, -3.9279 🏖🏝🚶

8 WILD PEAR BEACH, COMBE MARTIN
Sandy nudist beach beneath steep cliffs.
→ From Combe Martin 'Kiln' car park (EX34 0DH) take coast path up cliff. After ½ miles bear down to beach on L, by bench.
20 mins, 51.2112, -4.0328 🚫🏖🏝

9 BROAD SANDS, COMBE MARTIN
Dramatic double cove with caves, shingle beach, sheltered swimming and island.
→ 1½ miles W of Combe Martin (A399 dir Ilfracombe) turn R into Barton Hill. Park at Sandy Cove Hotel (EX34 9SR). Bear L / W on coast path and, near picnic area after 500m, drop down on steep steps. 🏕 Little Meadow with great views is a mile further on A399 (EX34 9SJ, 01271 866862).
15 mins, 51.2121, -4.0589 🏖🏊

13 Grunta Beach

North Devon: Woolacombe to Clovelly

North Devon's coastline was celebrated by the writer Henry Williamson, who settled in the village of Georgeham after the First World War. Here he wrote about the adventurous life of an otter, *Tarka*, who was in constant flight from danger.

It was in the sea caves of Baggy Point, just next to the now popular surfing beach of Croyde, that Tarka and his mate Greymuzzle hid their cubs when on the run from otter hounds. On a hot afternoon in July I set out to retrace their footsteps, following the path out along the edge of the headland, engulfed by the scent of tamarisk and rhododendron, with limestone ledges dipping to the sea and grasses wavering atop the knolls above. The route passed a tiny natural harbour with an old slipway hewn into the rock, a large mooring ring still attached. Here steps lead down into a natural lagoon and it was tempting to stop and swim but I had already spied caves set beneath a steep shoulder of rock where anglers gather to fish the deep waters off the point, about half a mile further on. Scrambling down I found the long cave tunnel and two smaller coves with caves as well.

Morte Point to the north, named after its many shipwrecked souls, also features in *Tarka*. There are several tiny coves here and Barricane is the most popular. It has a little island lookout, steep rocks from which children jump and gritty shell-sand washed in from the Caribbean. The whole scene is set aflame at sunset. After a day's swimming, buy a plate of delicious Sri Lankan curry from the beach shack here and imagine you are far away, staring out into tropical waters.

13

11

14

Grunta cove, a little further on, is less busy; it came by its curious name after a cargo of pigs was washed up here a hundred years ago. Further round you'll find remote Rockham Bay, with camping fields above and some of the best views in Devon. As you continue onwards the rock strata become ever more silvery, smoothed into perfect soapstone shapes at the secret beach near Lee Bay.

The southern part of Devon's coastline, between Hartland and Bideford, also has watery literary connections. Charles Kingsley, author of The Waterbabies, was brought up at Clovelly, and his fame and influence helped found the Bideford Railway and establish the pioneering seaside town of Westward Ho! Along this steep pebbly coast Clovelly is typical of many Elizabethan settlements that grew up around the herring industry. Incoming boats would bring 'culm' from Wales – a mixture of coal and lime that would be burned in kilns to fertilise or 'sweeten' the acid Devon soil. Outgoing boats would carry valuable cargoes of herring, but the eventual exhaustion of fish stocks brought poverty to the whole coast.

The tourist kitsch of perfectly preserved Clovelly is probably best avoided, but at Buck's Mills, two miles east, you get a sense of a once-bustling port. There is a ruined limekiln, a fallen quay and a sandy 'gut' blown out of the rock with gunpowder to help land boats. According to local legend, the devil began building a rock promontory here, the Gor, to help him to get to Lundy Island. He allegedly abandoned the project after some two hundred yards when his Devon-made shovel broke.

For a wilder experience, make the effort to reach the shingle beach at Peppercombe, another two miles east, with a delightful walk through wooded glades of bluebells and ramsons in spring; or search out the spectacular wild rocky beach at Blackchurch Rock two miles west of Clovelly. Follow the path along the stream down from medieval Brownsham Farm through thick forest to reach the old cottage in the woods. At high tide on a calm day you can swim under the massive angular rock arch, one of the most awe-inspiring sights on this coast.

North Devon: Woolacombe to Clovelly

10 TUNNELS BEACH, ILFRACOMBE

Victorian sea-bathing complex. Tunnels lead through cliff to two large tidal pools.

→ Bath Place, Ilfracombe,(EX34 8AN, 01271 879882). Cafe on site.
5 mins, 51.2100, -4.1287

11 LEE BAY, LEE, ILFRACOMBE

Silver shingle cove with soapstone rocks, small caves and low tide route across the beach to a secret cove. Good pub.

→ 3 miles W of Ilfracombe on lanes or walk coast path from Torrs Park. At low tide follow path L across rock pools to second cove, or follow path from top of the hill heading W out of village. Grampus Inn (EX34 8LR, 01271 862906) serves real and cream teas in the garden.
5 mins, 51.1994, -4.1815

12 ROCKHAM BAY, MORTEHOE

Large, wild beach with remains of a wreck just below campsite. Amazing sunsets.

→ Signed Rockham Beach down footpath alley, on L 300m before North Morte Farm (or from slopey camping field at the far left bottom of site, EX34 7EG, 01271 870381). Or 2 miles N, beautiful coastal walk from Woolacombe via Morte Point.
20 mins, 51.1934, -4.2070

13 BARRICANE BEACH, WOOLACOMBE

Sunset sand cove with little rock island and Sri Lankan curry beach shack.

→ From main Woolacombe beach head N along the Esplanade 300m. Cove is opp Devon Beach Court. Shack open May–Sept, except if raining (EX34 7DJ, 07969 189304). Bring a rug and drinks. Continue on N to Grunta Beach 3 mins
3 mins, 51.1784, -4.2118

14 BAGGY POINT CAVES

Long tunnel, empty at low tide or swim through at high tide. Care if there is swell.

→ Park in the NT car park (EX33 1PA) at end of Moor Lane, signed Baggy Point N from Croyde. Continue through gate up track 15 mins. Pass houses and whalebone sculpture. Look out for interesting little natural harbour with carved slipway and iron rings on L. 300m further, take faint path L to rock outcrop. Caves below to L.
20 mins, 51.1394, -4.2550

15 PORTLEDGE BEACH, PEPPERCOMBE

Remote shingle and sand beach with waterfall and ancient woodland paths.

→ 4 miles W of Bideford A39, at Horns Cross, park by Coach and Horses (EX39 5DH, 01237 451214). Walk N down lane, and bear R on footpath / private road to beach, 1 mile.
25 mins, 50.9950, -4.3073

16 BUCK'S MILLS, NR CLOVELLY

Tiny, unspoilt fishing village with pebble beach, sandy 'gut', waterfall and limekiln.

→ 7 miles W of Bideford (A39), turn R in Buck's Cross by post office. Continue down to parking. Summer cream teas at church.
10 mins, 50.9895, -4.3465

17 BLACKCHURCH ROCK ARCH

Dramatic triangular rock arch. Rock pools. Beautiful walk through Brownham Woods.

→ W on A39 (Clovelly) turn R off B3248 (signed Hartland Point) then first R (signed Brownsham) and find car park at road end. Turn R through farm, down through the woods for 15 mins, then bear L, keeping stream to R. High tide only swimming.
30 mins, 51.0142, -4.4271

25 Crackington Haven

North Devon: Hartland to Crackington

Hartland's buckled, contorted, waterfall-washed cliffs form one of the least-visited yet most spectacular shores in the South West. Sand and access are at a premium here, but when you do reach the sea the sense of grandeur is immense.

The switchback striations of shales and mudstone, folded and compressed into geometric chevrons and pinnacles, were created by tectonic collisions 320 million years ago. This same band of hard rock stretches right out to Lundy Island offshore, a constant landmark on the near horizon.

One of the most popular places to view the scenery is the lone pub and hotel at Hartland Quay, once a large bustling port that was destroyed by ferocious storms. Take time out for a pint of Wreckers ale and visit the Shipwreck Museum to read accounts of wreckers luring ships on to the rocks. Not everyone had evil intentions, however; the church tower at nearby Stoke was built to be the tallest in Devon and serve as a hazard warning to ships. This stretch of coastline, one of the most dangerous in the country, was also one of the most bountiful for the local residents who collected wood, rope and other booty for free from the beach.

Twenty minutes south down the coast path brings you to Speke's Mill Mouth. This bay has the tallest waterfall in the South West with precipitous plunge pools, a wide bay and

21

20

23

fingers of rock reaching out to sea. Sand here is precious, as in most of Hartland, and where it collects it drifts into the folds of the wave-cut platforms – the stumps of old seamed cliffs worn down to ground level by the constant gyrations of sea, pebbles and storms. Warm water also collects in these long channels, creating shallow pools that are perfect for paddling in at low tide.

Four miles north of Hartland Quay is the aptly named Shipload Bay, reminding us again of the great cargoes and lives lost on this coast. There were stairs to the bottom of this remote wild bay but recent landslips have washed away the path. Six miles to the south at Welcombe Mouth beach there is easier access and a sandier reception with a modest beach-side car park located down a bumpy track, and a small waterfall.

Over the county border to the south the eccentric pastor Robert Hawker was the self-appointed guardian of those drowned on the Hartland coast. In the charming Cornish village of Morwenstow he was well known for wearing a seaweed wig and scribing the Cornish anthem, 'Trelawny' or 'The Song of the Western Men'. He built a lookout hut on the cliff made entirely of salvaged timber and retreated there to either compose poetry, indulge his opium habit or converse with Tennyson. Right on the coast path, it is now carved with the initials of visitors over the years. When the Caledonia, a grain brig from Arbroath, was wrecked on rocks at Morwenstow in 1842, he not only buried its dead but also managed to rescue the figurehead – a Scottish girl brandishing a cutlass – which stands in the graveyard today. Remains of the Caledonia can still be found at remote Stanbury Mouth.

South from Morwenstow the cliffs retreat and the coast softens and flattens as the coves become sandier. Duckpool has a freshwater pool at the beach head, Sandy Mouth a National Trust café and car park, and Bude and Widemouth offer long surfing bays. At Millook Haven the cliffs rise up again, displaying the same extraordinary chevron fault lines and pinnacles witnessed in Hartland. Finally, at Crackington Haven the cliffs reach 500 feet and snorkellers jump and swim in the rocky Mermaid Pool under towering Pencarrow Head.

North Devon: Hartland to Crackington

18 BLEGBERRY BEACH, HARTLAND QUAY
Pebble beach and folded rock strata.

→ 1 mile N of Hartland Quay (⬛ Wreckers Retreat Bar, EX39 6DU, 01237 441218) on coast path. Return via the wooded banks of the Abbey River. ⛰ Loveland Camping and Pod nearby (EX39 6AT, 01237 441894). 20 mins, 51.0057, -4.5316 ⬛⬛⛰

19 SPEKE'S MILL MOUTH, HARTLAND QUAY
Wild low tide beach with dramatic waterfall with a deep plunge pool on lip.

→ On coast path 1 mile S of Hartland Quay, or pretty stream walk from ⬛ Docton Mill Tea Gardens (EX39 6EA, 01237 441369). 20 mins, 50.9848, -4.5297 ⬛⬛⬛⬛

20 WELCOMBE MOUTH, WELCOMBE
Sandy guts at low tide, rock pools, waterfall. Streams and pools above.

→ 6 miles S of Clovelly A39, signed Welcombe. In Darracott turn R down narrow lane by ⬛ Old Smithy Inn (EX39 6HG, 01288 331305). Parking above beach at end of track. ½ mile S is secret **Marsland cove**. Nature reserve above. 2 mins, 50.9338, -4.5444 ⬛⬛⬛⬛

21 STANBURY MOUTH, MORWENSTOW
A fantastic remote low tide sand beach. The long descent keeps most away.

→ 1 mile N of Duckpool (below) on lanes, past eerie GCHQ listening station, then turn L (dir Stanbury) to park at lane end. In nearby Morwenstow find good ⬛⬛ and basic ⛰ at Bush Inn (EX23 9SR, 01288 331242). Seaonsal ⬛ cream teas at vicarage and Hawker's Hut on coast path. 10 mins, 50.8918, -4.5612 ⬛⬛⬛⬛

22 DUCKPOOL, COOMBE
Low tide sandy beach with freshwater pool and stream. Woodland walks.

→ As for Sandy Mouth, but on to Coombe (EX23 9JN) and R down to beach. Upstream (via Stowe Mill) explore walks in Lee Woods. 2 mins, 50.8761, -4.5576 ⬛⬛⬛⬛

23 SANDY MOUTH, STIBB
Perfect family beach at end of little lane.

→ 4 miles N of Bude turn L off A39 (dir Stibb/Coombe). Then L for Sandy Mouth (EX23 9HW). ⬛ NT café & lifeguards. 5 mins, 50.8613, -4.5570 ⬛⬛⬛

24 MILLOOK HAVEN, WIDEMOUTH BAY
Extraordinary zig-zag fault lines in cliffs at this wild pebble cove.

→ Small hamlet (EX23 0DQ) in valley bottom, on narrow steep lanes 1.5 miles S of Widemouth Bay, signed Millook. 5 mins, 50.7726, -4.5766 ⛰

25 MERMAID POOL, CRACKINGTON
Popular beach cove. At low tide follow rocks on R 300m to the deep inlets of Mermaid Pool for jumping. Sunsets.

→ Off A39, 8 miles S of Bude. ⬛ Coombe Barton Inn (EX23 0JG, 01840 230345) or organic ⬛ Cabin Café (01840 230238). 10 mins, 50.7416, -4.6340 ⬛⬛⬛⬛

26 STRANGLES BEACH, CRACKINGTON
Fantastic wild beach under high cliffs. Huge rock arch of Northern Door at N end.

→ Follow coast path S from Crackington Haven 2 miles. Or follow lane (dir High Cliff), past seasonal ⛰ field and park just after ⬛ Trevigue Farm (EX23 0LQ, 01840 230418). Path is well trodden and bears down through scrub NW. 30 mins, 50.7287, -4.6520 ⬛⬛⬛⬛⬛

27 Bossiney

North Cornwall: Tintagel to Polzeath

I first visited Tintagel castle late one summer night. A full moon was beating down on a still sea and the castle ruins were laced with milky shadows. We climbed down to the rocky haven below the castle and scrambled into the deep, dark cave that runs beneath the headland.

According to legend, when young King Arthur was washed up here after a shipwreck the wizard Merlin nursed him back to health in these caverns and tutored him in the ways of magic and 'wyrd'. You can still explore the caves, clambering through with torches, feeling and touching your way over slippery dark pools and emerging by a narrow chamber into the opposite cove. The sloping rocks and many caves of Tintagel Haven are an ethereal setting for a swim in the crystal-clear sea. From here a mile-long dramatic walk eastwards leads to narrow Bossiney Haven, hidden among the cliffs and featuring a rock arch shaped like an elephant's trunk, a great sweep of low-tide sand and secret sunbathing rocks. Another mile and you're at Rocky Valley where waterfalls and giant plunge pools fall into the sea. Arthur is said to have baptised his knights upstream at St Nectan's Kieve before they set off on their long and arduous quest for the Holy Grail.

32

31

31

For more cave adventures head south to Port Quin and Lundy Bay. Port Quin was abandoned in the 19th century after its entire male population, all fishermen, was drowned at sea one stormy night. Now this tiny, timeless hamlet is owned by the National Trust. On the cliffs above you'll see Doyden Castle folly. Beneath is a rocky inlet where you can swim and flat rocks for scrambling and jumping. If you bear west on the coast path you'll quickly come to the low-tide sands of Lundy Bay. A short swim from the beach leads into great Lundy Hole with its massive skylight and various tunnels branching off to the right. On the other side of the cove a long dark cave leads through the headland to adjacent Epphaven Cove.

Neighbouring Port Isaac, to the east, had more luck with fishing than Port Quin and is one of the better-preserved traditional Cornish villages. Its whitewashed streets and alleys still bustle with fishmongers and pubs alongside the ubiquitous fudge and pottery shops, but neighbouring Port Gaverne has the best swimming. Steps lead down from its little headland to a rocky inlet with wonderfully blue water. From here, if you are feeling strong and the sea is calm, swim around through the narrow pass beneath the spot where local lads jump and enter the lagoon in the far right corner. There are also huge caves in the cliffs a little further on. The Port Gaverne Inn is a gem of a pub with log fires for drying out after your swim.

Heading west again, nearby Polzeath is known for its surf, loud bars and good times. Its tiny church of St Enodoc, lost in the dunes, is a world away. For hundreds of years the church was buried in the sand but once a year the vicar and parishioners descended into the sanctuary through a hole in the roof to perform the annual ceremony required for the tithes. The church has since been unearthed and poet laureate John Betjeman is buried there. The beach lying to the south is one of the best on the estuary. On a flood tide the waters cross the warm sands of the Doom Bar, creating extensive shallows with gentle ripples, and small rocky bays from which to swim or dive. North of here, below the large houses of the Greenaway, purple rock pools with hues of maroon and blue provide inlets to snorkel and explore, like an eel.

North Cornwall: Tintagel to Polzeath

27 BOSSINEY HAVEN, TINTAGEL

Beautiful cove under dramatic cliffs. LT connects to Benoath Cove too on R.

→ 1 mile E of Tintagel on B3263, car park on L by transmitter (PL34 0AY) then follow track down. Continue 700m E along coast path for **Rocky Valley** waterfalls and walk.

10 mins, 50.6722, -4.7380 🏊 🅱 🚶

28 TINTAGEL HAVEN, TINTAGEL

Swim from rocks and cove opposite castle or explore huge double-ended sea cavern beneath castle.

→ Haven beach is below and to R of castle.

10 mins, 50.6680, -4.7591 🏖 🏊

29 HOLE BEACH, TREBARWITH BAY

Isolated LT cove down steep goat track. Also explore quarries, Treknow cliff.

→ 1 mile N of **Trebarwith** beach (🍴 Mill House Inn, PL34 0HD, 01840 770200). Or footpath from Treknow (Penallick Hotel, PL34 0EJ), then R 200m. See bench below leading to steep descent. Or turn L 200m for path into quarry from S.

20 mins, 50.6525, -4.7596 🏖 🏔 🏊

30 TREGARDOCK BEACH, TREBARWITH

Long, wild low tide sand beach but with rocks and rip currents in swells.

→ 2 miles S of Trebarwith on coast path. Or turn R (dir Treligga) off B3314, S of Delabole, then first L (Caradoc) to lane end by farm (pod camping 🏕 PL33 9ED, 01840 213300).

20 mins, 50.6239, -4.7722 🏔 🏔

31 PORT GAVERNE, PORT ISAAC

Safe swimming cove but popular with lads who jump from the rocky promontories. Adventurers can swim through channel, around headland into the huge sea cave beneath the cliff, R.

→ 1 miles E of Port Isaac, signed off B3314.

2 mins, 50.5945, -4.8249 🏖 🍴 🏊

32 LUNDY BAY, PORT QUIN

Swim L into Lundy Hole cavern or explore R long cave tunel to Epphaven cove.

→ 1 mile W along the coast path from pretty and poignant **Port Quin** (PL29 3SU) or ½ mile N from NT car park on New Polzeath road (PL27 6QZ). Coasteering with Cornish Coast Adventures (01208 880280). Jumps from rocks 100m to L of Port Quin below Doyden Castle.

20 mins, 50.5825, -4.8861 🏊 🍴 🚶

33 PENTIRE POINT COVE

A lovely walk across the headland leads to secluded, sandy, LT double coves on NE side of Pentire Point.

→ Park at Pentire Farm (1 mile N of New Polzeath, beyond PL27 6QY). Bear L of farm into field and, after 300m, turn R down to coast path. Turn L and immediately on R find path leading down to cliff edge via hedge tunnel.

15 mins, 50.5888, -4.9159 🚶 🏖

34 DAYMER BAY & ST ENODOC

Idyllic sands with warm tidal waters. St Enodoc church is in the dunes behind.

→ From Trebetherick (S of Polzeath), bear R signed St Endoc, to car park (PL27 6EZ). Head S across beach, then around Brea Hill (L via St Enodoc church or R via coast path). 🏕 Tristram (PL27 6TD, 01208 862215). Hire 🚣 from Cornish Sea Tours (PL27 6LD, 07791 533569).

20 mins, 50.5550, -4.9281 🚣

North Cornwall: Padstow to Newquay

From Newquay to Padstow the Cornish coast bears the full brunt of westerly storms and swells. Great caves have been pummelled into the cliffs and blowholes forced up through the ground.

Nowhere quite captures this drama like Bedruthan Steps, a mile-long stretch of tidal sand dotted with rock stacks and 'statues', some pinnacled in sharp points, others with crooked apertures. According to local folklore, the 'steps' were the stacks which the giant Bedruthan used as stepping stones, but they are more likely to be the perilous steps hewn out of the cliff-face in the late 18th century when Bedruthan was a stopping point for poets and artists of the Romantic school. The original rock steps were washed away and replaced by a concrete set in the 1970s and still attract many visitors. Rip currents on this beach can be fierce, however, with large swells arriving unchecked from the Atlantic. At low tide these sandy pools are a good place for children to paddle; adults should only swim in the sea here when it is very calm.

The Victorians, who were always keen to conquer nature's wonders, also built steps down to the beach at Pentire, a continuation of Bedruthan to the north and an approach that is little known. You can walk here on the sands at low tide by the rock arch of Diggory's Island, or approach by road via the beautiful Pentire Farm. The old Victorian switchback track can still be seen but it now ends abruptly where the cliff has collapsed. Instead a faint footpath offers a route for the intrepid. The large, empty beach has no stacks and therefore fewer rips, but you should, nevertheless, always take great care when swimming in high swells in this remote location.

39

35

41

'Rude flights of steps, cut into the profile of the cliffs, and fortified here and there by a crazy iron or timber hand rail... The steps are ancient beyond knowledge, and have given a name to the place.'

Charles G. Harper, The Cornish Coast, 1910

A similar scramble leads to the hidden and unvisited northern end of Watergate Bay, the famous sands just north of Newquay. This alternative approach to the bay takes in fantastic cliff scenery and the alluring Beacon Cove, a deeply recessed beach with caves and cliffs that traps the afternoon sunlight like a prism. The approach to the cove is treacherous; descend a steep grass embankment to find a steel cable that leads you down into a large cave. Nimble-footed adventurers will no doubt relish the challenge. I swam here alone as the tide ebbed and an early evening sun broke from beneath storm clouds, body-surfing in perfect hollow waves, the white sand churning into blue below.

For a far more sedate swim nothing can beat the exquisite rock pool at Treyarnon, perched on a ledge above the sea like a great infinity pool. It's about 30 feet long and 8 feet deep with a wonderful array of bladderwracks and the occasional starfish. Treyarnon Bay is just one of the (somewhat overdeveloped) super-coves on the way to Padstow, one of north Cornwall's prettiest and most upmarket seaside towns. Situated in the Camel estuary, Padstow's sands are both a delight for swimmers and a hazard for boats. The infamous Doom Bar creates a beach for St George's and Hawker's coves, but has wrecked many a vessel.

If you head further out of Padstow, make your way to Trevose Head. Start at the dramatic new lifeboat station and work south towards the caravan parks of Mother Ivey's Bay. Wedges of white sand fill the inlets and places like Long Cove provide perfect opportunities for diving, jumping and exploring away from the crowds. Or, if you really want to get right away and test your rock scrambling and swimming skills, why not explore the famous Round Holes. These collapsed caves are like massive craters in the land with eerie passages out to the sea. One can be found on the west side of Trevose Head and on a flat calm day you can descend to the rocks about a hundred yards south and swim into the entrance. Another is east of nearby Trevone Bay and a steep, slippery descent into the hole itself provides access to the great ocean beyond.

North Cornwall: Padstow to Newquay

35 DOOM BAR, PADSTOW
Large area of sands at the estuary mouth, reached by a pretty walk through fields.

→ Follow B3276 W from Padstow (dir Newquay) and at T junction find Hawker's Cove / Crugmeer signed R down narrow lane. After 2 miles turn R down track into field (Car Park £2). Or 1 mile N of Padstow on coast path, past war memorial. Explore the coast a mile N to find **Pepper Hole**, a collapsed sea cave. Rick Stein's 🚉 Cornish Arms inn in St Merryn (PL28 8ND, 01841 520288). NB best 🔺 is Dennis Cove on S side Padstow, overlooking the Camel estuary (PL28 8DR, 01841 532349).
10 mins, 50.5565, -4.9485 🚶 🏊

36 TREVONE ROUND HOLE
Large crater in headland. Steep scramble leads down and out to the ocean.

→ 500m on coast path NE from Trevone.
10 mins, 50.5480, -4.9794 🏊 🅅

37 TREVONE TIDAL POOL, TREVONE
Rockpools and semi-natural plunge pool.

→ Rocky foreshore just SW of beach.
10 mins, 50.5446, -4.9809 🏊 🏊 🔺

38 TREVOSE HOLE, CONSTANTINE BAY
Dramatic collapsed sea cave on cliff path, adventure swim in from rocks 200m S.

→ Trevose Head (PL28 8SL) is at the end of a toll road from Harlyn. Bear S from car park, 200m, or walk a mile up from Constantine Bay. **Long Cove** with jumps on opp side of headland, S of lifeboat station.
5 mins, 50.5454, -5.0347 🏊 🏊 🍽

39 TREYARNON ROCK POOL
Huge natural rock pool above beach.

→ Just below the 🍽 YHA Café (PL28 8JR, 0845 371 9664), short walk from car park.
5 mins, 50.5291, -5.0255 🏊 🏊

40 FOX COVE, TREYARNON
Narrow LT only cove. Rocks for jumping.

→ S from Treyarnon on cliff path, beyond Trethias caravan campsite (🔺 PL28 8PL, 01841 520323). Descend on steep path on N edge of cove. Tricky final scramble.
20 mins, 50.5200, -5.0272 🏊 🍽

41 PENTIRE STEPS, BEDRUTHAN
The Victorian 'steps' at the remote N end

of this popular beach have washed away but there is still a goat track down.

½ mile N of the Bedruthan Steps B3276 turn L (Pentire Farm / Park Head). Head to coast path. Look L for a path down slope ending in a rocky scramble. Turn R to visit High Cove inlet with sea arch and caves. Basic 🔺 Bedruthan Steps - great sunsets.
10 mins, 50.4944, -5.0346 🔺

42 BEACON COVE, TREVARRIAN
Almost inaccessible cove. Ropes, cables.

As for Fox Hole (below) but bear R after stile, up to coast path. Descend on v. steep grass slope on N side of cove, traversing L at bottom to steel rope into cave.
20 mins, 50.4605, -5.0378 🏊 🏊 🔺

43 FOX HOLE, WATERGATE BAY
This access route brings you down to remote N end of popular Watergate Bay.

→ Follow grassy track by cottage from Trevarrian (by Shrub Cottage, near 'Kernow Trek', TR8 4AQ). After ½ mile, after stile, bear L along the field boundary to reach coast path, then down to Watergate Bay.
15 mins, 50.4547, -5.0397 🏊 🔺

48 Chapel Porth

North Cornwall: St Agnes to St Ives

The coast is harsh on Cornwall's northern seaboard. From St Ives to St Agnes are soaring cliffs, tin-mine tunnels and caves, as well as evidence of two women's saltwater passions: Lady Basset's bathing pools and Virginia Woolf's lighthouse.

During Woolf's childhood her family made frequent visits to their holiday home on the edge of St Ives, a place where she spent possibly the happiest days of her life. The elegant octagonal Godrevy lighthouse stood on the horizon, a constant beacon and the inspiration for her philosophical musings in *To the Lighthouse* – the story of a boy's dream to sail to the offshore island. The best viewpoint today is Navax Point, which also conceals the stunning Fishing Cove, set deep beneath the rock face and so well hidden that even some local people don't know it exists.

East from here the cliffs rise to giddy heights for at least five miles. In my search for swims there seemed little chance of finding a way down to the still blue waters. That night I camped, despondent, on the coast path on the high Carvannel Downs but woke early to see thick blankets of morning mist pouring down through a nearby gully on to the beach below, vaporising as they hit the purple sea. By following the narrow coombe I finally found a way down to Porth-cadjack Cove, via a steep path with a handy rope tied for support. The shady cliffs loomed above and the stacks of Samphire Island stood just offshore. Wondrously alone and unseen, my heart thumping, I

51

47

44

'Probably nothing we had as children was quite so important to us as our summers in Cornwall… to hear the waves breaking…to dig in the sands; to scramble over the rocks and see the anemones flourishing their antennae in the pools.'

Virginia Woolf in
Moments of Being

plunged into the sea just as the first morning rays broke over the cliff and touched the water.

If you fancy a long foreshore scramble and the tide is on your side, Basset's Cove, a sandier beach to the west of Porthcadjack, is a possible destination. It was once possible to descend to this cove from the high cliff above via a winch that Lady Basset had installed in 1800 to enable her to bathe here. She also had six multi-level bathing pools cut into the rock on the west side of Portreath Beach. Two are still just visible. There is another rock pool by the harbour wall; it was used until 1970 for swimming lessons.

This tumultuous coast has several bathing pools, mainly built as safe places to swim when the sea is dangerous. The most hidden, at Porthtowan, was built during the Second World War; the beach had been heavily mined by German bombers seeking to destroy the surrounding airfields. The pool had its own access steps cut into the cliff so people could reach it in safety via the coast path without crossing the beach.

A couple of miles to the north the spectacular Wheal Coates engine house is just one of many mining relics in the area and a reminder of the harsh working conditions in the tin mines of the 19th century. This engine pumped water from mines 70 fathoms deep with tunnels that extended almost a mile out under the sea. Today, on spring low tides, sand extends for a few miles along the cliff base between Porthtowan, Chapel Porth and Wheal Coates. The intrepid can access the numerous old sea caves, including one that connects with the old lift shaft and flooded mine workings. At high tide, on the cliff above, you may well hear the thunderous boom of waves entering the caves far below.

A tiny working remnant of the tin industry exists at Blue Hills Tin, where traditional tin jewellery is made. The old, ruined mine buildings are dotted among gnarled oaks and waterfalls. Trevellas Cove, below, is the rough neighbour of sandy Trevaunance and, on summer days, you can join local lads jumping from the sea stacks or, if the tide is low, try your hand at skin-diving for the delicious fat mussels growing on the jagged rocks.

North Cornwall: St Agnes to St Ives

44 VUGGA COVE, WEST PENTIRE
On wild southwest end of Crantock Beach.
→ On coast path below Goose Rock Hotel
(TR8 5SE) about ¼ mile to sea.
5 mins, 50.4065, -5.1312

45 PORTH JOKE, WEST PENTIRE
Popular 'secret' beach below meadows in
a little coombe. Stream and caves.
→ From West Pentire follow track towards
headland, then L down track after 200m.
Nearby △ Treago Farm is worth a visit out
of season (TR8 5QS, 01637 830277).
15 mins, 50.3981, -5.1298

46 HOLYWELL BEACH, CAVE AND WELL
Large cavern at the remote NE end of this
beautiful beach. Holy well spring inside.
→ Accessible at LT, ¾ mile from car park.
20 mins, 50.3985, -5.1459

47 TREVELLAS COVE, ST AGNES
Shingle beach at bottom of coombe with
dramatic mine ruins and giant sea stacks.
→ Signed Blue Hills Tin (TR5 0YW, 01872
553341) off B3285 just E of St Agnes.

After ½ mile at hairpin, turn R down track
to parking. Continue on to the stacks for
very high jumps and mussel collecting.
5 mins, 50.3251, -5.1957

48 CHAPEL PORTH, ST AGNES
Popular dramatic cove. LT reveals access
to sea cave (Towanroath Vugga) beneath
Wheal Coates engine house, connected to
tunnels beneath sea.
→ Cave is 400m NE of Chapel Porth
beach along the sands. Choose a spring
LT to allow plenty of time. Good NT
Café serves tasty toasted croques, or
'Hedgehog' ice cream, through a hole in the
wall (outside seating). △ Beacon Cottage
is above (TR5 0NU, 01872 552347).
10 mins, 50.3010, -5.2357

49 PORTHTOWAN TIDAL POOL
Wonderful, secluded tidal pool set among
the cliffs, 300m to NE of surf beach.
→ Follow coast path N, past Blue beach
bar (TR4 8AW, 01209 890329) climb hill
300m to find eroded steps down to L. At LT
sands open to Chapel Porth to R (1 mile).
15 mins, 50.2902, -5.2435

50 PORTH-CADJACK COVE, PORTREATH
Hidden, super-wild, LT pebble beach
beneath cliffs with rope scramble.
Explore Samphire Island or swim 300m
NE into the chasm of Ralph's Cupboard.
→ From Portreath take B3301 coast road
(dir. St Ives / TR14 0HQ) 1½ miles to rough,
cliff-top parking above Basset Cove. Walk
400m NE on coast path, then drop down
into obvious gully L, with steep scramble
(before Carvannel Downs).
20 mins, 50.2550, -5.3094

51 FISHING COVE, NAVAX POINT
Secluded, part-naturist double coves,
tucked away down a dramatic path to the
E of Navax Point. Seals may be seen here.
→ Follow B3301 coast road from
Portreath 4¼ miles or from Gwithian 1½
miles to find track to coast at top of hill.
Follow coast path 300m L (W) towards
headland, then find path on R winding
down to cove. △ Gwithian Farm (TR27 5BX,
01736 753127) or △ Churchtown (01736
753219) are by Gwithian beach. Also find
giant LT rock pool beneath Godrevy Point.
15 mins, 50.2379, -5.3726

© Porth Chapel

Land's End, Penwith and the Isles of Scilly

Granite outcrops and burial cairns rise up among heather and gorse. Far below a turquoise sea shifts, throwing up spray in the hot morning sun. The craggy granite peninsula of Land's End, at the furthest tip of England, is studded with secret coves, and further out on the Scilly archipelago are some of the finest white sand beaches.

For me, Nanjizal Bay is the real Land's End. One of the most inaccessible beaches in Penwith, the two-mile walk is a pilgrimage to a mystical and wild place. At the north end three sandstone caves are hunched like gnarled dinosaur feet. At the south a tall eyelet rock arch – Zawn Pyg, the 'Song of the Sea' – shields a low-tide, sandy plunge pool. The sand from Nanjizal, completely displaced by a violent storm in 1953, is slowly returning and there is a good stretch at low tide.

The sands that Nanjizal lost, Pedn Vounder, some three miles east, has gained. This dramatic bay is protected by towering granite outcrops; sandbars and lagoons form between them and shallow pools warm up in the sun. Bathers can swim in among little inlets or wade over to the Logan Rock headland, where a cantilevered rock once stood until some local lads tipped it into the sea as a challenge nearly a hundred years ago.

Pedn Vounder is mainly used by local people, campers and nudists and there's a great pub and cliff-top campsite above.

58

60

52

The beach is reached by a flower-lined track but a tricky descent keeps the crowds away. If you're staying in the area, try to catch a performance at the open-air Minack Theatre, continue up the lane to the church at St Levan, and perhaps also visit lesser-known Porth Chapel Beach.

Heading north from Nanjizal and Land's End a sleepy stream runs down through Cot Valley. Here the path leads down past great marble boulders to sands at low tide. The tiny Brisons islands stand half a mile offshore and each year an annual swimming race takes place between them and nearby Priest's Cove, with a flotilla of rowing gigs organised by the Cape Cornwall Slipway Association following on behind to pick up the stragglers. From here the north coast becomes steeper and rockier with breaks at little-known Portheras Cove and, at spring low tides, at the sands of Gurnard's Head and eventually Zennor, which has a great pub and a legendary mermaid.

Looking west from Penwith on a clear day you can sometimes make out the white shimmer of the Isles of Scilly, 28 miles offshore. The sea between covers the ancient mythical kingdom of Lyonesse and, according to Arthurian legend, when the final storm covered the land a knight rode out on a white horse. The sand on Scilly is iridescent, mixed with pulverised white sea-shells brought in from the Caribbean by the Gulf Stream. The crystal water is a diver's paradise. Stay on one of the off-islands to really soak up island life. Tresco's Pentle Bay is spectacular, while St Martin's has Great Bay. A single-track road to its tiny bakery is lined with stalls filled with garden tomatoes and orchard-fruit jam, with honesty boxes for payment.

The constant revealing and concealing of sea caves and causeways is part of the adventure of Scilly. A low-tide scramble over to White Island from St Martin's reveals deep inlets that are good for snorkelling and jumping, and a dark sea cave named Underland Girt. At the north end of Tresco you can explore Piper's Hole, a freshwater lake in a cavern that visitors often light with candles. And on a few special low spring tides each year this shallow archipelago almost joins itself back together as the seas recede and you wade for miles through turquoise water, from one beautiful island to the next.

Land's End, Penwith and the Isles of Scilly

52 GREAT BAY, ST MARTIN'S, SCILLY
Low-key, organic-food-friendly island. Tropical white sand bay with access to White Island at low tide by rock bar.

→ From St Martin's quay and hotel (currently closed) follow road a mile and turn L at community hall/reading rooms. Cross moor 400m down to bay. At far N end White Island can be accessed at LT by stone causeway. On NE side find deep inlets and a long sea cave (Underland Girt).
20 mins, 49.9693, -6.2910 ⛱

53 PENTLE BAY, TRESCO, SCILLY
Miles of sensational empty white sands.

→ ½ mile E of Gardens on straight path. At far NE tip of island find underground pool in Piper's Hole, an old sea cave just above HT line, hidden at top of an inlet.
10 mins, 49.9479, -6.3223 ⛱

54 RUSHY BAY, BRYHER, SCILLY
Sheltered sand bay on S side of island.

→ Head to hotel then S ½ mile. ⛺ Bryher (TR23 0PR, 01720 422559).
25 mins, 49.9454, -6.3558 ⛺

55 VEOR COVE, ZENNOR
Remote tidal cove beneath village with a mermaid legend. Bunkhouse, ice cream.

→ Follow track behind 🏠 Tinners Arms (TR26 3BY, 01736 796927) to coast. Bear L down to stream, up to top and find path to next cove on R. Excellent 🏠 Gurnards Head (TR26 3DE, 01736 796928) with LT Treen Cove and Porthmeor Cove below.
30 mins, 50.1949, -5.5815 ⛺ 🏠

56 PORTHERAS COVE, MORVAH
Superb 'locals' beach cove with stream, waterfall and shade under cliffs.

→ Walk E from Pendeen lighthouse ¾ mile. Or via track below Lower Chypraze Farm (TR19 7TU) signed off B3306, 2 miles NE of Pendeen. 🏠 Seasonal Morvah Gallery Tea Room (TR20 8YT, 01736 787808).
15 mins, 50.1641, -5.6571 🏠⛺

57 COT VALLEY, ST JUST
LT sands at base of pretty valley. July swimming race to The Brisons islands.

→ From St Just follow Cape Cornwall St, then first L by school (Bosorne Rd).
3 mins, 50.1192, -5.7007 ⛱

58 NANJIZAL / MILL BAY, TRETHEWEY
Spectacular tidal sands and caves with eyelet rock arch with plunge pool.

→ Between Land's End & Porthgwarra. Or take Porthgwarra road from Polgigga (B3315 / Land's End) then first track on R, bearing R through footpath gate at Higher Bosistow Farm. Some years no sand.
30 mins, 50.0537, -5.6929 ⛱🏊⛱

59 PORTH CHAPEL, PORTHCURNO
Pretty walk to cove, from tiny church.

→ Continue beyond Minack Theatre to parking / path by church (TR19 6JU). 🏠 Occasional farmer's market here.
10 mins, 50.0392, -5.6581 ⛱🚶

60 PEDN VOUNDER SANDS, TREEN
White sands and lagoons. Tricky descent.

→ From Penzance B3315, turn L 2 miles before Porthcurno, past 🏠 Logan Rock Inn (TR19 6LG, 01736 810495). Car park by 🏠 organic cafe. Follow farm track up past ⛺ Treen Farm Camping (TR19 6LF, 01736 810273, no booking) to coast path (½ mile) and then straight over and down.
20 mins, 50.0441, -5.6424 ⛱⛺🚫

North side of Kynance

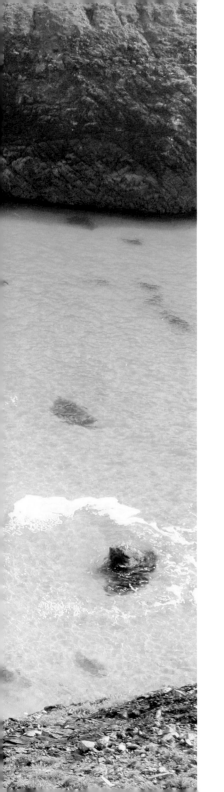

South Cornwall: Mount's Bay and The Lizard

Spectacular Kynance Cove on the Lizard was immortalised by the Romantic poets and painters of the 18th century. Shiny black serpentine rocks tower up in pinnacles around the beach and green and purple minerals colour the water.

This National Trust beach is very well known but the walk from the car park limits visitor numbers. The hidden parts are on the far beach by Asparagus Island, only accessible on a falling tide. Here the Devil's Letterbox blowhole hisses and bellows and several deep pools appear among the rocks. Daredevils jump from the high black crags and snorkellers explore overhangs and caves.

The dramatic serpentine scenery continues for six miles north up to Mullion Cove, which is surrounded by black cliffs and islands and features an old quay that is popular for jumping. Here I met a band of young local swimmers who regularly explore this coastline. I joined them on an expedition, scrambling along the south shore and around steep headlands to find sea caves and a tiny wedge of white sand. Jubilant, we waded ashore like modern Robinson Crusoes and lay exhausted in the sun, the towering cliffs condensing the evening light to heat on our bodies.

64

69

68

The indented shoreline of this area is full of secret places and has long been associated with the contraband trade. The area's most famous pirate family was headed by John Carter, the self-styled 'King of Prussia', who was part fisherman, part merchant and part Robin Hood. At Prussia Cove, to the north, you can still see the worn ruts of ancient cart tracks leading to the old smuggling slipway. With flat rocky ledges for sunbathing and sand at low tide this, and adjacent Piskies Cove, is an excellent spot for swimming, exploring and diving.

Find even more hideaways as you continue around Lizard Point. At cute and tiny Cadgwith you can visit the Devil's Frying Pan, an impressive blowhole that is best viewed from the coast path and into which local lads attempt to swim. If you want to try this wear a wetsuit, go in a group and choose a very calm day.

The coves of Lankidden and smaller Downas are perhaps the area's best hidden beaches. They are miles from anywhere, along a stretch of virtually untouched Cornish coastline, with large swathes of low tide sand and a dramatic hill fort above. It is a long but beautiful walk east from the surfing beach at Kennack Sands, or see if you can find the remote cliff-top field where locals park, down lanes from the tiny hamlet and chapel at Posongath, near Coverack. Walk further east to Downas and explore the wild valley above, with wooded copse, streams and moor. The area is open-access land.

The Manacles, beyond nearby St Keverne, are a famous granite reef and one of Britain's best-known diving sites. A trip from the dive centre at Porthkerris may yield sightings of cushion and spiny starfish and, in summer, you may even spot a pod of dolphins cruising by or be able to commune with sunfish and giant basking sharks.

You can also explore the series of tiny coves and old mine ruins to the south around the rather desolate 'wild west' cove of Porthoustock. Here giant concrete constructions tower above and there is an active aggregate quarry operation. This is an area tourists rarely visit so if you find Godrevy Cove, further south again, via Rosenithon, you'll likely have it to yourself. Beyond here are more old quarries and the disused quay at Polcries.

74 Polurrian

South Cornwall: Mount's Bay and The Lizard

61 BESSY'S COVE, PRUSSIA COVE
Famous smugglers' coves wth cart tracks.
→ 2 miles SE from Marazion on A394 turn R at Falmouth Packet Inn (signed). Continue to free parking (TR20 9BB) and descend on ramp. Coast path leads E 500m to long **Kenneggy Sands**. Tiny double Piskies Cove 600m to W. Cottages: 01736 762014.
15 mins, 50.1010, -5.4176

62 PORTHCEW / RINSEY BEACH
West facing cove, set beneath ruins.
→ Rinsey is signed 1 miles S of A394 at Ashton. Beach is below cliff-edge car park.
5 mins, 50.0935, -5.3668

63 CHURCH COVE, GUNWALLOE
Lone church on lovely cove. Gunwalloe beach to N, busier Poldhu 500m to S.
→ Signed Gunwalloe / Church Cove opp airfield, 2 miles S of Helston (A3083). For **Poldhu** take next turning. Barefoot Kitchen good for sundowners and glamping. (TR12 7QD, 07768 094686)
2 mins, 50.0379, -5.2670

64 MULLION COVE, MULLION
Jump from the quay, snorkel among the offshore rocks. Wet-suited adventurers swim 500m S to secret cove, Laden Ceyn.
→ Carry on through Mullion villlage (B3296) down to parking at Mullion Cove (TR12 7ES). 20min walk N on coast path leads to lovely, sandy **Polurrian Cove**.
3 mins, 50.0153, -5.2582

65 KYNANCE COVE, LIZARD
Busy but spectacular cove. Pinnacles, plunge pools and jumps for daredevils.
→ Signed off A3083 near Lizard. Head round to N beach at LT to find pools on far R for jumps. Good NT tea room.
5 mins, 49.9745, -5.2306

66 PENTREATH BEACH, KYNANCE
Wild inaccessible beach just S of Kynance.
→ Half way along Kynance access road, at bend, bear L down track (Holestrow). Henry's (TR12 7NX, 01326 290596).
10 mins, 49.9705, -5.2191

67 DEVIL'S FRYING PAN, CADGWITH
An adventure swim S from tiny fishing village leads to dramatic cave / blowhole.
→ NE of Lizard, off A3083. Cove too.
10 mins, 49.9848, -5.1804

68 LANKIDDEN COVE, PONSONGATH
Lizard's best secret cove? Remote LT cove under cliffs and hillfort, Carrick Luz.
→ 2 mile coast walk E beyond Kennack Sands (Kuggar). Or field parking at end of road / then track from Ponsongath church (TR12 6SJ). Little **Downas Cove** 1 mile E along coast beneath wooded valley.
35 mins, 50.0076, -5.1322

69 LEGGAN COVE, ST KEVERNE
Coarse dark sand falls away into crystal-clear waters. Hidden between two disused quarries, 1 mile E of St Keverne.
→ Follow signs dir Porthoustock to small hamlet of Rosenithon (TR12 6QR). Turn R at post-box in wall and continue on footpath through fields down to **Godrevy Cove** (10 mins). Leggan Cove is just to N. Love Lane (TR12 6NX, 01326 340406.)
15 mins, 50.0501, -5.0641

West from Polhawn Cove

South Cornwall: Roseland to Rame

By the time you reach the Helford River estuary, which is filled with little tidal inlets, the coast has softened. There are several secret wooded coves along the river with silver-shale beaches, perfect for exploring by kayak or on foot.

Bosham is my favourite cove. Self-drive boats can be hired from Helford Quay and a small ferry will take you across the water to Trebah Manor with its gardens and beach. Gear Farm, at the head of the estuary, is a wonderful place to camp, explore and swim. The owners sell cider, cured meat and superb pizza. But the most atmospheric place is Frenchmans' Pill or Creek, still as silent as it must have been when Daphne du Maurier wrote the book of the same name some 75 years ago. Navron, the strange yellow house, is down a track at the head of the wooded pill. Hidden from sunlight and seemingly trapped in time, the creek, which many say is haunted, is given a jungle-like air by the overhanging trees and green waters. This is a place to explore by open canoe in the dawn mist, or at dusk.

Across the water the luxuriant gardens and subtropical palms of the unspoilt Roseland peninsula opposite seem worlds away from the dramatic rocks and serpentine cliffs of the Lizard. The church at St Just is Roseland's jewel. A path winds down through ivy-clad mausoleums and vibrant rhododendrons to a jade-green tidal creek with an Edwardian boathouse. From here the south Cornwall coast opens out into Veryan Bay and the lanes are so deep, narrow and twisted they seem to swallow cars and cycles whole.

87

76

73

'Last night I dreamt I went to Manderley again...'

Daphne Du Maurier's *Rebecca*, inspired by Menabilly and Polridmouth Cove

Just to the west of Portholland on the coast path, I found a truly hidden wild beach near May's Rock, known only to a few locals who hide their surfboards here in the bushes. If you're alert you'll spot the goat track off to the left. It quickly opens up into a wide, roped path with steps down through low-growing hawthorn. Back in the village, John, who runs the café, explained that they strim the route every year to keep it open, but stop 50 yards short of the coast path to ensure it remains hidden.

Gardens offering cream teas, wooded castles and low-key family coves are spied through hedgerows, and bumble-bees and butterflies twirl and zip through the cow parsley as you head on to dramatic Dodman Point. Once round this headland, you come to the long naturist strand of Vault Beach and perfect little Hemmick Cove, its rocky ledges stretching into the sea. Porthluney Cove is a busy family beach, set beneath imposing Caerhays Castle and chosen by Alfred Hitchcock as the setting for his adaptation of Daphne du Maurier's *Rebecca* in 1940.

If you want to visit the real Manderley you'll need to head east to nearby Fowey, huddled around its riverside creeks. Daphne du Maurier spent her childhood holidays around Fowey and Gribbin Head, and it was here that she learned to sail. Du Maurier's family moved to Bodinnick, opposite Fowey, when she was 20, but it was to remote Polridmouth Cove that she went to bathe naked, and it was here she developed her infatuation with Menabilly – Manderley in *Rebecca*. During the war she rented a house at Readymoney Cove before leasing her beloved Menabilly. Readymoney, set beneath St Catherine's Castle and just a short walk from Fowey, has a bathing platform tethered in the middle of the cove – great fun to swim to and dive from. A half-hour's walk from Fowey you'll find the Menabilly estate, which has gardens running right down to the beach. Further along is the harbour cove of Polkerris; the Rashleigh Inn is 'Kerrith' in *Rebecca*.

The coast eastwards from Fowey to Polperro, one of the most beautiful and timeless parts of Cornwall, has a long association with smuggling. At the beginning of the 19th century, when the

87

South Cornwall: Helford to Roseland

70 SCOTT'S QUAY, NANCENOY
Small stone quay on remote N side of estuary. HT swim only.

→ Bear E on lane from Trengilly Wartha pub, Nancenoy (TR11 5RP) to find foot path on R after 300m. Walk 1 mile across fields, past beech woods down to quay. Continue on lane to find delicious 🍴 Potager Café (TR11 5RF, 01326 341258).

20 mins, 50.1027, -5.1644 🚶 ⛺

71 BOSAHAN COVE, HELFORD
Enjoy quiet inlets and shingle sand coves, fringed by woods with ancient oaks.

→ 1½ miles E of Helford village on coast path and continue onto Ponsence Cove too. ℹ️ Shipwrights Arms (TR12 6JX, 01326 231235). Wonderfully quaint 🍴 Down By The Riverside Cafe (TR12 6LB, 01326 231893). ⛺ Gear Farm is a mile E of Mawgan (TR12 6DE, 01326 221364). **Frenchman's Creek** is a mile to W via Kestle.

15 mins, 50.0950, -5.1143 ⛴

72 PORTHALLACK, MAWNAN
Shingle coves with lovely walk on N side of Helford estuary with many gardens.

→ From Mawnan Church (TR11 5HX) follow bridleway ½ mile. Continue on to Porth Saxon cove and return up wooded stream valley into Carwinion House garden, or on to Grebe and Durgan beaches. ℹ️ Ferry Boat Inn (TR11 5LB, 01326 250625). ⛴ Helford Passage, TR11 5LB, 01326 250770.

10 mins, 50.1012, -5.1032 ⛴ 🚶

73 MOLUNAN COVES, ST ANTHONY
Tiny sheltered coves under lighthouse with views out across the Carrick Roads.

→ As you enter St Anthony's Head car park (TR2 5HA) find path R by gate and descend.

10 mins, 50.1450, -5.0150 🚶

74 PORTHBEOR BEACH, ST ANTHONY
Fabulous long wild sand beach with rock pools. Explore to N for secret cove.

→ Heading N from St Anthony's Head, just before turn-off to Bohortha (TR2 5EY), find path on R to cliff and path down.

5 mins, 50.1494, -4.9919 ⛴ ⛺

75 TOWAN BEACH, ST ANTHONY
Long beach; sandy at HT with many rock pools at LT. Easy access.

→ NT car park/toilets at Porth Farm, ½ mile N of Porthbeor. Just before Froe.

10 mins, 50.1579, -4.9823 ⛴ ⛺

76 PETERS SPLASH, PORTSCATHO
Series of sandy LT coves beneath Treloan campsite.

→ Follow coast path S from pretty Portscatho (past Plume of Feathers, TR2 5HW) to find first small cover after ½ mile. Continue past gate for Treloan ⛺ (TR2 5EF, 01872 580989 children can help collect eggs and feed the rabbits) and go on another 300m for Peter's Splash, access from far S end.

10 mins, 50.1750, -4.9723 ⛺

77 PORTHCURNICK, PORTSCATHO.
Pretty cove just N of town. The Hidden Hut Café operates out of a green shack and has excellent simple food and regular summer evening 'feast nights.'

→ ½ mile N of Portscatho on coast path, or via Rosevine Hotel (TR2 5EW) off A3078, to parking at bottom of lane. 🍴 Open daily 10am–5pm (hiddenhut.co.uk).

10 mins, 50.1870, -4.972 🅱

78

Napoleonic wars were raging and French goods were heavily taxed, landing brandy, tobacco and lace was a major local enterprise. Once on the beach the illicit goods would quickly disappear, to be hidden in caves or transported inland along well-trodden paths to secret hiding places. Generations of seafarers brought contraband goods ashore and you can find out much more about this at the Polperro museum, situated near the harbour mouth, where there is a beautifully restored, natural tidal plunge pool.

For a real glimpse of the smuggling coves, however, visit beautiful Lansallos, which has an organic farm shop and campsite. From here a wooded glade leads to a tiny beach with a smugglers' passage, complete with cart tracks worn into the stone. Or you can swim from adjacent Palace Cove – its old 'quay' is just steps hewn from the rock.

South Cornwall: Veryan to Fowey

78 CELLAR COVE, W PORTHOLLAND
Secret surfers' beach. Hidden path, ropes.
→ Follow coast path W from West Portholland (PL26 6NA), up hill then turn down L after 500m at junction. After 100m find hidden path on L which cuts back and down, becoming clearer with ropes after 50m. Refuel at the seasonal Journey's End kitchen café or walk 2 miles W to delightful Portloe for crab sandwiches at ⬛ Ship Inn (TR2 5RA, 01872 501356). Also popular **Porthluney Cove** below Caerhays Castle, on lanes 2 miles to E (PL26 6LY).
15 mins, 50.2316,-4.8718 🧍🏔️🌊🏕️

79 HEMMICK BEACH, GORRAN HAVEN
Lovely W-facing sandy cove. Parking is back up the hill, so it's never too crowded.
→ Between Boswinger and Penare, 2 miles W of Gorran Haven. Easily accessed from back of family-friendly 🏕️ Treveague Farm (PL26 6NY, 01726 842295) with pigs, wildlife lookout, playground, and story time for the kids. Can be busy but there are secluded pitches at the far end up the hill.
5 mins, 50.2299, -4.8144 🌊🏕️

80 VAULT/BOW BEACH, GORRAN HAVEN
Long, isolated wild beach with fine white pebble beads. Semi-naturist.
→ Access to beach is on NE / Gorran side of bay. Park at Lamledra Farm (PL26 6JS) up Lamledra Hill. Or kayak or walk around from Gorran Haven, 20 mins. On the way, look out for the beautiful rock pools and lagoons beneath Cadythew Rocks.
20 mins, 50.2347, -4.7869 🏔️🏔️🏔️🚫

81 HALLANE COVE & BLACK HEAD
A wooded path leads down from the headland to a little 'lost in time' cove with mill, stream and rock pools. Not sandy.
→ Follow lanes behind Pentewan N to Trenarren. Park and walk through hamlet, following coast path signs. Intrepid can continue ½ mile to cove below W side of Black Head (scramble down to 50.29997,-4.7556).
20 mins, 50.2998, -4.7565 🧍🌊

82 KILMARTH COVE, POLKERRIS
Polkerris is a popular little beach with pub /cafe. Secret Kilmarth / Booley cove is 15 mins N (dir Par) on coast path.

→ Polkerris is off A3082 between St Austell and Fowey. Beach side ⬛ Rashleigh Inn (PL24 2TL, 01726 813991). 🍴 Sam's serves wood-fired pizzas and sea food (01726 812255). 🚣 hire 01726 813306.
15 mins, 50.3410,-4.6868 🌊

83 POLRIDMOUTH, MENABILLY
Daphne du Maurier's swimming cove, below her home, Menabilly / Manderley.
→ Continue past Polkerris to park at road end. Take path beyond farm down to cove.
15 mins, 50.3230, -4.6656 🌊🚫

84 READYMONEY COVE & CASTLE
A pretty cove with an offshore bathing platform in season. Castle ruins.
→ 30 mins E of Polridmouth on coast path, or well signed 1 mile S of Fowey. No parking
15 mins, 50.3291, -4.6445 🌊

85 ST. WINNOW, LOSTWITHIEL
Remote basic orchard campsite on river Fowey. HT swim only. Tractor museum
→ St Winnow 🏕️ (PL22 0LF, 01208 872327)
3 mins, 50.3822, -4.6519 🚣

86

South Cornwall: Fowey to Whitsand

86 LANTIC BAY, POLRUAN

Stunning wild, grass-backed sand beach, just W of Pencarrow Head. Swim around into Little Lantic cove.

→ 1½ miles E from Polruan (dir. Lansallos / Polperro) find car park on L, footpath on R. Steep walk up then down fields to coast path, then R on steps down to beach.

20 mins, 50.3283, -4.6036 ▲ ⛺

87 LANSALLOS COVES, POLPERRO

Enchanting walk down a pretty coombe from a charming hamlet. Smugglers' passage hewn from rocks, waterfall and snorkelling.

→ Take path by church down through woods 15 mins to cove. Continue 500m W on the coast path to find tiny Palace Cove, where steps have been carved from the rocks to create a mini-quay. Or walk 200m E to find Parson's Cove. Excellent NT ⛺ Highertown Farm (PL13 2PX, 01208 265211). 🍴 Cream teas and local beef / lamb at Barton Farm (PL13 2PU, 01503 272293). Lansallos is signed 2 miles W of Polperro by The Crumplehorn Inn.

15 mins, 50.3319, -4.5785 🥾 🐕 🚶

88 POLPERRO TIDAL PLUNGE POOL

Tiny LT plunge pool among rocks on the W side of the harbour mouth.

→ From harbour climb steps by the Blue Peter Inn (PL13 2QZ) to coast path. At bench drop down off the path to L, then find steps down on R (before white hut).

15 mins, 50.3294, -4.5157 🏊 🐕

89 DONKEY BEACH, TALLAND

Tiny LT sand cove just W of Talland Bay

→ Pass beach cafe / car park, turning L for coast path. 🍴 Smugglers Rest (PL13 2JA, 01503 272259) with evening barbecues.

15 mins, 50.3329, -4.4994 ⛺

90 PORTNADLER BAY, TALLAND

Remote stretch of beach with LT sands and views out to St George's Island.

→ 2 miles E of Talland on the coast path

30 mins, 50.3367, -4.4719 ⛺

91 OLDHOUSE COVE, PORTWRINKLE

Secluded coves on W end of Whitsands.

→ From Portwrinkle car park (PL11 3BP) climb lane 200m and join coast path on

R. After golf course / gate (10 mins) path descends to cove. At LT continue along the sand a mile to reach the lifeguard station below Tregantle Fort and cliff and return via coast path above. Several secret coves just W of Portwrinkle on coast path (Britain Cove and Eglarooze Cove).

10 mins, 50.3583, -4.2921 🚶 🐕 ⛺

92 THE GROTTO, FREATHY, WHITSAND

Series of sandy coves connected at LT.

→ Just W of Freathy find car park on R and a path straight down. Local lads jump from rocks below coastguard hut at HT. Delicious lunches at nearby 🍴 The View (PL10 1JY, 01752 822345).

5 mins, 50.3476, -4.2613 🐕 🍴

93 POLHAWN COVES, RAME HEAD

Series of secret beaches on W side of Rame, including one below Polhawn Fort.

→ From triangle car park (50.3313, -4.2219, near PL10 1JD) on coast road N of Rame, bearing L along coast path. After 400m, before old lookout hut, find path to beach on R. Or 500m to Polhawn Cove.

15 mins, 50.3227, -4.2201 🚶 ⛺

Soar Mill Cove

South Devon: Plymouth to Salcombe

I first swam out to the Thurlestone Rock arch when I was 12 years old. To my brother and me back then it seemed an awfully long way – about 200 yards of shallow water, bladderwrack floating like a forest beneath us.

A 'thirled' stone is an Old English term for a stone that has been naturally pierced and is therefore imbued with supernatural powers. We climbed through the arch and it felt exciting, like a rite of passage. You need a high tide to actually swim through the hole and by the time we headed back the ebbing waters were revealing the weedy rock ledge that connects the stack to the beach. We arrived back to our towels, shivering but full of our adventure.

West from Thurlestone beach you'll find peace and tranquillity at Cowry Cove beneath the golf course and coast path. The shells on this wild beach are beautiful and down below the cliff you are well away from Devon's hustle and bustle. There are views to glorious Bantham Sands and tiny art deco Burgh Island. During the roaring 1920s and indiscreet 1930s the island's hotel was a sophisticated 'party pad' where London society, most famously Agatha Christie, came to enjoy seaside

100

98

96

life. When playwright Noel Coward visited for three days in the 1930s he loved it so much he stayed for three weeks. According to local folklore, floating bars were moored in summer at various points offshore for swimmers and there is still an annual round-island swimming race with cocktails served to the winner by waiters in black tie. Today you can cross the sands to the island and explore Herring Cove just to the north. Afterwards, have a refreshing drink at the Pilchard Inn.

Another hotel, also founded in the 1920s, can be found on the steep grassy slopes that lead down to tiny, sandy Soarmill Cove. This is a wild and empty piece of coast. As I strolled through fields, butterfly orchids nodded among the heather and purple moor-grass and yellow rattle were flourishing by the wayside. The cove has a small island and caves for exploring, a few hundred yards to the left. From here a three-mile walk takes you to Bolt Head at the south of Salcombe Harbour. Starehole Bay sits far below, its tiny, double sandy coves sheltered beneath the pinnacles of Sharp Tor and the wooded inlets of Salcombe beyond.

At low tide you can see three masts from the older wrecks submerged in this bay. In nearby Sharpitor you'll come across Overbeck's, an elegant Edwardian house with luxuriant subtropical gardens and featuring a range of the most curious artefacts and inventions, many of nautical bent. A hostel and excellent tea shop provide accommodation and refreshment with views over the sand flats of the harbour. Why not hire a little boat at Whitestrand Quay in Salcombe and explore Stink Cove and Splatcove Point, or land on the sandbars of Sunny Cove on the harbour shore opposite.

If you are looking for liquid refreshment in this part of Devon you are definitely spoilt for choice. To the west of Bigbury and Burgh Island you can visit the 13th century Journey's End Inn above the silver rocks and shale of remote Ayrmer Cove. Two miles further, at Kingston, is the well-loved, oak-beamed Dolphin with a track down to the sparkling sands of the Erme Mouth Estuary. Finally, at Newton Ferrers you'll find Wadham Rocks and Devon's most hidden cove with its wonderful rock formations.

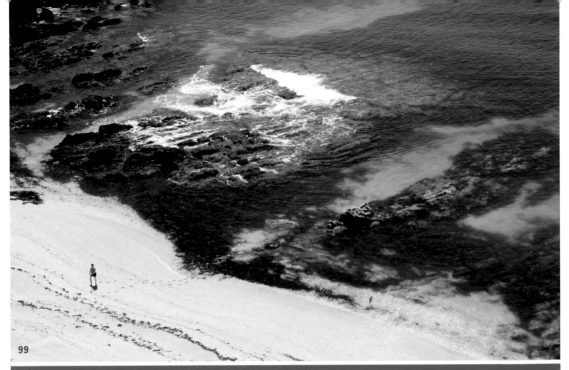

99

South Devon: Plymouth to Salcombe

94 CELLAR BEACH, NOSS MAYO
Small pebble sand beach on Yealm estuary. Continue on for other tiny coves.
→ From waterside 🍴 Ship Inn (PL8 1EW, 01752 872387) head to end of Passage Rd then coast path seawards, dropping down below Battery Cottage to beach. Or approach from Warren car park (PL8 1EL) S of Noss and complete coast loop back.
30 mins, 50.3098, -4.0644 🚶🚻⛺

95 WADHAM ROCKS, NEWTON FERRERS
Tiny silver-sand naturist cove. Coloured rock formations and crystal-clear water.
→ From B3186 / Newton Ferrers turn R by church, dir. Membland. After 1½ miles L at T-junction dir Mothecombe, (PL8 1HQ) and after ½ mile find footpath on R between hedges. R at coast path, then descend L.
10 mins, 50.3054, -3.9968 🚫🚭

96 ERME MOUTH, MOTHECOMBE
Beautiful sandy tidal river mouth.
→ As for Wadham (above) but continue to Mothecombe (PL8 1LB). Park and walk down lane. Coast path leads S 500m to **Meadowsfoot Beach**. Continue on coast path to Bugle Hole (50.3050, -3.964), a small inlet with a sea cave and tunnel. Excellent 🍴 Dartmoor Union in Holbeton (PL8 1NE, 01752 395078). Opposite bank accessed from Kingston (🍴 Dolphin Inn, TQ7 4QE, 01548 810314).
10 mins, 50.3116, -3.9478 ⛺🏊

97 AYRMER COVE, RINGMORE
Pretty walk down through orchards and valley to silver rock and sand cove.
→ Descend from NT car park on edge of Ringmore (dir Challaborough). Continue W along coast for Westcombe Beach. Good 🍴 Journey's End (TQ7 4HL, 01548 810205).
15 mins, 50.2937, -3.9102 🏄🚶

98 BANTHAM SAND & BURGH ISLAND
Well-known surf beach on mouth of the river Avon with shallow lagoons at LT.
→ Narrow lanes off the A379, S of Aveton Gifford. Swim across to Bigbury for 🍴 Oyster Shack (TQ7 4BE, 01548 810876).
5 mins, 50.2799, -3.8876 🚶🏊⛺

99 YARMER BEACH, THURLESTONE
Lovely sand beach beneath golf course.
→ From car park by golf clubhouse bear R on coast path W, passing Leas Foot cove to drop down just before the green hut.
20 mins, 50.2666, -3.8679 🚫

100 THURLESTONE ROCK ARCH
HT snorkel out across reefs to tall arch.
→ Signed off A381 W of Kingsbridge.
20 mins, 50.2579, -3.8611 🚶🚫🏊

101 SOAR MILL COVE, BOLT HEAD
Pretty NT cove below Soar Mill Cove Hotel. Island and caves to explore at LT.
→ From Malborough (A381, W of Salcombe) follow signs for Soar and then hotel. Pay for parking or eat at the hotel (TQ7 3DS, 01548 561566).
20 mins, 50.2229, -3.8275 🚶🏊🚶

102 SUNNY COVE, EAST PORTLEMOUTH
Pretty cove on E side of Kingsbridge estuary, overlooking Salcombe Castle.
→ Park at Mill Bay, East Portlemouth (TQ8 8PU). Walk 300m on to Sunny Cove. (🏊 TQ8 8ET, 01548 843818.)
15 mins, 50.2280, -3.7707 🏊🏄🏄

Moor Sands in rising mist

South Devon: Prawle and South Hams

It was the late afternoon of a hot summer's day and the sun was casting a soft, golden glow over the rocky landscape. Our group set off down the remote vale, picnics stuffed into bags, towels trailing in the long grass.

Prawle Point is a wild and rugged headland with tiny white coves strung along the coastline like pearls. Marsh fritillaries and silver-studded blue butterflies flitted on the warm breeze, meadow pipits and skylarks darted among the heather, while kestrels and buzzards circled above searching for unwary voles and lizards. As we neared Moor Sands we could see the Bronze Age field ridges along Deckler's Cliff. Down below a solitary figure was braving the blue surf, his wet body glinting in the sun and the spray.

A track leads down the cliff-side and you drop on to the beach with the help of a rope. Several offshore rock islands make this a fun place to play. It's remote and clothes are definitely optional. The beach surface is made up of tiny round white beads of quartz, smooth and wet under foot, that blind you in reflected light and grind as the surf chases them up the beach and back down into the sea.

That afternoon we continued on to remote Gammon Head and Elender Cove – easy to miss if you come from the west – nestled deep in the east side of Prawle Point. As we arrived the afternoon shadows were already stretching across the sands and the tide was rapidly reclaiming the beach. To the west of

103

103

105

Moor Sands you'll find the excellent beach under the new Gara Rock resort with its modern cliff-top restaurant.

This exposed coastline picks up any Atlantic swell so you need to be careful in the surf. The lighthouse at Start Point, five miles to the east, is testament to the number of shipwrecks and the force of the sea. There's a beautifully remote beach below Start Point (Great Mattiscombe Sands) but nowhere is the sea's power more evident than at Hallsands to the north. Here an entire village was washed away by storms in 1917. Today only 2 of the original 37 houses remain, together with the foundations of the 16th century chapel. The villagers, however, blamed not the storms but the dredging operators, who had been extracting hundreds of thousands of tonnes of shingle to expand Plymouth's harbour. Over time the village beach had been lowered until it was eventually washed away altogether, leaving the community totally exposed to the sea.

At the north end of Start Bay in Dartmouth restorers are working to re-open Castle Cove, also damaged by the sea. This dramatic shingle cove sits in the shadow of the castle and café, owned by English Heritage, at the mouth of the estuary. It has several caves, great views and was a favourite sea-bathing spot. Now funds are being raised to repair the bathing ledge along its east side. From here the coast path leads to Compass Cove, plunging down a steep grass embankment and then snaking through trees. It's best to swim in Compass Cove at high tide to avoid the slimy green rocks that are revealed at low water. Another mile brings you to little-known Western Combe Cove near the Dancing Beggars, with steps, shingle, an island and caves at the south end. Again, seaweed is a problem, so swim at high tide.

North of Dartmouth near Kingswear, Scabbacombe and Man Sands are two hidden gems with long bays featuring sheltered coves. Further on, the developments of Torbay begin in earnest. On the north side of Torbay we are almost at the limit of the West Country. Before you leave, try the red cliffs of Watcombe Head, hung with tropical vegetation. Adventurers in wet suits or with boats can swim and scramble north and find great slabs of red rock and extraordinary sea caves beneath the cliffs.

107

South Devon: Prawle and South Hams

103 ELENDER COVE & MACELY BEACH
Two tiny LT sand coves on opp side of bay.
→ See below. Both are steep. Macely is trickiest. Elender is shaded in afternoon.
10 mins, 50.2087, -3.7297 🏖️🅰️

104 MOOR SANDS, EAST PRAWLE
The best of a trio of wonderful white coves along this dramatic, hidden coast.
→ Drive through East Prawle to parking at bottom of lanes (Prawle Point). Follow coast path 1½ miles W, past Macely and Elender Coves, 10 mins past Gammon Head. Also via bridleway / stream path from lane W of Prawle (TQ7 2DB). 🍺 Pigs Nose Inn (TQ7 2BY, 01548 511209). 🍴 Gara Rock (TQ8 8FA, 01548 844810).
20 mins, 50.2143, -3.7368 🚶🏖️

105 HORSELEY COVE, PRAWLE
Beautiful walk to long wild sand and pebble beach. Rock pools / reef at LT.
→ Follow lane down from village. Half way, at sharp R (🔺 Mollie Tuckers camping field, Little Holloway, 01548 511422, TQ7 2BY) turn L down bridleway to beach.
20 mins, 50.2120, -3.7016 🔺🚶🏖️

106 LANNACOMBE BEACH, START POINT
Sand shingle cove down very narrow lane.
→ Signed ½ mile S of Kellaton. Seasonal 🔺 at farm (TQ7 2NH, 01548 511158).
5 mins, 50.2228, -3.6807 ⛵

107 GREAT MATTISCOMBE, START POINT
Fabulous sand beach on dramatic headland. Ravens cove cave 400m to E.
→ Follow signs to Start Point lighthouse from A379 / Stokenham. Take path in back corner of car park SW down through fields to beach ½ mile. 🍺 Tradesmans Arms, Stokenham (TQ7 2SZ, 01548 580996). 🔺 Beryl's field, Beeson near Beesands Beach (TQ7 2HN, 01548 580527).
15 mins, 50.2204, -3.6595 🚶🏖️

108 LANDCOMBE COVE, STRETE
Isolated cove at bottom of stream.
→ ¾ mile on coast path E from Strete, or layby parking above A379 (TQ6 0RQ).
5 mins, 50.3142, -3.6159 🏖️

109 WESTERN COMBE, COMBE POINT
Tiny rocky cove with secret steps.

→ Park at NT Little Dartmouth car park, 1 mile E of Stoke Fleming (TQ6 0JP)). To coast path, then L for 400m to W side of Combe Point. Continue on lower coast path ¾ mile NE to remote **Compass Cove** (down grass slope, rocky at LT) or **Castle Cove** (🍴 (TQ6 0JN, 01803 833897).
20 mins, 50.3264, -3.5728 🚶🏊

110 MAN SANDS, WOODHUISH
Long sandy bay on remote stretch of coast between Brixham and Dartmouth.
→ At Hillhead / A379 follow signs to Coleton Fishacre but after 1½ miles bear L. First car park on R after 1 mile leads to **Scabbacombe**. Continue through farm (TQ6 0EF), park on L and take track down to main beach.
20 mins, 50.3708, -3.5165 🔺🚶

111 REDGATE BEACH, TORQUAY
Swim or kayak from Anstey's Cove round to isolated Redgate beach.
→ Anstey's Cove Road, Torquay, TQ1 3YY (off A379, near Kent's Cavern). 🏖️🍴 Anstey's Cove Café (07780 554603).
20 mins, 50.4739, -3.5010 🏖️

Durdle Door to Scratchy Bottom

South and East

Dorset is dominated by the remote fossil-filled bays of the Jurassic coastline and the grand sandstone arches, caves and rock pools of Lulworth and the Purbecks. Heading east, the lagoons and chalk cliffs of Sussex, the desolate shingle spits of Kent and Suffolk and finally the sweeping sandy coastline of north Norfolk combine to offer a rich and diverse array of wild-swimming gems, all of them well away from busy resorts and coastal development.

Highlights
South and East England

Our favourites include:

114-116 A string of remote south-facing beaches from Seatown to Sidmouth beneath the fossil-studded Jurassic coastline cliffs of Lyme Bay in west Dorset.

121-122 Dramatic limestone cliffs, caves and jumps are characteristic features of the Isle of Portland.

126-128 Swimming through Durdle Door archway is a classic wild swimmer's rite of passage, while Stair Hole lagoons and sea catacombs are a snorkeller's watery paradise.

131 Follow Britain's only snorkel trail at remote Kimmeridge Ledges where the shallow bay is teeming with amazing underwater wildlife.

135 Lounge on hot rocks and pretend you are in the Mediterranean at Dancing Ledge, a man-made rock pool under dramatic cliffs where Ian Fleming learned to swim.

143-144 You can reach tiny oldfashioned Steephill Cove on the Isle of Wight only by foot. Visit the beach shack selling crab sandwiches and walk to Mount Bay.

152 Head for the superb shell-white sands at East Head spit and remote Pilsey Island, a short cycle ride from Chichester.

155 Wild Cuckmere Haven was where Virginia Woolf and the rest of the Bloomsbury Group bathed. There are iconic views to the Seven Sisters and access to a little-known walk beneath the cliffs to Beachy Head.

174 Eat the best and freshest seafood in Britain at the Company Shed, then swim from the oyster-shell beach at the Mersea Stone.

196 Scolt Head Island with its pristine white beaches is accessible only by wading at low tide.

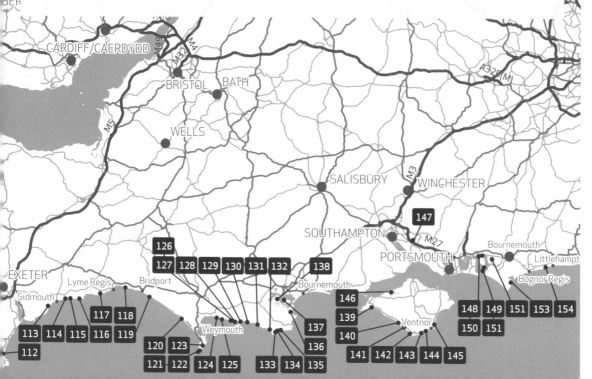

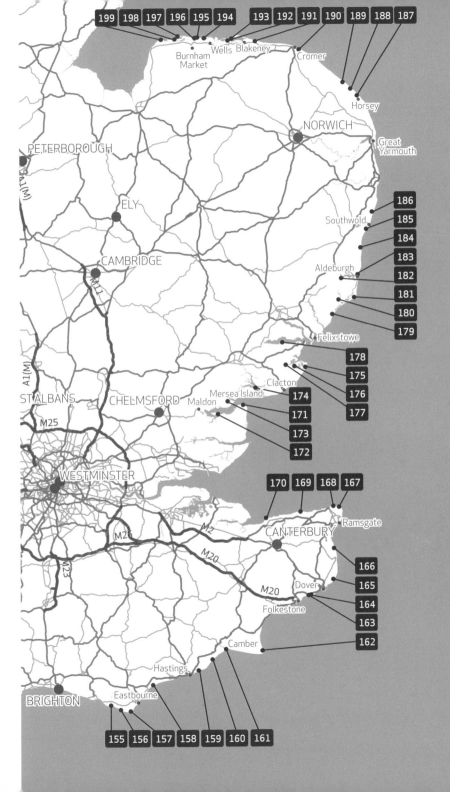

Weston Mouth

West Dorset and Lyme Bay

On Christmas Eve 1839 a massive 45-acre chunk of land came sliding down the cliff into Lyme Bay after a few days of intense rain. A great chasm then appeared – more than 300 feet across, 160 feet deep and three-quarters of a mile long.

As the land hit the sea a huge reef was pushed up, yet the crops of wheat and turnip remained intact on the top of what became known as Goat Island. This strange phenomenon attracted many visitors, even Queen Victoria, and the canny farmers charged sixpence for entrance and held a grand reaping party when the island wheat ripened.

The area of the avalanche is today known as the 'undercliff', a nature reserve and site of a unique ecology. Though Goat Island has long gone, an overgrown hillside jungle of great floral diversity remains, concealing one of the south coast's most hidden beaches. Residents and friends of the Rousdon Estate holiday cottages have exclusive access to this beach, via a short steep footpath. The track emerges into sunlight at the cliff-top and then you descend through wild rose bushes and rhododendron. The sandy strand has the air of a desert island, hidden away far below beneath such dense foliage. We spent the morning there undisturbed, feeling like castaways, and made a Robinson Crusoe-style swing with jetsam rope on a fallen tree bough that had been naturally polished by sand and sea.

Just a few miles to the east is Lyme Regis, once a major wool port. Like many coastal towns it reinvented itself in the 19th century by promoting the health benefits of sea bathing. Now it is most famous for its horseshoe Cobb, featured in two novels: John Fowles' *The French Lieutenant's Woman* and Jane Austen's *Persuasion*. The Austens were particularly keen swimmers and bathed here for a whole season in 1804. Today local youths jump from the Cobb at high tide and there is a newly 'restored' beach, complete with sand from France and rocks from Norway.

113

117

116

'The bathing was so delightful this morning and Molly so pressing with me to enjoy myself that I believe I staid in rather too long, as since the middle of the day I have felt unreasonably tired...'

Jane Austen writing in Lyme Regis, September 1804

The unstable green sandstone, limestone and watery clay of this coast are a perfect preserving medium for its abundant fossils. One of the most famous fossil-hunters of the area was 12-year-old Mary Annings, who sold her treasures on the beach and who was probably the inspiration for the tongue-twister 'she sells seashells on the seashore'. In her explorations, Mary discovered an almost complete 30-foot ichthyosaur skeleton that changed the course of palaeontology. Today some of the most popular ammonite hunting spots are the beaches beneath Golden Cap, three miles to the east of Lyme Regis. The auburn-tinged summit – the highest on the south coast – can be accessed from quaint Seatown with its convivial beach-side Anchor Inn. Alternatively, explore the remote west hillside via St Gabriel's church and beach.

More wild beaches below cliffs can be found at the west end of the bay. Beautiful, pastoral Weston Mouth, five miles west of Seaton, is reached after a walk of about a mile, down through woods and fields following a stream. Easier to access is the charming National Trust beach at Branscombe, where you'll find the oak-beamed village pub set right on the remote beach. West, beyond Sidmouth, the coastal geology changes abruptly, this time into towering red sandstone cliffs. These are spectacular, especially at Ladram Bay where they have formed into sea caves, stacks and giant rock pools.

The waters of Lyme Bay have incredible ecological diversity. Its offshore reefs are home to around 300 recorded species of plants and animals, including the pink sea-fan, the rare sunset coral, sponges and starfish. For many years this habitat was threatened by scallop dredging but recent campaigns and the growth of diving and angling have afforded the area a high degree of conservation. An increasing appreciation of the sea for its beauty, as well as its food, will surely safeguard its wildlife.

At Ladram Bay adventurers can escape the caravan park by swimming round the headlands and scrabbling into adjacent Sandy Cove or Chiselbury Bay. Be careful, though, for while there may not be landslips here, the stacks are in a constant process of erosion and one sailor told me how he had watched a one-tonne lump of red rock crash down near his boat sending a mini tidal wave crashing over his stern.

119

West Dorset and Lyme Bay

112 WATCOMBE BEACH, TORQUAY
Dramatic red cliffs and sea caves.

→ Signed off A379, 2km N of Torquay (TQ1 4SH). Beach 🍴. Swim / scramble N around headland to Whitsand Beach or coasteer 500m N to Bell Rock sea arch.

10 mins, 50.4961, -3.5144 🏊🏕️🤿🅱️

113 LADRAM STACKS, OTTERTON
Red cliffs, stacks and sea caves, best explored by kayak or adventure swims.

→ Access via caravan park (EX9 7BX) near Otterton. 🛶 from beach kiosk or adventure swim N around stacks, to Sandy Cove (400m), or S around S headland 200m to Chiselbury Bay.

5 mins, 50.6595, -3.2777 🏊🅅🅱️

114 WESTON MOUTH, SIDMOUTH
NT beach at bottom of secluded, steep valley with shingle, sand and rock pools.

→ There's a small NT car park in Weston (signed off A3052, E of Sidmouth). Follow path along valley edge to coast then bear R down to beach. Also on Cycle Route 2.

20 mins, 50.6849, -3.1847 🚲🚫

115 LITTLECOMBE SHOOT, BRANSCOMBE
Empty pebble beach near pretty village.

→ Follow footpath (dir Berry Cliff) from Berry Barton Farm Caravan Park (EX12 3BD) to coast path to find beach below. Or approach / return via Branscombe Church inland, and a mile to the E. Open fires at medieval 🍴 Masons Arms (EX12 3DJ, 01297 680300). Campfires at 🏕️ Coombe View (EX12 3BT, 01297 680218).

30 mins, 50.6861, -3.1582 🏕️🚶

116 HOOKEN BEACH, BRANSCOMBE
Long pebble beach below lush undercliff.

→ From Branscombe beach (crab sandwiches at the 🍴 Sea Shanty, EX12 3DP, 01297 680577) follow coast path E up cliff (dir Beer, Hooken Cliff) then bear down through huts to undercliff and wild beach beyond. Or approach from Beer (car park at top of Common Hill, EX12 3AH).

30 mins, 50.6859, -3.1082

117 CHARTON UNDERCLIFF, ROUSDON
Remote, isolated, long sand beach below verdant coastal forest. Nature Reserve.

→ Access on coast path via long walk

from Lyme Regis or Axmouth (3 miles). At Rousdon Cliff (ruins of Allhallows pump station) cross gate / stile (warning sign) and follow boardwalks / steps down to beach.

60 mins, 50.7054, -2.9950 🏕️🚶

118 ST GABRIEL'S MOUTH, SEATOWN
Remote fossil beach beneath Golden Cap peak and ruins of St Gabriel's Church.

→ Steep walk from Seatown (🍴 Anchor Inn, 01297 489215) via Golden Cap, or from Stonebarrow Hill car park (take lane by Charmouth Caravans DT6 6QZ). 🍴 Felicity's Farm shop (A35, DT6 6DJ, 01297 480930). Nearby 🏕️ Downhouse Farm, Eype Mouth beach. Cream teas and home-grown produce (DT6 6AH, 01308 421232)

40 mins, 50.7265, -2.8575 🚶🏕️

119 COGDEN, BURTON BRADSTOCK
Honeycomb cliffs and fab seafood café.

→ From Burton (B3157) turn R signed **Hive Beach** (cafe 🍴 DT6 4RF, 01308 897070) or a mile on to roadside parking and more remote Cogden beach. 🏕️ Graston Copse (DT6 4PQ, 01308 422139).

2 mins, 50.6965, -2.7230 🏕️

121 Red Crane, Portland

South Dorset: Chesil, Portland and Ringstead

Hard, bright Portland limestone was used to build St Paul's Cathedral and to clad the UN headquarters in New York. This limestone isle offers some of the most spectacular clear-water snorkelling in Britain, and there are sea caves and stacks for swimming around with aquatic rock gardens to explore.

The Isle of Portland is also renowned for its great tidal currents, some of the fiercest in Britain. The peninsula and its long underwater ridge create swirling eddies and standing waves that have terrified sailors for centuries. Thankfully these currents don't operate near to the shore, but you should chose a neap (half-moon) tide for swimming or stay in close – within a hundred yards of the shore. And remember, the currents on the east side of Portland Bill always pull south, whatever the tide.

Start your exploration at Portland Bill lighthouse, then head north to explore the old hand-worked quarries with wooden cranes that dot this industrial coastline. The first derrick you come to is still used to haul fishing boats up and down the low white cliffs. This spot is popular for jumping and the water below is crystal clear, almost indigo blue when the sun shines and reflects off the bright stone. Carry on walking past further quarries and another crane. There's an old iron ladder down to the sea here, small stacks to explore and several sea caves.

120

124

125

'Yet I love to see it best when it is lashed to madness in the autumn gale, and to hear the grinding roar and churn of the pebbles like a great organ playing all the night.'

Chesil Beach, described in J. Meade Falkner's *Moonfleet* (1898)

Look out for shoals of orange wrasse and enjoy the colourful pink anemones and purple kelp.

For a more traditional beach swim try nearby Church Ope Cove, located down a steep path beneath the ruins of St Andrew's church and Rufus Castle. There is a white shingle beach here and a scattering of colourful, ramshackle gardening huts. The beach looks out over the south Dorset coast where the quiet beaches at Ringstead Bay and below Eweleaze Farm – with its superb seasonal campsite open during July and August – are also recommended.

On your way back to the mainland you can't help but notice amazing Chesil Beach stretched out beneath you. Over the years hundreds of ships have been wrecked here, beached by violent south-westerly storms. This 18-mile-long, 600-year-old 'tombolo' or isthmus is naturally graded. Pebbles at the west end are the size of a pea, while the cobbles at the east end are more like potatoes. Smugglers landing on the beach at night knew which way to walk by the size of the pebbles. The steeply shelving gradient of the beach gives it a notorious undertow when the surf is up. When the sea is calm, of course, it is safe to swim and one of the easiest access points is quaint Abbotsbury where there is parking, a swannery and the excellent Ilchester Arms.

An alternative is to test the shallow waters of Fleet Lagoon itself, subject of J. Meade Falkner's classic tale of smuggling and child heroism, *Moonfleet*. You can visit the ruined church and crypt at East Fleet near Chickerell but the best pace to swim is Gore Cove by Moonfleet Manor Hotel or follow the track through the fields beneath Langton Herring. This last section is opposite the most central and remote part of Chesil Beach, a place frequented only by the occasional fisherman. The waters of the Fleet – warm, shallow and brackish – are remarkable for their midnight phosphorescence. So why not make the journey to the cove on a clear night, ideally under a full moon. Everything around you will be glowing and when you reach the massive empty beach, it will be just you, the shimmering milky light, the stars above, and the souls of a thousand shipwrecked sailors in silent communion with the sea.

South Dorset: Chesil, Portland and Ringstead

120 GORE COVE, CHESIL BEACH

The Fleet lagoon is a 10 mile lake behind Chesil Beach. Its water is warm, shallow and brackish, with phosphorescence at night. The adventurous can canoe or swim across to the most remote, central section of Chesil beach.

→ Follow signs for Moonfleet Manor Hotel (DT3 4ED, 01305 786948) ·via East Fleet (from Chickerell, B3157). Note the tiny chapel ruined by storms in 1824. Join the coast path via track on L, 200m before the hotel, and follow shore for about 15 mins N to reach the cove, or continue up the Fleet to Herbury Bay and Langton Herring slipway. Smugglers' tales at 🍺 Elm Tree Inn, DT3 4HU, 01305 871257). Chesil Beach N end can also be accessed directly from Abbotsbury, or the S end from Weymouth, Chesil Beach Centre.

20 mins, 50.6258, -2.5452 ⬛⬛

121 RED CRANE, PORTLAND BILL

There are wonderful deep, clear waters for snorkelling, caving, swimming and jumping on the E shore of Portland Bill, but stay close to the shore as offshore currents are strong.

→ From Portland Bill lighthouse and car park head up the NE coast 300m past café to old crane. To R is a popular inlet for jumping at high or low tide with ladder out (or exit on slab rock).

5 mins, 50.5152, -2.4531 ⬛⬛⬛⬛

122 CAVE HOLE, PORTLAND BILL

Peer into the sea cave from grill above then climb down ladder and explore, snorkelling among the sea stacks.

→ Continue on ¾ mile up coast to Cave Hole and Bob's Crane / Longstone Ope Quarry, and find an iron ladder below that allows easy entrance and exit to the sea, the sea cave and a little island stack. Also accessible from lighthouse road on track footpath, signed Longstone Ope Quarry.

20 mins, 50.5206, -2.4433 ⬛⬛⬛⬛

123 CHURCH OPE COVE, EASTON

Pretty pebble cove with beach huts set beneath the ruins of castle and church.

→ From Easton on the Isle of Portland, take Church Ope Road, next to the Portland Museum, and follow path down to beach, under old archway, past Rufus Castle ruins,

then past those of St Andrew's chapel.

15 mins, 50.5377, -2.4282 ⬛

124 RINGSTEAD BAY, OSMINGTON

Quiet family beach with smooth pebbles and offshore reef for snorkelling. Cafe.

→ From Weymouth on A353 turn R for Upton, 1½ miles after Osmington Mills. Turn R again after ½ mile for toll road down to beach (Good 🍺 café, serving fresh mackerel and chips in the garden DT2 8NG, 01305 852427) Redcliffe Point (50.6344, -2.4083) has lively seasonal ⬛ above Eweleaze Farm (DT3 6ED, 01305 833690)

2 mins, 50.6312, -2.3532 ⬛⬛

125 WHITE NOTHE, RINGSTEAD

Very remote tiny beach backed by dramatic white, striated cliffs. Reached by precarious Smugglers' Path through the steep, lush undercliff.

→ As for Ringstead but continue up to hilltop and NT car parking. Follow bridleway towards Holworth House (15 mins) then beyond the abandoned brick watchtower. A stone marker indicates Smugglers' Path.

40 mins, 50.6252, -2.3241 ⬛⬛

Man O' War

South Dorset: Lulworth and Durdle Door

The Lulworth coast, from Kimmeridge to Bat Hole, is one of the most dramatic in Britain, featuring the famous cathedral-like rock arch of Durdle Door and a host of lesser-known caves and hidden bays.

On a hot sunny day, Stair Hole is one of my favourite snorkelling venues in the whole of Britain. This catacomb of collapsed sea caves and tunnels has created a shallow lagoon with three routes out to the ocean. The first is a great archway that you can climb and jump from. The second is a series of smaller holes including the Blue Door – a deep, narrow lateral chasm that only becomes negotiable at low tide. In the middle is the cavern, open on both sides, with ledges for sitting, jumping or diving.

For many, however, the greatest draw on this Jurassic coast is nearby Durdle Door, gnarled and scaly like an old dinosaur. To swim through this ancient archway is a rite of passage. The distance is not great but the scale is awe-inspiring: when the watery chasm below you deepens into purple and indigo and the limestone columns above you veer skyward, you'll feel a

127

128

129

sense of absolute wonder. The beach can become busy, despite the long walk from the car park, so for a more peaceful location visit nearby Man o'War beach on the opposite side of the Durdle Door headland. Its offshore rock ledges are excellent for jumping and snorkelling. Or escape the crowds altogether by heading west down the beach via Scratchy Bottom towards Bat Hole with its tiny keyhole arch. Should it rain there are several caves in the cliffs that will provide shelter on the way. The quietest beaches, however, are to the east of Lulworth Cove. A half-hour's walk from Lulworth past fossilised tree stumps and calcified dinosaur prints brings you to tranquil Mupe Bay, a wide white curve of shingle with a backdop of marram grass, high cliffs and the Mupe rock pinnacles.

A few miles on, via country lanes to the east, the ruined village of Tyneham has an eerie feel. In 1943 the unfortunate villagers were evicted from their idyllic location by the army who wanted to set up a temporary training ground for the war effort. They were never allowed to return. Now the woods and fields are havens for wildlife. Worbarrow Bay, below, is a great, perfect semicircular sweep of pale blue water and yellowish shingle. To the right is tiny Pondfield Cove with a chalk cave, clear water for snorkelling and masses of luminous yellow thongweed with spaghetti-like strands.

For the best chance of spotting underwater wonders, Kimmeridge Bay is the place to visit. Here, great ledges of slate are home to abundant rock pools and marine life. The area is under the protection of the Purbeck Marine Wildlife Reserve, the longest-established marine nature reserve in Britain. Owing to the unusual double low tide, Kimmeridge Bay is empty of water for much of the afternoon during spring tides and is great for rock-pooling. If you want to snorkel and swim, however, neap (half-moon) tides offer the best opportunities. A unique snorkelling trail was created here in August 2006 and the visitor centre will provide a waterproof guide-sheet and route map. If you don't fancy getting wet, then try your hand at fossil-rubbing, identify wildlife in the centre's aquarium or grab the joystick and go 'virtual snorkelling' using the remote-controlled sea-bed camera.

128

South Dorset: Lulworth and Durdle Door

126 DURDLE DOOR, WEST LULWORTH

Huge, ancient sea arch on dramatic Purbeck coastline. Long steep, shingle beach (undertow in surf conditions) with caves in cliffs.

→ Signed West Lulworth from A352, then 5 miles. Park in the huge Lulworth visitor centre car park and follow signs up hill (30 mins). For a shorter approach, park at Durdle Door Holiday Park (BH20 5PU, 01929 400200, turn R before West Lulworth and continue up hill). There is a wooded tent only ▲ section here – the only one near the beach for miles. For tranquility, arrive evening or morning, or continue W on coast path 500m to **Scratchy Bottom** to descend to a quieter section of beach. Or continue W on beach to **Bat Hole sea arch**.

20 mins, 50.6217, -2.2767   ▲ ⛵ ⛱ B

127 MAN O'WAR BEACH, W. LULWORTH

To the E side of the Durdle Door headland, this cove is sheltered and quieter, with offshore reefs for snorkelling and jumps.

→ As above but descend L on steps
20 mins, 50.6212, -2.2716   ⛵ ⛺ ⛱ B

128 STAIR HOLE, WEST LULWORTH

Scramble down to inland lagoon with sea caverns and arches. Amazing rock formations and great swimming (HT only).

→ From Lulworth car park (see above) bear R on the track by the coastguard hut, just behind the visitor centre, 200m. From path scramble carefully down the loose slope. Or hire kayaks ⛵ from Secondwind, Lulworth Cove, (DT3 6RY, 01305 835301).

2 mins, 50.6180, -2.2524   ⛴ ⛵ ⛱ ⛴

129 MUPE BAY, WEST LULWORTH

Remote, beautifully sheltered hidden cove with good snorkeling at Mupe Rocks.

→ Follow coast path heading E past Lulworth Cove (high route via coast path or low route via beach). Pass 'Fossil Forest' and old concrete lookout to find stairs down to bay after 1 mile.

30 mins, 50.6187, -2.2225   🚶 ▲ ⛱

130 WORBARROW BAY, TYNEHAM

Wonderful wide crescent of sand and shingle through fields and woods, near ruined village of Tyneham. Pondfield Cove is adjacent on L, with a sea cave.

→ Heading N from West Lulworth back to Wool/A352 turn R towards East Lulworth (B3070), then R (straight ahead) on entering the village, at the army range warning sign (NB no access on army firing days, weekdays). After 3 miles take hard R down to Tyneham. Footpath signs to sea.

20 mins, 50.6170, -2.1844   ⛵ ⛺ B

131 KIMMERIDGE SNORKEL TRAILS

Small shingle beach with a large expanse of reefs and rock pools. Small visitor centre provides waterproof route map of underwater trails.

→ BH20 5PF, 01929 481044. Continue on from Worbarrow, or head W from Corfe village via Church Knowle passing Clavell's Farmshop (🍴 BH20 5PE, 01929 480701).

5 mins, 50.6094, -2.1300   🍴 ⛱

132 CHAPMAN'S POOL

Grey-shingled perfect crescent at bottom of remote wooded vale.

→ Drive through Worth Matravers 1 mile W and park at Renscombe Farm. Explore W on beach to waterfall at **Freshwater Steps**.

20 mins, 50.5935, -2.0634   ▲ 🚶

South Dorset: The Purbecks and Poole

The Purbeck Hills form a stately upland sweep of land with sea on three sides. To the north is Poole, which has the second-largest natural harbour in the world, and to the east are the sandy expanses of Studland Bay. To the south is a series of rugged limestone sea caves, inlets and rock pools, including the famous Dancing Ledge.

The small-scale quarrying along these limestone cliffs calls to mind the workings on Portland Bill, and throughout the 18th century many of these supplied high-quality limestone for the rapidly increasing Georgian squares of London. From cliff-edge quarries, massive stones would be lowered down to waiting boats. In some places the entire profile of the coast was altered when new inlets, pools, ledges and lagoons were excavated this way. Some of these new features are ideal for wild swimming.

Winspit is one of the most spectacular examples, a natural cove at the end of rolling fields beneath pretty Worth Matravers. An old bridleway passes through wildflower meadows and medieval hillside ridges, then a small waterfall leads down to a large rocky ledge extending to the edge of the

134

138

137

sea. There's a lagoon to the left, rock ledges for jumping, plus several impressive limestone pillars.

Remains of the old quarries stretch up and along the cliff edge, their slopes now overgrown with purple ragwort and their caverns filled with bats. The coast path heading west carries on to a similar set of quarries known as Seacombe Cliff. This cove and ledge also provide opportunities for jumping and diving, though the ocean drop-off is deeper. Another mile brings you to the most famous of the Purbeck quarries. Here at the bottom of rolling downs a great sea-level platform, as in an amphitheatre, has been hewn from the cliffs. Dancing Ledge is so called because it has the standard dimensions of a ballroom. On a hot day, lie on the ammonite-studded rocks until you are well and truly baked, then tiptoe to the edge of this deep-blue abyss and dive straight down. Feel the sea soothe your hot, prickly skin, watch the sun's rays filter through layers of green and listen to the guttural groans of the heaving sea moving on the distant sea bed.

If the sea is too rough, then you can always take a dip in the natural rock pool, blasted from the rock ledge for use by pupils at nearby Spyway boys' prep school at the turn of the century. Ian Fleming, creator of James Bond, reminisced about the invigorating early morning swims here and film-maker Derek Jarman, also a former pupil, was so moved by his swims that he entitled his autobiography *Dancing Ledge*.

Around the next headland, in the waters of Poole Harbour, Lord Baden-Powell was keen to promote the health benefits of sea bathing for growing boys. The first Scout camp was held on Brownsea Island in August 1907. There were lessons in woodcraft, observation, life-saving, patriotism, chivalry and endurance, with daily sea bathing at midday. The Scouts swam below the Baden-Powell memorial where the original camp was held but you'll find the beach is sandier a little to the east. The island is still an exciting destination for youngsters, with stands of Scots pine, and red squirrels and peacocks roaming free. Jump in one of the yellow ferry boats from Poole Quay or Sandbanks and experience the traditional outdoor pursuits of yesteryear.

135

South Dorset : The Purbecks and Poole

133 WINSPIT, WORTH MATRAVERS
Rocky limestone lagoon under cliffs with low jumps to L. Huge old quarry caverns.

→ Follow signs to Worth Matravers via Langton Matravers (B3069 between Corfe or Swanage). Park at quirky ☐ Square and Compass (BH19 3LF, 01929 439229). Walk into village, past green, and turn L (Winspit Rd, blue-painted cottages) and continue down valley to sea (1 mile), descending by waterfall to Winspit rocks and lagoon.
20 mins, 50.5843, -2.0332 🖼️🏊🏻🐟🍴🚶

134 SEACOMBE, WORTH MATRAVERS
Rocky limestone platform with good rock jumping ledges and caves.

→ Turn first L by duck pond / telephone box, and follow footpath signs to Seacombe, climbing before descending. Or continue on coast path E from Winspit ¾ mile and lovely loop back up to village.
20 mins, 50.5894, -2.0236 🏊🏻🐟🍴🚶

135 DANCING LEDGE, LANGTON M.
Great sea-level plateau hewn from cliff by quarrymen, with rectangular plunge pool. Several adjacent sea caves for exploring.

→ Continue 1½ miles E along coast from Seacombe. Or from Langton Matravers, turn into Durnford Drove (signed Langton House) and park at road end. Footpath signed to Dancing Ledge. △ Tom's Fields (next L after Durnford Drove) is popular (BH19 3HN, 01929 427110) also △ Acton Field next door (01929 424184).
20 mins, 50.5917, -2.0046 🏊🏻🐟🚶

136 STUDLAND BEACH, SWANAGE
Three mile long beach and dunes. The N stretch is nudist. Knoll Beach to S has a large car park, facilities and is favoured by families. Shell Bay is far N end with parking by chain ferry.

→ 4 miles N of Swanage, or via the chain ferry from Sandbanks, Bournemouth. A wealth of wild flowers, sika deer and rare heathers in dunes and heath behind. 🍴 Joe's Café with local organic and fairtrade produce (BH19 3AN, 07931325243). Kayak out to Old Harry rocks and sea arches with 🏊 Studland Watersports (BH19 3AX, 01929 554492, 07980 559143).
5 mins, 50.6519, -1.9527 🏊🐕♿🅱️

137 BROWNSEA ISLAND, POOLE
Red squirrels, peacocks and shingle.

→ From Branksea Castle pier bear L towards S beach – a mixture of shingle, sand and seaweed with woods behind. Sandier at E end but deeper towards W. For deepest swimming bear L at memorial, along coastal path, to Pottery Pier. Brownsea Island Ferries (01929 462383) from Poole Old Town quay (£9.50, BH15 1BQ) or Sandbanks (£5.75, BH13 7QN).
20 mins, 50.6926, -1.9884 🏊🅿️

138 ARNE RSPB RESERVE, WAREHAM
A pretty path through heathland and ancient beechwoods (look out for deer), leads down to a remote peninsula, with a small sand and mud beach. Poole Harbour lagoon is one of the world's largest natural harbours, with flocks of waders.

→ From Wareham town centre, head S over the causeway to Stoborough and turn L, following signs (4 miles). Or hire 🚲 Purbeck Cycle Hire (01929 556 601) near the station. Swimming HT only but watch for currents in tidal channel.
20 mins, 50.6956, -2.0245 🏊🅱️

139 Watcombe Bay

Isle of Wight

Officially the sunniest place in Britain, the Isle of Wight has been a popular holiday destination since the eighteenth century when the aristocracy flocked to its beaches and Queen Victoria eventually settled there. Today the isle is enjoying a resurgence in popularity and, thankfully, retains large stretches of undeveloped coast. There are white cliffs and landslip jungles as well as remote ravines or 'chines' and sleepy coves.

One of the best ways to get a sense of the isle's varied scenery is to join the annual round-island cycle tour along miles of spectacular coast roads. The south-west section is without doubt the most impressive. High cliffs protect around 12 miles of shingle and sand with access only possible by descending the sheer ravines or chines that streams and waterfalls have cut through the soft clay and chalk cliffs. Shepherd's Chine and Whale Chine are the most dramatic – perfect places to watch the sun set over the western Needles and swim in the bronze-hued twilight.

The most remote end of this long strand and the most southerly tip of the isle is Rocken End. It lies below dramatic Gore Cliffs, ancient sea cliffs that became landlocked when sea levels fell and landslips accumulated. There are several interesting coves on the east coast too. Luccombe Chine, with yellowed rocks and low-tide sand, is reached by a series of stairways down through tumbling

141

143

144

foliage. Shanklin Chine, its better-known neighbour, is illuminated with fairy lights on warm summer nights.

Steephill Cove, just outside Ventnor, welcomed many royal visitors in its heyday but has reverted to a backwater with a handful of deck chairs, beach huts and crab shacks serving freshly caught and dressed crab in sandwiches. A short walk west brings you to the coast path below Ventnor Botanic Garden and to Orchard and Woody Bays. Lord Jellicoe, Admiral of the Fleet, swam almost daily in Steephill Cove, and Queen Victoria and Queen Mary were frequent visitors. Tennyson, Dickens, Keats, Swinburne and Alfred Noyes are among the literati who immortalised this romantic and rugged stretch of coastline in their writings.

The Needles are probably the most famous coastal landmark around the Isle, and the cold-war rocket-testing station behind them is its most unusual site. The best approach is the three-mile blustery walk along Tennyson's Down from Freshwater Bay. At neighbouring Watcombe Bay look out for the locked metal door – behind it is a tunnel leading down to the cove. Adventurous swimmers can access this cove, its tunnel and the adjacent sea caves by traversing the coast from Freshwater Bay's west side using a mixture of swimming and scrambling. Once on the beach, chalk caves at head height lead into the remains of the old tunnel. Towards the end of the beach you'll find more caves, and another short swim leads to further sea caves around on the west side. If scrambling and swimming along the coast doesn't appeal you can take a tour with Isle of Wight Sea Kayaking, located behind the beach car park at the Sandpipers Hotel. On a calm day you can be taken all the way to the Needles and even make a landing in Scratchell's Bay alongside the famous pinnacles.

The sleepy hamlet of Newtown, on a remote tidal estuary in the north-west of the Isle, is a good place to end your explorations. In the 13th century Newtown was the Isle's biggest town and harbour. Today only its crooked town hall remains, perched alone on the village green, a relic of a once-thriving port that slowly silted up. The old port, a mile's walk across the wetlands, has long since been submerged under marsh grass and mud but it still has a quay and now provides a peaceful and magical place to swim.

Isle of Wight

139 WATCOMBE BAY, FRESHWATER
The adventurous can swim around Fort Redoubt to Watcombe Bay with sands, stacks and many sea caves to explore. A secret tunnel connects to the cliff above.

→ Freshwater Bay is a fun family beach with waterside ▮ Red Lion (PO40 9BP, 01983 754925). Scramble along rocks to far W end of the bay, past the timber staircase, then swim, wade or scramble to headland, followed by 150m swim into Watcombe Bay. Raised cave leads up into a smugglers tunnel emerging on cliff-top. Many more interconnected caves and lagoons at far end. Hire ▲ Isle of Wight Sea Kayaking by beach (01983 755838).
30 mins, 50.6682, -1.5162 ▨▨▨▨

140 SHEPHERD'S CHINE, CHALE
Small stream leads to shingle beach below cliffs on wild Brighstone Bay.

→ On A3055, 8 miles from Freshwater, find foot path to coast from road, 500m beyond ▲ Chine Farm (PO38 2JH, 07929 765747). Good ▲ Grange Farm (PO30 4DA, 01983 740296) also on A3055.
5 mins, 50.6164, -1.3702

141 WHALE CHINE, CHALE
Wooden steps used to lead down beach.

→ 2 miles beyond Chine Farm (above) find lay-by on R (600m before turning for Atherfield Green). Main steps have collapsed at bottom but an informal path exists along stream.
10 mins, 50.6021, -1.3395 ▨▨▨

142 ROCKEN END, ST CATHERINE'S
The Isle's most remote beach, at the bitter end of Chale Bay, Blackgang cliffs.

→ Heading downhill E out of Niton A3055, turn R signed for lighthouse and ▮ Buddle Inn (PO38 2NE, 01983 730243). Continue 'all traffic' past pub then L to parking at end of Old Blackgang Road. Bear down to sea R, crossing stream at bottom. Scramble across mud and rock slide to find beach.
10 mins, 50.5801, -1.3086 ▨▨▨▨

143 MOUNT BAY, VENTNOR
Shingle beach beneath Botanic Gardens.

→ Pass E through St Lawrence /A3055 and park in Inglewood Park on L. Cross road and follow path to coast and then bear R 300m. Or ½ mile from Steephill or from Botanic Gardens (PO38 1UL, 01983 855397).
5 mins, 50.5862, -1.2349 ▨

144 STEEPHILL COVE, VENTNOR
Old-fashioned cove with crab shacks, sand and deck chairs. No cars.

→ Heading into Ventnor from W (A3055) look for tiny Love Lane on R by cricket club. Park on main road. Small path, signed ▮ Crab Shed (PO38 1AF, 01983 855819) leads off lane to cove.
5 mins, 50.5888, -1.2235 ▨

145 LUCCOMBE CHINE, VENTNOR
Steep path. LT sand cove beneath cliffs.

→ A mile E of Ventnor park at Smuggler's Haven car park (The Landslip) and descend.
10 mins, 50.6105, -1.1768 ▨▨

146 NEWTOWN QUAY, SHALFLEET
HT swim at remote historic quay.

→ From Old Town Hall, Newtown (PO30 4PA) bear L, past church to road end and across meadow ½ mile to quay. ▮ New Inn (Shalfleet, PO30 4NS, 01983 531314).
20 mins, 50.7183, -1.4083 ▨

152 East Head, West Wittering

West Sussex

Chichester Harbour's wide expanses and intricate creeks are major wildlife havens and here is the ancient site of King Canute's stand against the incoming tide. One of the least developed sites on the south coast, this is a paradise of muddy tidal creeks and perfect white sandbars.

Pilsey Island is perhaps the most remote of the harbour's beaches and Sussex's very own answer to a desert island. It's actually an acre of cockle beds, mud flats and shingle, fringed by white beaches on its east side and accessible only by boat or via a very long walk across military land. Pilsey Island borders the deep Thorney Channel and has a steeply shelving beach for a refreshing plunge at any state of the tide. Beachcombers will find little treasures such as pearl-lined limpet shells, razor clams and whelks. The bird life is also outstanding.

Easier to access but much busier on hot summer days are the famous West Wittering beaches, probably the most spectacular of any beaches within two hours of London. If you do come exploring here make for East Head, a long spit of white sands and dunes that, through a gradual process of erosion and deposition, is forming itself into an island within the harbour mouth. This is a paradise of silver sand dunes and green marram grass with burrows and hollows where you can stretch out and listen to skylarks sing overhead. The extreme tip is a popular anchorage for dinghies and yachts on summer days and, owing to its depth, it's also great for swimming. To the left of the head, on the seaward side, the beach is shallow. As the tide goes out sparkling water flows in rivulets around your ankles, tugging you towards the sea.

152

154

153

To the right of the head there is a wonderfully squishy mud lagoon where children make ramps and mud slides. After a sunny day the water becomes exceptionally warm, almost tepid, and as the tide ebbs people wallow in the river channel, throwing mud pies, administering mud packs and swimming with summer abandon.

By far the best way to reach the Witterings is to take the train and then use the brilliant new 11-mile Salterns rural cycle route from Chichester train station (driving can mean long frustrating tailbacks). The route follows dedicated paths across wheatfields, passing flint-walled cottages and waterways covered in lily pads before it arrives at the dunes. On the way, stop off at some of the pretty villages that border the harbour, such as beautiful medieval Bosham where King Canute set down his throne and failed to hold back the tide. Bosham still has problems with the tide and its main road is inundated daily. There is a beautiful church here, a fantastic pub and an ancient quay from which the local children practise their leaps and jumps at high tide and when the harbour is not too busy.

Pagham is a much smaller natural harbour, but rich in wildlife and a place of solitude. It is best accessed from the south, via ancient Church Norton. The harbour itself is now too silted and shallow for swimming but the unspoilt shingle beach, with its colonies of sea kale and sea lavender, feels wonderfully isolated.

On the far side of Bognor you can find Sussex's last 'rural' beach before the urban onslaught of the south coast begins in earnest. Climping is at the end of a lane with only a pub and a mobile café in the tiny car park for sustenance. Here, a dedicated group of sea-swimmers gathers every morning to dive from the groynes, swim the length of the beach and then huddle together in front of steaming mugs of tea. The fields and woodlands around are alive with birdsong and offer a small oasis to those seeking solitude. From here you can glimpse Littlehampton, yet this surprisingly rural place provides solace for those of us who yearn for land without buildings and a coast without concrete.

149

West Sussex

147 RIVER HAMBLE, HEDGE END
Tree-lined shingle beaches, HT only.
→ J8 off the M27, signed 'Manor Farm Country Park', then first R. Park at Barnfield carpark, then to river upstream of pontoon (SO31 1BH, 01489 787055).
10 mins, 50.8935, -1.2892 🔺

148 EMSWORTH HARBOUR
Steps lead down to estuary for HT swim.
→ Follow Thorney Island / Thorney Rd for Emsworth Yacht Harbour (PO10 8BP) then follow harbour wall S 500m to steps.
10 mins, 50.8381, -0.9333 🏊

149 PILSEY ISLAND, THORNEY ISLAND
Very remote beach and nature reserve.
→ Continue past yacht club (above) then next L (300m) to Thornam Marina (PO10 8DD). Follow coast path 2½ miles S, crossing onto SE tip of remote Pilsey Island
60 mins, 50.8003, -0.9066 🔺🏊🔺

150 PRINSTEAD COVE, SOUTHBOURNE
HT only cove, warm water as tide rises.
→ A mile E of Emsworth (A259), look for Prinstead Lane on R (PO10 8HS).
1 mins, 50.8401, -0.9134 🏊

151 BOSHAM QUAY
Ancient harbour village of King Canute. Kids enjoy jumping from quay at HT.
→ 3 miles E of Emsworth (A259). Signed to Bosham. Head down Shore Road, past 🍺 Anchor Bleu (PO18 8LS, 01243 573956) to far end of quay, by black building. Do not impede boats. Also Ferry Barn HT shingle beach at ferry for West Itchenor, 2 miles S.
2 mins, 50.8280, -0.8609 🍽🏊🚻

152 EAST HEAD, WEST WITTERING
A sand dune peninsula to the N of popular Witterings. Lagoons, crabbing and mud slides. A new rural cycle route – the Salterns Way – links to Chichester centre.
→ Head S from Chichester bypass on A286 following signs to Birdham, then West Wittering beach (PO20 8AU). Often very busy here. Park at far end of beach car park (½ mile) and walk R onto dunes N ½ mile, past crabbing pools and away from main beach, onto East Head. To the L waters run fast over the 'Winner' sand flats on the harbour mouth – accessible at LT. At the spit head a deep shelving beach creates a popular anchorage for boats and the best swimming. To the R the lagoon can be warm and the ebb tide drains via a warm muddy channel, good for swimming and mud slides. Good 🔺 Stubcroft Farm (PO20 8PJ, 01243 671469).
20 mins, 50.7892, -0.9134 🏊🔺🚴🅱

153 CHURCH NORTON, SELSEY
Wild shingle beach beyond tiny church next to Pagham Harbour nature reserve.
→ Turn off B2145 for Church Norton 2 miles before Selsey. Park by church (PO20 9DT) and follow path to R alongside natural harbour / mud flats to shingle sea beach.
15 mins, 50.7483, -0.7621 🔺🚶🏃

154 ATHERINGTON BEACH, CLIMPING
A quiet rural shingle and sand beach.
→ Between Bognor and Littlehampton (A259), signed Climping Beach by the farm shop. Palm-decked 🍺 Black Horse Inn (BN17 5RL, 01903 715175). Walk E up to a mile for rural dunes and sand (West Beach).
1 mins, 50.7978, -0.5721 🅱🚶🚻

101

155 Cuckmere Haven

East Sussex

The famous Seven Sisters chalk cliffs halt abruptly at Cuckmere Vale where the broad green meanders of the River Ouse roll out across the valley floor. A lone house sits on the hill and in the distance the shingle beach of Cuckmere Haven churns between the waves, sun and sea.

Arriving here brings a welcome sense of relief: open countryside prevails after 30 miles of south-coast conurbations. There is something quintessentially English about the Sussex Downs. Vanessa Bell, Duncan Grant, Virginia Woolf and the rest of the artists and writers who made up the Bloomsbury Group spent time at Charleston, the famous house two miles up the vale, and came to Cuckmere Haven to picnic and bathe on summer days.

There are four ways to reach the beach. It's possible to take the right bank of the river's new cut via the Golden Galley pub, but the classic route follows the left bank from Exceat past the oxbow lakes, now gleaming and disconnected from their stream. You can also camp in Foxhole Dale, where there is a medieval camping barn.

A less well-known but more dramatic route is via Seaford, where a stairway brings you down to Hope Gap, a rocky ledge puckered with pools and caves carved out by wind, rain and sea. But the very wildest approach is from Birling Gap and along the foot of the Seven Sisters themselves – an inter-tidal no man's land of tiny coves and cliff tunnels. Here you'll find some of the most remote beaches in southern England. Make sure

155

159

156

you leave three hours before low tide to give yourself plenty of time for the slow three-mile return scramble to your starting point, or you'll risk being cut off.

Birling Gap itself is a good place to swim. At this remote spot a narrow gut of sand opens up among the rock pools at low tide and there is now a National Trust cafe, perched high on the cliff. A metal stairway leads down to the beach next to a vertiginous boat-launching ramp with hoists and winches. Local people have swum here for decades and hardy types will enjoy the rugged rocky scene.

It's also possible to walk east from the gap to Beachy Head, Britain's tallest chalk sea-cliff. The name comes from *beau chef*, or beautiful head(land). You can visit its beach by climbing down via Cow Gap to explore the small low-tide zone with its lighthouse. If you wish, wade out across milky bedrock and sticky sand into the shallows of the Channel and swim out towards France.

Past Eastbourne the chalk turns to shingle. Those in search of peaceful shingle beaches to swim from could do worse than Cooden, with its lone station and hotel, or Norman's Bay two miles west, the site of the famous 1066 Norman landings. But if you continue on to Fairlight Glen on the east side of Hastings, you'll find a magical rocky haven beneath a wooded glade. Situated at the bottom of a shadowy chine with a waterfall and pools, access down the final section of the path can be difficult, but this wild naturist beach has wonderful bronze-coloured sand at the lowest spring tides.

For the best sand in East Sussex, though, head to Camber on the border of Romney Marsh. Long considered a tacky resort, the west end of Camber is, however, undergoing a minor renaissance led by the stylish bar, grill and hotel – The Gallivant – offering good quality food and wine just minutes from the beach. Across the road there is an uninterrupted stretch of fine sand to the water's edge, with shallow swimming over the warm flats. And you can always escape among the dunes, bounded in late summer by sea buckthorn with golden berries.

161

East Sussex

155 CUCKMERE HAVEN, SEAFORD
Rough shingle and sand beach at base of the iconic Seven Sisters chalk cliffs.

➜ Park at Exceat, 2 miles E of Seaford (A259). Follow valley past meanders (on L Foxhole) to E end of beach. Access W beach via Golden Galley pub (BN25 4AB) on other side of bridge. Also access via Hope Gap ¾ mile W (from Seaford follow signs for golf course, go to end of Chyngton Road BN25 4JE, then R to South Hill Barn). Avoid river mouth in high swell.

30 mins, 50.7591, 0.1486 🅰 🅰 🅰

156 BIRLING GAP, EAST DEAN
Wild rocky beach below cliffs, accessed via steep steps beneath faded hotel.

➜ Signed from Friston (A259). Park at 🍴 NT cafe (BN20 0AB, 01323 423163).

3 mins, 50.7426, 0.2009 🅰

157 FALLING SANDS, BEACHY HEAD
LT sands and rocks beneath famous cliffs.

➜ From Beachy Head visitor centre car park (BN20 7YA), cross road and descend hill to beach at Cow Gap, then S 500m.

25 mins, 50.7375, 0.2556 🅰 🅰

158 NORMAN'S BAY, BEXHILL
Shingle and sand beach remarkable for absence of buildings, except for train station (1hr 40 min to London) and hotel.

➜ Just W of Bexhill, turn by **Cooden Beach** Hotel (TN39 4TT, 01424 842281) to follow coast road to Norman's Bay (1066 landing site) with large windy 🅰 (BN24 6PR, 01323 761190).

5 mins, 50.8220, 0.3820 🅰 🅱

159 FAIRLIGHT GLEN, COVEHURST
A beautiful LT rock and sand cove (Black Rock) below woody stream glade in the unstable greensand cliffs between Hastings and Winchelsea. Path is sometimes blocked by landslips. The rocks have fascinating patterns. Popular with pleasant naturists.

➜ Follow A259, 2 miles E out of Hastings and turn R at church up Fairlight Rd. After a mile park at the Fairlight Road picnic site on L. Cross road, down track 800m and just before Place Farm (TN35 5DT), by green, bear R then L to find Fairlight Glen footpath sign leading down through woods with stream. Also explore beach to E to

Fairlight Cove and W back to Hastings.

20 mins, 50.8652, 0.6317 🅰 🅰 🅰 🅰

160 WINCHELSEA, PETT LEVEL
Groynes and shingle / sand expanses.

➜ Continue on road 4 miles past Fairlight Cove and park near lakes a mile before Winchelsea to climb shingle banks to beach. Luxury 🅰 at Lunsford Farm (Feather Down Farm), Pett (TN35 4HH, 01420 80804)

5 mins, 50.9011, 0.7083 🅰

161 CAMBER SANDS WEST, CAMBER
Great expanse of sand and dunes. Sea is mainly shallow and warm at HT.

➜ Approaching from Rye, choose the first car park and park at near end for path through dunes to beach. Don't swim too near the river mouth. The Gallivant, further along on the L, is a trendy place to 🍴 or stay (TN31 7RB, 01797 225057). 3 miles on, heading E out of Camber, is **Broomhill beach** at Jury's Gap. More desolate with LT sand.

10 mins, 50.9331, 0.7837 🅰

105

157 Botany Bay

Kent

The Royal Sea Bathing Infirmary – a grand Palladian palace built in 1791 – is one of the first buildings you see as you drive into Margate. Its size is testament to the huge popularity of sea bathing and the central role played by the Kent coast in developing this national pastime.

Established by a Quaker physician, the Infirmary originally opened to treat scrofula, associated with tuberculosis. Sufferers were not only given sea water to drink but were also immersed in it on a regular basis. It wasn't long before the healthy were also visiting Margate, many to escape the squalor of London and enjoy an invigorating summer dip.

Margate still thrives as a resort and has two impressively large tidal bathing pools but the real treasures are its chalky coves to the east. Botany Bay is an unlikely find, hidden behind residential streets on the way to Broadstairs. There are no facilities here except the delightful café that Alison, a local resident, sets up in her cliff-side garden every summer. Below, white sand stretches out beneath low chalk cliffs and, in the next bay to the right, which you can only access at low tide or by wading, you can try to climb into the cliff chambers where smugglers once hid their booty. Broadstairs is said to have grown prosperous on the proceeds of smuggling and was once so fashionable that luminaries such as Charles Dickens chose to live there. In Roman times, however, the area was a remote island – the Isle of Thanet – separated from the mainland by the Wantsum channel.

The island marshes of Kent and the Thames Estuary have long yielded delicious oysters. Once consumed only by the poor, oysters are now considered a luxury and this fashionable shellfish has been central to the resurgence of nearby Whitstable, which has beach huts for rent as well as hip, art-deco oyster bars. The steep, shingle harbour beach is perfect for a refreshing morning plunge or a midnight dip.

162

164

167

Shingle predominates as the coast curves around to the south of Kent through the desolate open flats of Sandwich before reaching the famous white cliffs of Dover. Here you can explore one of Britain's newest landforms, Samphire Hoe. The foreshore here was once a no man's land, home to those on the fringes of society, housed in ramshackle shelters and living on fish and chalky spring water beneath the cliffs. The construction of the Channel Tunnel brought radical change as the tailings removed from the tunnel were dumped on this shore. A new country park, Samphire Hoe, has been created and is accessible by a steep road tunnel off the A20. The area still manages to retain its air of wild, frontier territory and you can find several miles of beach under the cliffs at Lydden Spout, with some outback huts surviving. Smoke trails up from their chimneys and you come across the odd ancient digger, used to help shore up the huts with primitive sea defences.

There is a similar 'edge-of-the-world' air about Dungeness, a place frequented by gulls, terns and gadwalls as well as artists and philosophers who established retreats in the old railway cabins and fishing huts on the bleak shingle spit. This is one of the largest and most important shingle beaches in Europe, a unique habitat that is incredibly sensitive to disturbance.

Prospect Cottage, once owned by film-maker Derek Jarman, has been lovingly preserved here, its famous driftwood garden imaginatively decorated with iron and wooden *objets trouvés*. I follow the track opposite across the shingle and towards the sea. The landscape is littered with rusting railway machinery, old sheds and peeling wooden boats in pastel pinks and greens. As I scramble down the steep shingle bank to the beach, the sand is silver and wet and dark clouds are rolling in from the east. This is where I swim, among the quiet bleakness of a beautiful wasteland. On the far horizon Dungeness nuclear power station hums and glows, and the new lighthouse flashes intermittently through the dusk, warning wise sailors to stay away. Despite this, the whole shingle mass is moving eastwards at two yards a year (or it would be if trucks were not constantly moving the shingle back to where it came from to ensure the nuclear power station does not fall into the sea).

167 Kingsgate Bay

Kent

162 DUNGENESS EAST, LYDD
Bleak but atmospheric shingle spit. Fishing huts, lighthouse and nuclear power station make for an eerie mix.
→ From Lydd roundabout follow signs to Dungeness and ☐ Pilot Inn, built from shipwreck timber (TN29 9NJ, 01797 320314). 200m before pub turn R for 'RH&DR Dungeness' and continue to black-and yellow-painted Prospect Cottage, R (TN29 9NE). Park beyond and cross shingle to L (E), through old boats and sheds 300m to reach the sea. Explore coastline to N via the Romney Hythe and Dymchurch miniature railway (01797 362353).
5 mins, 50.9225, 0.9816 ▲

163 ABBOT'S CLIFF, FOLKESTONE
Isolated rock and sand beach beneath the verdant cliffs and woods of 'The Warren'.
→ Park in Helena Road (Capel-le-Ferne) for the ☐ Clifftop Cafe (CT18 7HT, 01303 255588). Follow path down through cliffs and over railway (footbridge). Turn L and walk 200m to the stairs down to the seawall, then L for 15 mins to beach.
30 mins, 51.1007, 1.2446 🚶▲⚓

164 LYDDEN SPOUT, DOVER
Remote undercliff just E of Abbot's Cliff.
→ Leave Dover W on A20. After 1 mile Samphire Hoe is signed to the L after last roundabout. Continue down through tunnel to car park. Walk 15 mins to W end of park to find beach extending 800m to cabin and Abbot's Cliff. Shingle at HT, deep rock pools and sand at LT. Avoid sea wall area.
20 mins, 51.1022, 1.2594 ▲ 🖼

165 ST MARGARET'S AT CLIFFE, DOVER
Small shingle bay under white cliffs.
→ From A258 head straight through St Margaret's down Bay Hill to beach and ☐ Coastguard (CT15 6DY 01304 853176).
2 mins, 51.1499, 1.3847 🍽 B

166 CHEQUERS, NORTH DEAL
Desolate shingle strand with sea kale.
→ From N Deal follow 'dead-end' Golf Rd a mile N from Ethelbert Rd, past golf club to park at ☐ Chequers Inn (CT14 6RG 01304 362288). Footpath to beach is just after inn on R, across golf course
5 mins, 51.2525, 1.3971 ▲ ⚓

167 BOTANY BAY, BROADSTAIRS
Sandy bay with white cliffs and caves.
→ From Broadstairs follow B2052 N past **Joss Bay** (surfing), **Kingsgate Bay** (caves and Captain Digby ☐ CT10 3QH, 01843 867764) then R after a mile, Botany Road. Park at bottom (lovely Botany Bay Tea Gardens CT10 3SD, 01843 867662). Bear R at LT to second bay and smugglers' caves.
3 mins, 51.3893, 1.4352 🏄 B 🖼

168 TIDAL POOL, MARGATE
Huge tidal pool on Queen's Promenade.
→ Beneath Palm Bay Ave (CT9 3DH).
3 mins, 51.3930, 1.4042 🏊 B

169 BEACH WALK, WHITSTABLE
Shingle beach and yummy oyster hotel.
☐ Continental (CT5 2BP, 01227 280280).
1 mins, 51.3650, 1.0320 B

170 RECULVER, HERNE BAY
Medieval remains, bear E for quiet beach
→ Off A299 (Reculver / Hilborough). ☐ King Ethelbert (CT6 6SU, 01227 374368)
10 mins, 51.3796, 1.2215 🍽 B

177 Beaumont Quay

Essex

St Peter-on-the-Wall, one of the most ancient churches in England, stands on the edge of the remote Essex marshes looking out to sea. St Cedd, who was ordained at the monastery on Holy Island, landed here by boat in 653 on a mission to convert the heathen East Angles.

The great saint began to build his great church from the remains of an old Roman fort and it continued to be a place of worship for over 600 years. But eventually the church fell into neglect, probably owing to its remote location. Its original purpose forgotten, it became variously a grain store, cattle shed and smugglers' hideaway until the building was rediscovered in the 1920s by a passing rambler. In 1946 the Othona Community was established here and it became a sacred place again.

Today you can stay within the community and there are regular swimming sessions from the sandy strip by the sea wall. The beach closest to the church borders on the Dengie Flat, but the water is shallow and the only satisfactory swimming is at high tide. Look out for markers that show where old stakes protrude from the mud. It's better to continue a mile up to Sales Point where there is a beach with shells and sand that shelves deeply into the estuary mouth.

Despite the nuclear power station at nearby Bradwell, the Blackwater and Colne rivers have some of the cleanest waters in the South East; Mersea Island, between the two rivers, has been famous for its oysters since Roman times, when they were supplied to the garrisons at Colchester. Today the Company Shed is one of the finest and yet most unpretentious

111

174

176

171

eateries in the region. Bring your own wine and bread, sit down at one of the plastic-topped tables and enjoy freshly prepared, unadulterated seafood. Start with a dozen flat oysters and lashings of tabasco sauce, some succulent local cockles or maybe a superb lobster washed down with cheap, ice-cold wine. Almost everything on the menu has been caught within an area of a few miles.

Mersea's best beach is at the Mersea Stone at the end of the island's only road, across an area of ponds and marsh grass. The beach here is made up of thousands of oyster shells with pearly linings that give the place an ethereal white glow. As at other estuary mouths the beach is deep at the spit head, perfect for swimming but with more gently shelving sections to the sides. Remember that currents will be strong here at mid-tide, between low and high tide, especially on spring tides.

From Mersea Stone you can take the ferry over to Brightlingsea and its beaches. Off Mersea Island you can also swim in the tidal harbour pool at Tollesbury – a lovely setting among old boathouses. But for an adventure straight out of *Swallows and Amazons*, make for Hamford Water and Horsey Island, an Essex archipelago of tiny creeks and islands and the setting for Ransome's delightful book *Secret Water* published in 1939. In this, his eighth book, the Swallows and Amazons sail their new boat, Goblin, to one of the islands. Once there they fend for themselves, chart the many creeks, fight a local band of sailor-children and nearly drown on the Wade, a tidal causeway to Horsey Island.

You can still get across to Horsey by road via the Wade, or swim from the pontoon at high tide, but the best places for summer dipping are Beaumont or Kirby tidal quays. At Kirby-Le-Soken a walk across two fields leads to a pontoon and beach. Even better is Beaumont Quay near Thorpe, built in 1831 using the 12thcentury stones of the old, dismantled London Bridge. From here, brown topsails drifting out across the flat marsh skyline, flat-bottomed barges would set sail loaded with haystacks for London's horses, and return with manure for the Essex fields: 'Hay out, muck in', as the saying went. Now, at high tide, this is an idyllic swimming spot.

Essex

171 ST PETER'S, BRADWELL
Remote cockle-shell beach by one of our oldest chapels, St Peter's on the Wall.

→ From Bradwell-on-Sea, follow East End Rd from church 2 miles. Park then continue on foot to chapel (CM0 7PN). Bear L and follow coast N ½ mile past Othona community huts to Sales Point. Watch out for old submerged stakes here; an area free of them has been marked. Or continue N along sea wall to estuary mouth beach.
30 mins, 51.7443, 0.9338

172 OSEA ISLAND, STEEPLE
Shingle beach facing Osea Island.

→ From Steeple follow Stansgate Road to Marconi Sailing Club (CM0 7NU, 01621 772164). Beach is 200m to L. Or try nearby Ramsey Island.
5 mins, 51.7177, 0.7929 **B**

173 TOLLESBURY & SHINGLEHEAD
Tidal swimming pool in old harbour.

→ 10 miles S of Colchester on B1026. Turn L signed Marina, Woodrolfe Rd (CM9 8TB). Or walk out 2 miles E to Shinglehead Point.
3 mins, 51.7590, 0.8495

174 MERSEA STONE, EAST MERSEA
Famous oyster island. Superb oyster-shell beach with deep swimming.

→ Immediately after crossing onto island turn L dir East Mersea. Continue 3 miles to road end and find limited parking (near Ivy House, CO5 8US). Walk 500m to sea wall, then R, then L to cross to beach. Follow beach around to tip at mouth of estuary to find steep oyster-shell beach. Careful of currents at mid-tide. Also reached by ferry from Brightlingsea (CO7 0AP, 01206 302200). No visit to Mersea Island is complete without ¶ Company Shed, West Mersea (CO5 8LT, 01206 382700). Bring your own white wine and bread. Massive Waldegraves Holiday Park (CO5 8SE, 01206 382898) does at least have beach-side pitches and a boating lake.
20 mins, 51.7998, 1.0066

175 THE NAZE, WALTON-ON-THE-NAZE
Beach and cliffs beneath tower.

→ From promenade follow signs 'The Naze' a mile to parking (CO14 8LG) then bear N.
5 mins, 51.8663, 1.2907 **B**

176 KIRBY-LE-SOKEN JETTY
HT wooden jetty in fields and meadows.

→ 2 miles W to Kirby-le-Soken (B1034) park in village and turn R near post office (CO13 0DS) down Quay Lane to waterside. Cross bridge to L 50m before quay, cross two fields, 300m, to reach jetty and small beach. HT only. Road 500m E of Kirby is Island Road for The Wade, **Horsey Island**.
20 mins, 51.8649, 1.2256

177 BEAUMONT QUAY
High tide creek and barn made from London Bridge stone.

→ Head N out of Thorpe-le-Soken (B1414) then turn R into farm (CO16 0BB) after 1½ mile. Pass through yard 200m to find Beaumont Quay written on wall R. Walk 50m to quay. Two hours either side of HT.
3 mins, 51.8716, 1.1794

178 WRABNESS, HARWICH / R STOUR
Stone / silt estuary beach with huts close to train station. Swimming platform.

→ Follow Black Boy Lane from station entrance to sea, then bear L
20 mins, 51.9474, 1.1657

Dunwich Heath

Suffolk

Suffolk's sand and shingle coastline is one of the least developed in England. Its villages and resorts, set among woods and marshland rich in wildlife, have an unspoilt charm as well as a slightly eccentric air.

One of the prettiest places is Orford, complete with ancient castle, medieval pub and shop selling home-made baskets. From here several walks radiate out along the tidal creeks, my favourite being the westerly path to Butley Creek. At the old ferry crossing a telephone number allows you to summon the rowing boat from the west bank, but when I arrived the ferryman had vanished so I decided to swim between the two wooden pontoons. Easing myself into the deep water, just able to touch the creamy silt with one toe, I glided around among the moorhens and admired the bucolic scene.

The main attraction at Orford, however, is its Ness, the largest shingle spit in Europe. In the Middle Ages the spit choked and closed Orford's port and it is still growing, extending its long tentacles southwards. A top-secret military base in the Second World War, it is now a precious ecosystem where sea lavender and sea kale flourish. The National Trust runs ferry trips to the spit from Orford and from here an extensive network of paths unfolds. For a similar shingle experience but with a shorter walk to the sea, visit the settlement of Shingle Street at the southern tip of the Ness. This remote beach community has

182

185

180

a handful of flint-fronted coastguards' cottages and several Napoleonic Martello towers, but little else.

Heading up the coast you'll pass through classical-music-lovers' paradise, Aldeburgh, and funky 1920s Thorpeness and come to the nuclear reactor at bleak Sizewell, where the power station actually heats up the sea water via two cooling towers. Some say this is the best wild beach on the Suffolk coast because no one goes there. The next treat is Minsmere, near Dunwich – two miles of sand and dunes backing on to heathland. In summer you can watch avocets and marsh harriers or hear booming bitterns; in autumn and winter you will see many wading birds and waterfowl. Listen for nightingales singing in the scrub from mid-April, and for great spotted woodpeckers drumming. Little terns nest in a designated, fenced area on the beach, and water voles swim in the adjoining ponds. Under an evening sky at low tide, with the surf rushing over the sand, the sea fades into a soup of pink and mauve, making this a mesmerising place to swim.

Of Dunwich village itself only a few cottages, a ruined abbey and a pub remain. It's amazing to think that 900 years ago, before the waters closed over it, this village was a city boasting twelve churches and extending a mile out to sea. Longshore drift is still eroding the coast at over three feet per year and depositing the debris downstream on spits such as Blakeney or Orford. It's the same story at many places along this coast: the road ends abruptly and runs straight over the cliff at remote Covehithe, which has a dramatic ruined church, a beautiful beach and a lagoon.

At nearby Walberswick the proceeds of the British Open Crabbing Championship are donated to the Sea Wall Defence Fund. Fortunately for the fund the championship attracts over a thousand participants each year and is the largest crabbing competition in the world. Everyone pays a pound and has 30 minutes to catch the largest possible crab. You're only allowed to use a simple line and bait and the casting techniques and bait recipes are closely guarded secrets. This is an addictive sport that children, in particular, will love, so get here early in the season and start practising!

Suffolk

179 SHINGLE STREET, HOLLESLEY
A remote shingle beach with Martello towers. Strong currents at river mouth.

→ From Woodbridge (A12) take A1152 2 miles, then B1083 dir Sutton 1km before turning L across Sutton Common to reach Hollesley, 4 miles. Go over crossroads and follow narrow lanes 2 miles to Shingle Street (IP12 3BE). Initial beach, before the cottages, has currents so continue on and park closer to the Martello tower (700m).
15 mins, 52.0331, 1.4516 🏕️🏔️

180 BUTLEY RIVER, ORFORD
Wooden jetty on tidal creek among fields.

→ Take Gedgrave Road (Orford) 2 miles then bear R (cycle path sign) down to Butley River (500m) and bear L to ferry.
15 mins, 52.0804, 1.4905 🍴

181 ORFORD NESS, ORDFORD
Pretty Orford with ferry across to the mysterious military 'ness' and beach (NT).

→ Follow paths to the black tower. Wild, steep shingle beach. Only swim in calm seas and stay close to shore.
40 mins, 52.0858, 1.5788 🚶🏕️🏔️

182 IKEN CLIFF, SNAPE
Quiet, old-world tidal backwater beach. HT swim in water warmed over hot mud.

→ Turn off B1069 just S of Snape Maltings, signed Orford. Then L after a mile (Iken), first L to picnic parking then bear R 200m. Good 🏔️ High House Fruit Farm, Sudbourne (IP12 2BL, 01394 450263).
5 mins, 52.1511, 1.5110 ⛴️🏔️

183 THE HAVEN, ALDEBURGH
Beautiful medieval Aldeburgh's shingle beach is never too crowded and offers great food. Or head N for remote beach.

→ For fish and chips 🍴 try 226 High Street (IP15 5DB). Head 1 mile N by road to the scallop-shell sculpture or 1 mile S by road to the Martello tower. Funky Thorpeness is 2 miles N.
5 mins, 52.1606, 1.6057 🅱️

184 DUNWICH HEATH, MINSMERE
Beautiful sand and shingle beach bordered by lagoons, heather and birdlife.

→ 1 mile W of Dunwich (🍺 Ship Inn IP17 3DT, 01728 648219) turn L signed Dunwich Heath. Continue 1½ miles past

excellent 🏔️ Beach View / Cliff House (IP17 3DQ, 01728 648282) to NT car park with 🍴 tea room (01728 648501).
5 mins, 52.2506, 1.6290 🌊

185 WALBERSWICK AND MARSHES
Arty Walberswick has a sandy village beach with dunes and vast wild marshes.

→ Tiny seasonal 🏔️ on the beach. The Anchor is the best 🍺 with excellent beer / food (IP18 6UA, 01502 722112). Crabbing competitions take place in the shallow channels behind the beach. Swim in the Blyth upriver from the row-boat ferry jetty, or near the windmill on Tinker's Marshes (2km). Head W on Lodge Road and take bridleway on L after ¾ mile for really wild beach, 20 mins, beyond ruined wind pump.
2 mins, 52.3112, 1.6665 🚶🏔️

186 COVEHITHE, SOUTHWOLD
Ruined church on cliffs above wild beach.

→ From Wrentham (A12) turn off for Covehithe. Take footpath R, 100m before church (NR34 7JW). Follow field edge to beach, next to Covehithe Broad.
15 mins, 52.3669, 1.7048 🏔️

Horsey Gap

East Norfolk: Blakeney and Stiffkey

North-east Norfolk has miles of coast shaped and funnelled into creek-filled harbours, shingle spits and towering dunes. Here you can swim with seals, ride the tides, wade out to uninhabited islands and return home with cockles and samphire for supper.

I began my explorations late one night at Horsey Corner, a remote lane that leads down through scrub to a car park among sand hills. The sea was thrashing about in the keen wind as I set up my billowing tent. That short summer night brought whistling rain, but as dawn broke the sky was blue, the sun was shining and the surf was up, peaked with silver caps.

These north-eastern beaches take the full brunt of the prevailing winds and tides from the North Sea. This is where longshore drift hits full on, turning left to drag south to the Thames or right to run into the Wash. Feeling hot in the tent and with the sun beating down, I ran to the beach, silky sand underfoot, but swell still crashing on the groynes. The sideways tow was instant, dragging me along the beach at about three knots. As I struggled with the waves a seal popped up almost within reach and swam with me and around me, appearing and disappearing. For about five minutes it watched me wide-eyed as it ducked in and out of the waves.

Two miles up the beach at remote Waxham – just a medieval barn, church and farm shop – I warmed up with tea and creamy

193

191

192

scrambled eggs and heard stories of the North Sea flood of 1953. A freak combination of tides and winds came together to create the worst peacetime disaster in British history. Over 500 people died and 1,000 miles of coastline were devastated as a huge wall of water surged down. Here at Waxham and Sea Palling the dunes were breached and a church entirely washed away. Today a concrete sea wall extends along the entire Norfolk coast; its huge iron sea gates can be clamped shut at a moment's notice. From here all the way to Blakeney along the winding B1159 coast road you'll find evidence of the sea's gradual onslaught. This is a battered, conquered coastline with whole villages relentlessly eroded, cliffs crumbling and tree-stumps floating – a place of shipwrecks and lighthouses but not one single safe harbour.

A sense of relief returns for the sailor, and swimmer, from Cley beach onwards. The coast turns west and a succession of creeks offers refuge. Harbours since medieval times, these inland quays or 'staithes' are reached via tortuous winding inland tidal channels that empty and fill with the ebb and flow. At Blakeney, one of the finest and richest villages in Norfolk, local boys make good use of these flows, swimming and floating up the channel as the tide comes in. At Morston, now the main harbour for boat trips to see the seals, you can make the long walk out across the harbour's low-tide marsh and cockle beds to swim in the channel off Blakeney Point. Here, among the shingle and sand and against a backdrop of elegant old lifeboat houses, you will be closely observed by basking seals.

A simpler route to Blakeney Point is via Stiffkey, below the popular campsite. This walk borders Patch Pit Creek with its six wooden footbridges, and then heads out for a mile across the low-tide sands. The sea is so far away and so shallow that the best places to swim here are the creeks. At high tide you can swim anywhere, but at low tide head for Stiffkey pool, which is always reliably deep. Watch children jump and slide in this endless flat land, muddy samphire marshes on one side, sand flats stretching out on the other – a true interface between land, sky and sea.

East Norfolk: Blakeney and Stiffkey

187 HORSEY GAP

Remote NT beach, with 4 miles of dunes and heath between Winterton and Waxham. Seals regularly swim here.

→ ¾ mile N of Horsey turn R at sharp L bend down unmarked track (NR29 4EQ). ▲ Walnut Farm (NR12 0EG, 01692 598217) or beach-side ▲ Waxham (NR29 4EJ, 01692 598325) just beyond.

3 mins, 52.7593, 1.6534

188 WAXHAM, SEA PALLING

Historic Great Barn with excellent cafe. Sandy lane leads through dunes to beach.

→ 2 miles beyond Horsey. 🍴 (NR12 0EE, 01692 598824). Adjacent Sea Palling is much busier (jet-skis) with offshore rock reefs and artificial coves for swimming.

10 mins, 52.7801, 1.6203

189 NORTH GAP, ECCLES

Dunes, sandy bays and tombolos out to the new rock island breakwaters.

→ From Lessingham (Happisburgh Rd) turn off for Eccles then third L, signed North Gap (limited parking at end).

5 mins, 52.8037, 1.5786 🅱

190 OVERSTRAND, CROMER

Seasonal beach campsite in quiet village.

→ From Cromer Rd, follow Paul's Lane opp school, to Beach Close on L after ½ mile, by car park (NR27 0PJ, 01507 343909). If closed, try ▲ Woodhill Park, East Runton, Cromer (NR27 9PX, 01263 512 242).

1 mins, 52.9210, 1.3394 💬 🅱

191 SALTHOUSE MARSHES, CLEY

Quiet shingle sand beach. Nature reserve.

→ 100m E from popular 🍴 Dun Cow (NR25 7XA, 01263 740467) find beach footpath opp Grouts Ln, through nature reserve. Also Cley beach with parking (NR25 7RY). ▲ Foxhills on Weybourne Rd (NR25 7EH, 01263 588253)

10 mins, 52.9570, 1.0921

192 BLAKENEY POINT POOL

Dramatic low-tide walk across the cockle beds and salt marshes to sand banks and pool at Blakeney Point. Many seals.

→ Know your tides. Set off 1-2 hrs before LT. From Morston harbour (A149) follow the path along the creek N, past the boats, crossing two tributary footbridges (500m),

then curving L to skirt the edge of Morston salt marshes. Continue for ¾ mile with Blakeney Channel on your R. Once well past the old lifeboat station on opposite (N) bank, bear off path R towards Blakeney Point, across cockles, mud, sands and shallow water for ¾ mile. Reach the steep sand banks of the point and continue on to find a place to swim in the deep pool as the channel turns N out to sea. Never approach seals on foot: allow them to come to you in the water.

40 mins, 52.9696, 0.9583 ▲ 🏖 📷

193 STIFFKEY, GARBOROUGH CREEK

Popular LT swimming hole in the tidal creeks of Stiffkey marshes and flats.

→ Leave Stiffkey dir Wells, and turn R after 🍴 Red Lion (NR23 1AJ, 01328 830552) into The Greenway. Pass Highsand Creek ▲ (NR23 1QF, 01328 830235) and park at bottom of track (700m). Bear R (E) along woods 700m, joining Garborough Patch Pit Creek, then follow path to L, crossing six mini footbridges, to arrive at sand flats. Follow creek (L) 200m to find sharp bend and pool to the R. Mud on L side, sand on R.

20 mins, 52.9634, 0.9366 ▲ 🍴 💬

West Norfolk: Burnham to Brancaster

Scolt Head is Britain's very own desert island. A whaleback of white sand and dune hills, decked with green marram grass, it is accessible only by small sailing boat or by swimming.

To the north of the island is the sea but the south side is a network of snaking sandy channels and pools which, with the help of a little local knowledge, you can navigate. The best routes out are from Burnham Overy Staithe, one of the prettiest harbours on this coast and also where Nelson, whose father was a rector at nearby Burnham Thorpe, learned to swim and sail. The raised path follows the right-hand side of the creek up to Burnham beach, a dazzling stretch of sand with panoramic views from the dunes atop Gun Hill. A channel empties across the beach to make a warm paddling and swimming pool at low tide, but head west up the beach to arrive at the deep pool that separates you from Scolt Head Island. Brightly coloured dinghies are stored safe on the Island's sands opposite: this is a favourite local swimming hole and a sheltered spot for learning to canoe and sail. It makes a great swimming pool on a turning or rising tide but watch out for seaward currents on a spring falling tide.

The Island is also accessible from Burnham Overy Staithe at low tide via the old cockle path used by cockle pickers on the creek's left bank. The journey consists of a shallow wade, then a very muddy path – great fun in bare feet – with several mud

195

198

195

slides made by children along the way. The flows up and down the creek here are relatively gentle and safe, so if you have never ridden a tide, this is a a great place to learn. In one spot the creek almost meets one of its upper tributaries, in a tight meander. Hop out of the water, cross the grass, and jump back in its upper reaches for another tidally assisted circuit. You can keep going round until the tide turns.

The west side of Scolt Head Island is more remote and the channel deeper and larger than that at Burnham Overy Staithe, owing to the much larger body of water that rushes in and out. From Brancaster you can see the iconic shipwreck of the 1894 *SS Vina* steamship, sitting like a beacon on the western edge of the island. Originally used for trade with Baltic ports, *SS Vina* was sunk on the sand flats by the military in 1944 for use as a target for bombing practice. Every day the waters reveal and then submerge the wreck as they ebb and flow across the sand flats. Her mast is, in fact, a beacon and the great limpet-fringed holes in her midriff and broken, rusting hull are a stark reminder of the power of the sea,

Visiting the ship from Brancaster beach is a great adventure, but one that requires planning and caution. As with many of the channel swims in this chapter, understanding the flow of the tides will create a deeper connection to the wild Norfolk world between land and sea. The channel that crosses Brancaster beach is deep (and fun to swim in at low tide) but there is also a ford where it becomes shallow at low tide and from there it's just a short splash and 300 yards to the wreck.

When I first made this crossing my guide taught me three golden rules about channels. First, always set off two hours before low tide and ensure the channel is still flowing to the sea as you cross. Second, mark your crossing point in the sand using a stick well above the water level, in case the rising tide makes finding your fording point difficult on the return. Third, if you miscalculate the tide times and are forced to swim, don't panic and don't fight the current. The rising tide will be taking you into harbour not out to sea, and you will still be able to swim across the channel and reach the safety of the landward side upstream.

West Norfolk: Burnham to Brancaster

194 HOLKHAM BEACH

A huge expanse of forest-backed sand and dune. Good swimming only at HT.

→ Turn R 1½ miles W of Wells (A149) and park in Lady Ann's Drive (NR23 1RJ) opp The Victoria. Cross dunes through forest. Bear L for naturist section and to connect to Burnham Beach (2 miles). Bear R for forested stretch to Wells. ⓘ Victoria (NR23 1RG, 01328 711008) gastro-pub with rooms.

15 mins, 52.9758, 0.8032 🅱 ⊗

195 BURNHAM BEACH

Creek path with swimming holes and mud slides leads to superb dunes and beach with access to Scolt Head Island.

→ Park in Burnham Overy Staithe harbour (PE31 8JE). Bear R on path along E edge (R bank) of Overy Creek passing various swimming holes / mud slides. Continue 1½ miles to high white sand dunes and beach below. Swim in the channel or at sea edge. Take care at HT ebb as the emptying channel can create a strong L to R seaward current.

35 mins, 52.9789, 0.7663 🅰 🅰

196 SCOLT HEAD ISLAND EAST

Classic swimming and sailing spot on desert island.

→ Bear L (300m) along Burnham beach to reach pool opposite Scolt Head Island E and swim across. Or reach beach from the harbour at LT/MT via the 'cockle path'. Wade across harbour, follow muddy path ¾ mile N, crossing bridge, reaching flats. Turn L for 'creek riding' or straight on for deep wade to Scolt Head beach.

20 mins, 52.9779, 0.7502 🅰

197 BRANCASTER BEACH

White beach with views to Scolt Head west and wreck of SS Vina. Deep channel at E end of beach makes a great swimming pool at LT.

→ Brancaster is 4 miles W of Burnham Overy Staithe on A149. Turn R at church, just after ⓘ The Ship (PE31 8AP, 01485 210333) and park at golf club (PE31 8AX). Also ⓘ Jolly Sailors (PE31 8BJ, 01485 210314) and good views from ⓘ White Horse (PE31 8BY, 01485 210262) in Brancaster Staithe.

5 mins, 52.9755, 0.6362 ⬇ 🅰

198 SCOLT HEAD WEST, BRANCASTER

Crossing to SS Vina wreck/Scolt Head Island West is possible with extreme care.

→ Shallowest ford is at far E end of Brancaster beach (1 mile from clubhouse) on cockle beds, beyond wreck and between transmitter and church tower landmarks. Depart 1-2 hours before LT and ford the channel while water is still flowing seaward. Mark the best crossing point in sand to assist your return.

60 mins, 52.9852, 0.6543 🅰 ◨

199 HOLME DUNES, THORNHAM

Beautiful remote beach with lake and forest.

→ 2 miles W of Brancaster (A149) turn R into Staithe Lane and continue 1 mile to park at end (PE36 6LT). Bear L then R along marshes to dunes and lake. Good swimming at all tides with deeper tidal channel on R. ⓘ Lifeboat Inn (PE36 6LT, 01485 512236) with rooms.

20 mins, 52.9763, 0.5570 🅰 🅰 🅻

231 Dunstanburgh Castle

North

The famous Northumberland coast has some of the grandest, wildest beaches in Britain, bordered by ancient castles and holy islands. To the south the extensive dunes and skyscapes of Lincolnshire and Cumbria contrast with the dramatic caves at Flamborough Head and the high cliffs of the Yorkshire Moors. Here you will find secluded wykes, goblin holes and settings for stories of *Count Dracula*.

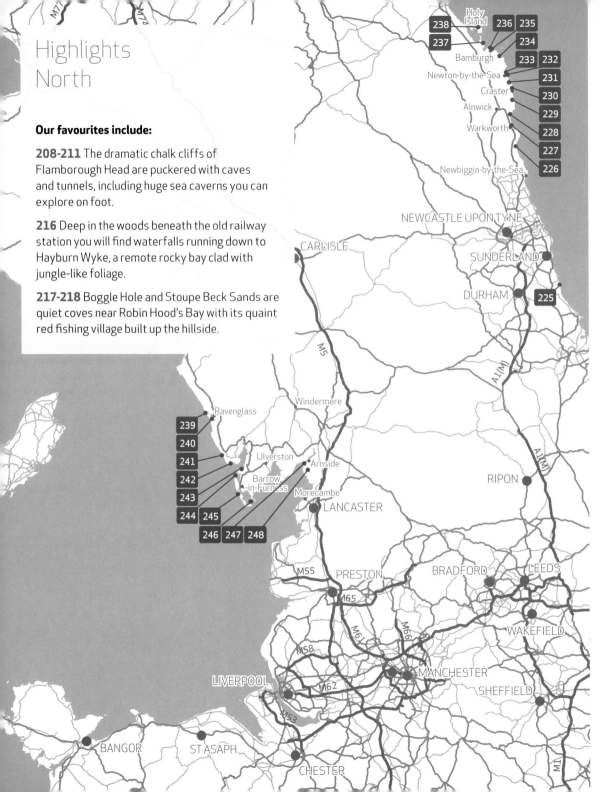

Highlights
North

Our favourites include:

208-211 The dramatic chalk cliffs of Flamborough Head are puckered with caves and tunnels, including huge sea caverns you can explore on foot.

216 Deep in the woods beneath the old railway station you will find waterfalls running down to Hayburn Wyke, a remote rocky bay clad with jungle-like foliage.

217-218 Boggle Hole and Stoupe Beck Sands are quiet coves near Robin Hood's Bay with its quaint red fishing village built up the hillside.

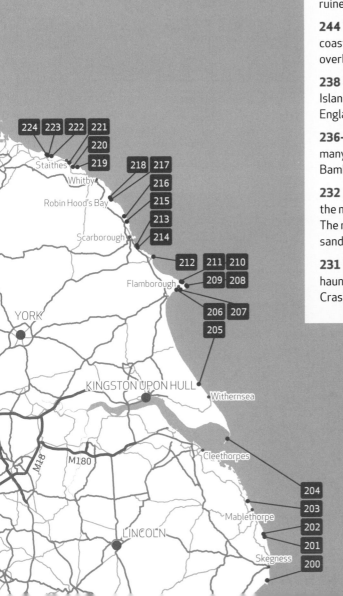

220 At Runswick Bay the long stretch of sand has a backdrop of high cliffs with 'Hob Hole' caves – old hobgoblin lairs.

223 Skinningrove is a run-down old mine village. It attracts few visitors but has a stunning beach and an amazing old pier.

346 Visit the King of Piel with his pub and ruined castle on Piel Island.

244 This remote sand beach on the north coast of Walney Island has a deep tidal pool overlooked by Black Combe in the Lake District.

238 Cross the tidal causeway and visit Holy Island (Lindisfarne), birthplace of Christianity in England.

236-237 Take a refreshing dip in one of the many beautiful rock pools near dramatic Bamburgh Castle's beach.

232 Football Hole cove is set between two of the most beautiful bays in Northumberland. The nearby Ship Inn serves excellent crab sandwiches.

231 Dunstanburgh Castle is one of the most haunting ruins on the coast and is close to Craster village, famous for its seafood.

theddlethorpe

Lincolnshire and Humber

Lincolnshire, famous for its vast skies and endless beaches, is the site of Britain's first official cloud-spotting station, complete with parabolic mirrors, roof-top loungers and 'cloud-bar' menu. There are also dunes and wildflower meadows galore at Gibraltar Point and Theddlethorpe.

When the Cloud Appreciation Society was established in 2005 few thought it would develop such a cult following. With a manifesto pledging to fight the banality of 'blue-sky thinking' it aims to rekindle an appreciation of Britain's clouds and skyscapes. What better place than Lincolnshire – where endless fens merge with marine horizons inspiring painters and stargazers alike – to take a disused beach hut and construct a rooftop observatory. Anderby Creek is one of five beach access points along the surprisingly empty stretch from Skegness to Mablethorpe. Here, at this rather jaded and low-key coastal spot, you'll find a larch Cloud Bar. Instead of stools there are sky loungers, instead of a cocktail menu there's a cloud menu. Choose a cloud you'd like to see, grab yourself one of the parabolic mirrors on hinges then lie back and search the sky until your chosen cloud floats into view above you.

This isn't the only wacky venture to take root on this coast. In 1936 ex-showman Billy Butlin established Britain's first seaside holiday camp here, and it's still going strong. More recently, in Mablethorpe, the Bathing Beauties Festival was established: not a pageant for beautiful bodies but a line-up of

200

202

201

colourful and quirky beach huts, with cabins and shacks of all kinds, celebrated here each year.

For simpler pleasures Gibraltar Point Nature Reserve offers rare seasonal flowers such as yellow lady's bedstraw, cowslip and the tiny white, meadow saxifrage. Flocks of migrating birds also gather here: up to 10,000 dunlins at a time may break from their migration, descend from the clouds and come to feed upon the shore. The sea here is shallow but when you run out through the breakers – the huge expanse of the Wash to the south, dunes and meadows behind – you're reminded of the immensity of nature and the vast tracts of open space still left in Britain.

To the north at Theddlethorpe St Helen there are more dunes and an undulating beach with deep, wide furrows, so the depth can vary quite suddenly and rips can develop in rough conditions. It's best to swim here at low tide when large sandy bathing channels emerge, or on a rising tide as the channels fill from the sea. The dunes extend for five miles and are prettiest in midsummer when the sea buckthorn bushes bear golden berries and the sea pea forms violet carpets. In spring, whitethroats and linnets breed in the hawthorn scrub and skylarks nest on the saltmarshes. And at night the rare natterjack toads begin to search for each other with loud booming calls.

Looking north towards the Humber Estuary, it's almost possible to make out the southern tip of Yorkshire – Spurn Head, a low, narrow three-mile spit of beach and shingle growing inexorably south-westwards into the sea. Gaining several yards per year by 'recycling' material eroded from further up the coast, it represents a perfect balance between destruction and deposition. A toll road snakes through the dunes and marsh flats, there is a beach with groynes on the east-facing side, and at the very tip of the spit are two abandoned lighthouses. This location, right out at sea, is a windy place on most days and once in the water you can feel the pull of the swell tugging you southwards. But when the sun is shining and the surface of the sea lies flat and reflective, the huge expanse of water and sky all around you is humbling.

201

Lincolnshire and Humber

200 GIBRALTAR POINT, SKEGNESS

3 miles of fine sandy beach with gently shelving sea close to Skegness. Accessed via a long walk over nature reserve with dunes and ponds.

→ Entering Skegness from Boston A52, at train station gyratory take exit for sea front, then turn R after church (700m) into Drummond Rd. Continue straight (S) out of town for 2 miles, via Gibraltar Rd, to end of golf course. Park in the beach car park (L), ¾ mile before visitor centre. Follow path past mere and lagoons, over Mill Hill, and down to sands. Some L–R cross-shore current in surf conditions. Home to huge numbers of breeding, wintering and migratory bird species often in vast flocks; also natterjack toads and pyramid orchids. The visitor centre includes the Wild Coast exhibition, Nature Discovery Centre, shop and ⬛ Point Café, open every day 11–4 (PE24 4SU, 01507 526667). ⬛ Salem Bridge Brewery windmill pub in nearby Wainfleet (PE24 4JE, 01754 882009).
20 mins, 53.1002, 0.3387 🚶⛺️⛺️

201 WOLLA BANK, ANDERBY

A 5-mile stretch of undeveloped coastline N from Chapel St Leonards, accessed via breaks in the sea wall. Fine sands, some dunes and good swimming.

→ Continue N of Skegness (A52 coast road) past Butlins and Ingoldmells, and turn R into and through Chapel St Leonards after 4 miles. Follow Skegness Rd, Church Lane, St Leonard's Drive to Chapel Point, 2 miles, with its greasy-spoon ⬛ Point Café by beach (PE24 5UZ, 01754 871670). Continue N on coast road 1½ miles to remote Wolla Bank beach, a mile before Anderby Creek (PE24 5XT).
2 mins, 53.2488, 0.3317 ⛺️

202 ANDERBY CREEK

Small rural resort with Cloud Bar for sky-gazing (parabolic mirrors and loungers on top of a larch-clad hut).

→ Continue a mile from Wolla Bank. The tiny ⛺️ Grove is 10 mins walk from the beach on Sea Road (PE24 5XY, 07415 230847).
2 mins, 53.2582, 0.3266 🐦

203 THEDDLETHORPE, MABLETHORPE

Vast expanse of sand and dunes with wood and heath in nature reserve. Some channels cross the beach to create warm tidal pools. Seaward currents on outgoing tide; safest on rising tide.

→ Take A1031 N from Mablethorpe. After 2 miles reach Theddlethorpe St Helen (atmospheric thatched ⬛ Kings Head LN12 1PB, 01507 339798). From A1031 turn R (LN12 1NW, Sea Lane) then R again (Crook Bank) to parking after 1 mile. Mablethorpe holds a Bathing Beauties Beach Hut Festival in September.
10 mins, 53.3720, 0.2396 ⛺️⛺️⛺️

204 SPURN HEAD, WITHERNSEA

Extraordinary, 5 mile sand and shingle spit growing into mouth of Humber. Strong currents run S down shore in surf conditions, so don't swim from S end.

→ From Hull take A1033 to Patrington, then B1445 to Easington. Toll road leads to lighthouse (HU12 0UG). Good ⛺️ Elmtree Farm, Holmpton (HU19 2QR, 01964 630957).
2 mins, 53.5885, 0.1353 ⛺️⛺️⛺️

Cathedral Cave

Flamborough Head and Filey Brigg

Protected by high cliffs, deep caves and steep coves Flamborough Head – literally the 'dart-shaped headland' – has long been a place of defence and retreat.

An ancient earth wall and ditch still leads down through woody glades to the sheltered, chalk-pebbled beach at Danes Dyke – a relic of King Ida's Viking invasion of the seventh century. Today the area is a popular holiday destination with caravan sites and beach car parks, but don't be put off. If you persevere you will soon discover its celebrated wild caves and archways.

It was an early summer evening when I first visited. The cliff walls of Thornwick Bay are riddled with numerous dark caves and I decided to reach one by swimming across the bay. Through the calm ripples, the chalky reef beneath me was casting a blue light amid the turquoise haze. As I swam nearer, seaweed forests floated in the water below and the cave walls loomed up, displaying pastel-pink and white hues, streaked with green algae. I began to explore, half in the water and half out of it, like some primordial wading creature. I counted eight caves along this cliff wall and, peering into their dim recesses, partly illuminated by shafts of light, I realised the caves were all interconnected and formed a labyrinth of deep passages that was, sadly, too dark and cold to explore.

209

208

210

Flamborough Head has more cave habitats than any other place in Britain and some extend underground for more than 50 yards. It also has some of the largest populations of nesting birds: gannets, guillemots, kittiwakes, puffins, razorbills, fulmars, herring gulls and shags gather on the sides of the sheer cliffs around Bempton and Scale Nab rock arch, a few miles to the north. From Thornwick Bay an eroded coastal footpath leads out on to adjacent Thornwick Nab, a headland of rock platforms and ledges now pitted with thousands of glinting rock pools. The chalky rock here, laid down millions of years ago, is composed of the corpses of trillions of tiny white-shelled sea creatures that lived in much warmer seas.

At North Landing, the next cove towards the head, a steep slipway leads from the café and car park to a pebble beach. More than 80 fishing boats – known locally as 'cobbles' – used to operate from this cove, though today's boats are mainly used for pleasure trips. The bay boasts around 20 interconnected caves and many, unlike those at Thornwick Bay, are accessible on foot at low tide. The most impressive among them is Cathedral Cave, a short scramble of about 100 yards along the right-hand edge of the bay. The entrance leads into the back of a massive cavern, which then shelves down to a large, arched opening facing out to sea.

Selwicks Bay, another mile down the coast path, is a popular bathing spot with a lighthouse and various cafés. To the right of the bay a scramble and swim leads to a cavern with a blowhole, formed when the roof of the sea cave collapsed. Further to the south, a few hundred yards along the footpath, is High Stacks, an isolated headland with a sea arch that is almost a stack.

The tidal currents can be ferocious in the open sea around Flamborough – the headland serves to 'funnel' the tidal flows. If you aren't a strong, experienced swimmer stay within the relative safety of the bays and coves since these are protected from the currents. If you choose to venture out under the cliffs chose a neap tide and go when the tide is on the turn. Remember that the tide flows from the north as it is rising (the flood), and from the south as it is lowering (the ebb). Do take care.

Flamborough Head and Filey Brigg

205 MONKWITH, TUNSTALL
Rapidly eroding cliffs, miles of deserted shingle sand. Coast road falling into sea.
→ From Tunstall (5 miles N of Withernsea) follow lane past church (HU12 0JF) as far as you can go, then scramble down cliffs.
5 mins, 53.7794, -0.0241 🏔️ 🏖️

206 DANES' DYKES, FLAMBOROUGH
Walk down through woods along ancient defensive Danes' Dyke to sand beach with large white cobbles.
→ 2 miles E of Bridlington on B1255, car park signed on R (YO15 1AA). Or 2 mile walk from Bridlington's North Sands.
15 mins, 54.1043, -0.1413 🚶

207 SOUTH LANDING, FLAMBOROUGH
Sand and chalk cobbles. Lifeboat station.
→ Signed on R from Flamborough village (YO15 1AE). Lifeboat visitor centre.
1 min, 54.1045, -0.1174 🚗 🅱️ 🏖️

208 HIGH STACKS, FLAMBOROUGH HD
Isolated pebble cove with sea arch.
→ 500m to the S of Selwicks (below) via

coast path. Descend on S side. Beware tidal races; choose slack water, neap tides.
10 mins, 54.1148, -0.0770 🏖️ 🏔️ 🏔️ 🏊

209 SELWICKS BAY, FLAMBOROUGH HD
Pronounced 'Selix', a wide popular sandy bay with rock pools galore plus several secret coves, tunnels and caves.
→ From Flamborough follow signs to Flamborough Head (2 miles) and park by 🍴 lighthouse/cafe (YO15 1AR, 01262 851020). On beach bear L and scramble round into deep inlet cove with further tunnel out to sea. Further swims/ scrambles around the headland and many more coves. At the R end of beach a LT scramble (HT swim) leads to a cave with skylight (100m).
5 mins, 54.1183, -0.0818 🏔️ 🏊 🔵 🅱️

210 CATHEDRAL CAVE, NORTH LANDING
A popular white chalk cove with HT sand, LT pebbles. Giant Cathedral Cave on R.
→ From Flamborough follow signs to North Landing (1 mile). Park by café (YO15 1BJ). Plenty of rock pools and caves to explore on L but largest cave is on R, after first

inlet (50m) beyond arch. The narrow cave entrance leads to a major cavern with access to sea. Strong tidal races offshore, so stay close if you swim.
5 mins, 54.1300, -0.1055 🏔️ 🏊 🏔️

211 THORNWICK BAY, NORTH LANDING
Riddled with caves, particularly on E side. Walk around to Thornwick Nab, the eroded headland of pyramids to L, to find rock arch plus many ledges and inlets.
→ Just to the NW of North Landing. Basic 🏔️ Wold Farm, Bempton (YO15 1AT, 01262 850536) is a mile W along coast.
15 mins, 54.1317, -0.1133 🏊 🏖️

212 FILEY BRIGG, FILEY
Arch on Filey Brigg, accessible by boat
→ Dramatic, narrow headland descends to many rock ledges and pools. Follow signs for Country Park from Filey (YO14 9ET). Very difficult LT scramble W along N base of cliffs leads to Black Hole rock arch (boat required). Cliff-side 🏔️ Crow's Nest, Gristhorpe (YO14 9PS, 01723 582206).
25 mins, 54.2192, -0.2745 🏖️ 🏊

213 Cornelian Bay

North Yorkshire: Scarborough and Robin Hood's Bay

Scarborough, the great Yorkshire resort that introduced sea bathing and the bathing machine, is the gateway to a dramatic coastline of high cliffs, goblin coves, rocky bays known as 'wykes', and the picture-perfect old smuggling village of Robin Hood's Bay.

Cloughton Wyke is one of the area's most secret and verdant coves and can be found just a few miles north of Scarborough down a narrow, dead-end lane. A short walk leads to a stream, and then a steep path descends into a rocky bay with a backdrop of steep cliffs and vegetation. Water drips from the deeply layered, fern-covered rock face, and huge green boulders mark the site of past cliff falls. On a calm day the water is clear and it's a quiet place to snorkel among the ledges or look for the fossils of ammonites, sea-lilies and fish-lizards, for which this Jurassic coast is well known.

About two miles to the north, Hayburn Wyke, a wider bay, is hidden beneath a wooded valley and a double waterfall. Bracken and mistletoe run rampant on the slopes above and when the sea is calm this is a magical place to swim and admire strata upon strata of sandstone, mudstone and ironstone laid down through Yorkshire's various geological incarnations – desert, river basin, forest and ice sheet. The old railway station above the Hayburn Wyke Hotel was a minor stop on the Scarborough to Whitby railway line, now a stunning cycle route.

Old rolling stock in the sidings was turned into self-catering 'camping coaches' for holidaymakers, with fresh eggs supplied by the local farmer. The coaches proved so popular with families that camping continued until well after the railway line eventually closed.

215

218

216

This whole area attained its peak of popularity in Victorian times, but Scarborough first attracted tourists in the early seventeenth century when a local naturalist discovered mineral springs, which then featured in Dr Robert Wittie's 1660 book on British spas. Soon health-conscious bathers were venturing on to the sands and into the sea as well. Over the next 200 years doctors continued to promote the health benefits of sea bathing, which they recommended was performed naked so the skin could more readily absorb the water's beneficial qualities. An entire industry grew up around bathing machines, attendants and operators. Bathing was considered particularly good for chest infections and the young Anne Brontë took the waters on numerous occasions to improve her deteriorating health. During the Victorian era the resort flourished. Bathing for leisure replaced bathing for health, bathing suits replaced bathing machines and, when Scarborough was finally connected to York by railway and the Grand Spa Hotel opened (at that time one of the biggest hotels in the world), Scarborough became the undisputed queen of British watering holes, even surpassing its celebrated southern rival, Brighton.

Such was Scarborough's success that developers were keen to open hotels and create new settlements along the shore. To the north at the vertiginous Ravenscar Cliff, the highest point on the Yorkshire coastline, a plan was laid out for an entire resort with views over Robin Hood's Bay and its tightly packed smuggling village. (This Robin Hood wasn't the legendary hero from Sherwood Forest but a local name given to forest spirits and elves who were said to inhabit the wooded cliffs, coasts and coves.) The investors, however, pulled out, fearful of potential cliff erosion and ground instability, and the secluded woody beaches of Stoupe Beck Sands and Boggle or 'Goblins' Hole still remain likely places to meet the tree sprites. Walk a mile or two beneath the cliffs at low water from Robin Hood's Bay village or drop down on country lanes from Ravenscar to Stoupe Beck Sands. You can swim from the sand or snorkel around the rocky ledges, with the pretty red-tiled village making a perfect backdrop.

217

North Yorkshire: Scarborough and Robin Hood's Bay

213 CORNELIAN BAY, SCARBOROUGH
Long sand beach beneath forested cliffs with deep rock pools and WW2 ruins.

→ From A165 South Cliff roundabout take Filey Rd, then L into Cornelian Dr (YO11 3AL). Take second L to pumping station. Bear L on coast path and find wide gravel track down to beach, rough at end.
10 mins, 54.2592, -0.3741 🅻🅰🅰

214 CAYTON CLIFF, OSGODBY POINT
Beautiful sand bay below wooded cliffs.

→ Continue SE along Filey Road to find footpath on L next to Knipe Point homes (YO11 3JT). Parking next R, Osgodby Way. At coast path bear R then first L to beach.
15 mins, 54.2515, -0.3682 🅻

215 CLOUGHTON WYKE, CLOUGHTON
Remote, verdant but rocky bay with cobbles and rock ledges. Tricky descent.

→ From Cloughton A171 turn onto Newlands Rd (YO13 0AP, signed Staintondale) then imediately R into Newlands Lane. Park at road end. Descend to coast path and bear R for 500m to find stream flowing down to Cloughton Wyke.

Follow path down stream, using chains to help you down slippery ledges. Explore far R of bay to find ledges good for snorkelling. Good access from Cycle Route 1.
15 mins, 54.3409, -0.4307 🅻🤿

216 HAYBURN WYKE, CLOUGHTON
Stony bay set beneath jungle-like foliage with double waterfall. Beautiful walk down from hotel through glens.

→ Turn off A171 at Cloughton as for Cloughton Wyke (see above) but continue towards Staintondale. After 1½ miles turn R for 🍺 Hayburn Wyke Inn (YO13 0AU, 01723 870202). Beach path is just before car park on R. Follow this across fields down to NT woodland (200m), and path down to sea (200m). Continue on Ravenscar Rd 4 miles for a posh drink with a view at 🍺 Raven Hall Hotel (YO13 0ET, 01723 870353). From here a 2 mile walk leads along coast down to Stoupe Beck Sands (below), or return to the corner by ruined windmill and take the dead-end road, signed to Stoupe Brow, for 2 miles. Good access from Cycle Route 1.
20 mins, 54.3589, -0.4454 🅰🤿🍺🚶

217 STOUPE BECK SANDS, ROBIN H B
Small sandy stretch in most remote section of Robin Hood's Bay.

→ As above, continue to Stoupe Bank Farm pay parking, then 300m down pretty path and steps, or from Boggle Hole (below).
10 mins, 54.4174, -0.5226 🅰🅰🚶🚲

218 BOGGLE HOLE, ROBIN H B
Small, sheltered sandy cove at the bottom of a wooded valley. Wave-cut platform for snorkelling and swimming.

→ 4 miles N of Cloughton (A171) take R signed Boggle Hole. Continue 2½ miles to parking at corner (YO22 4UQ), where there is very basic camping at 🅰 Mill Beck Farm in their field down the track. Continue on foot to 🅰 Boggle Hole Youth Hostel (YO22 4UQ, 0845 3719504) and cove. Walk L under cliffs ½ mile at LT to reach village of **Robin Hood's Bay** (delightful 🍺 Laurel YO22 4SE, 01947 880400). Walk R ½ mile to reach Stoupe Beck Sands. Nearby 🅰 Hook's House Farm (YO22 4PE, 01947 880283) or 🅰 Middlewood Farm (YO22 4UF, 01947 880414).
10 mins, 54.4242, -0.5284 🅱🅰

Kettleness

North Yorkshire: Whitby, Runswick and Skinningrove

A night-time cliff-top walk among the graves and ruins of Whitby Abbey may well have inspired Bram Stoker to write the celebrated story of Count Dracula, who survives a shipwreck and is washed up on the sands below.

In the book, the mystery ship Demeter is later recovered but the log shows that members of its crew have been gradually disappearing since the ship left Varna in Russia. Further examination of the ship's hold gives the reader an insight into the shipwrecked Count's dark passions: it is full of coffins. Is it a coincidence that a few years before Stoker wrote the book a ship, the *Demetrius*, ran on to the rocks near Whitby harbour and its cargo of coffins tumbled into the sea?

Other writers have also been inspired by Whitby. Melville's Moby Dick is set during the town's whaling boom in the late eighteenth century and you still pass through a whalebone arch when you enter it. The famous seafarer, Captain Cook, also lived and sailed from here. Today Whitby's sands are enjoyed by thousands of tourists, but leave the crowds behind as you head out to the wide, wild sweep of Runswick Bay. The village of the same name has a delightful and popular family beach with a fine café, but fewer people visit Kettleness at the southern end of the bay, reached by walking down winding narrow lanes past a remote chapel and farm. Here, the slippery mudstone and silvery-blue

143

221 Staithes

220

222

shale cliffs shimmer in the evening light, feathers of rock extend in an arc out to sea, a steep path leads down to the sands and a network of rough trails fans out across a lunar plateau bearing the scars of old alum mine workings.

Between the seventeenth and nineteenth centuries alum was one of the most important industrial chemicals in Britain, and was used to tan leather, make paper and dye fabric. One hundred tons of cliff shale had to be mined to extract a single ton of alum powder and the unpleasant process involved relentless kiln firing and then further treatment with pungent-smelling human urine. Local inhabitants supplied urine by means of a night-time jar system and stocks were supplemented by public urinals in Hull and London.

From Kettleness you can walk north towards Runswick Bay and pass the 'Hob Holes'. Said to be inhabited by hobgoblins, these are the remnants of tunnels from ancient mine workings for jet, a semi-precious stone that became popular when Queen Victoria wore it in mourning. More mine holes can be found beneath the high cliffs of Boulby via the sand and reef beach at Hummersea, beyond Staithes. The finest swimming, however, is at Skinningrove, another struggling mining community. Apparently, the village sits on top of more than 200 miles of old iron mines, many of them sites of catastrophic mining accidents. You can still explore some tunnels with the help of a guide, but beware, they are considered the most haunted mines in Britain.

More heartening is the superb and little-known bay at the bottom of the village – Cattersty Sands – with clear water and an old jetty built by the Skinningrove Iron Company in 1886 for loading ore on to steamers bound for Middlesbrough. Long since abandoned, the jetty is in good repair and adventurous swimmers can dive off it and swim in the deep water. There are plans to re-open the jetty as a visitor attraction, but funds have not yet been found. There's an air of decay about the whole of Skinningrove, but if you swim on a calm hot day you can see rippled sand beneath shimmering clear water that is as blue as the Mediterranean. On such days when local boys sail through the air as they practise their swallow dives, the place is vibrant again, its raw beauty a reminder of an industrial past long gone.

North Yorkshire: Whitby, Runswick and Skinningrove

219 KETTLENESS, GOLDSBOROUGH

Beach and rock scars beneath plateau cliffs with old mine ruins. Superb views.

→ 2 miles NW of Whitby (A174) turn R to Goldsborough just after Lythe. Bear R for Kettleness, past quirky bistro 🍴 Fox and Hounds (YO21 3RX, 01947 893372). Park at bottom near Kettleness Farm (YO21 3RY). By bench bear L on path through long grass (not coast path) down on to headland with landslips and mine workings. After 300m find very steep path L down landslip to beach. Rope provided for final descent.

15 mins, 54.5306, -0.7204 🏖️📷🏃

220 HOB HOLES, RUNSWICK BAY

Old mine tunnels and caves on beach.

→ Continue along A174 and turn R for pretty Runswick. Walk 500m S on sand, beyond sailing hut, to caves.

10 mins, 54.5318, -0.7482 🏖️

221 PORT MULGRAVE

Fascinating ruined harbour with rock and sand beach and fishermen's huts.

→ Turn at off A174 in Hinderwell, signed Port Mulgrave. Parking at end of road on cliff (TS13 5LH) after 1 mile, then descend on path. Sandiest at N end near old pier.

10 mins, 54.5467, -0.7693 🏃

222 HUMMERSEA, SKINNINGROVE

Dramatic, remote location under cliffs with old alum mine tunnels beneath cliffs. Rocky ledges and scars with sandy 'guts'. Very steep descent on stairs.

→ Turn off A174 in Loftus opp Golden Lion Hotel/church (TS13 4HG), down narrow North Rd. Continue over 1 mile to and through Hummersea Farm (TS13 4JH) and park by gate on L (200m). Follow track to coast path and steep NT steps to beach. A new 'gut' was blasted through the rocks to allow a sandy landing passage for boats. Explore R to find old gut and tunnels.

20 mins, 54.5702, -0.8770 🏖️

223 SKINNINGROVE JETTY AND SANDS

Old ironstone-mining town with beautiful sands and amazing old ruined quay.

→ As above, but turn L down lanes before Hummersea Farm to reach beach car park with tractors (TS13 4BJ). The jetty has deep, clear water over sand. Go to far end to find rusty steps down to water in R corner – difficult but not impossible. Eerie but interesting place, though watch out for old metalwork and uncovered hatches. Jetty good for fishing. Also visit Cleveland/Tom Leonard Mining Museum, with haunted tunnel tours (TS13 4AP, 01287 642877).

10 mins, 54.5729, -0.8992 🍴

224 CATTERSTY SANDS, SKINNINGROVE

Cross to far side of Skinningrove jetty to find immaculate stretch of empty beach.

→ A walk 3 miles W along the coast path will also bring you to Saltburn-by-the-Sea for the beautifully sited nautical-themed 🍺 Ship (TS12 1HF, 01287 622361).

10 mins, 54.5766, -0.9069

225 HAWTHORN HIVE, EASINGTON

Wild and remote sand shingle bay at end of woodland walk and stream.

→ Approach from Seaham on B1432 and turn L signed Hawthorn. Continue to road end (SR7 8SJ). Bear R on track, following purple footpath signs to coast/Dene, eventually passing beneath viaduct.

35 mins, 54.8063, -1.3117 🏃🏕️

231 Dunstanburgh Castle

South Northumberland: Druridge to Embleton

Our Northumberland cycle expedition picked up again beyond Seahouses at a tiny pub on the edge of empty Embleton Bay. The salt spray blowing in on a light midsummer breeze added the perfect seasoning to our lunch of crab sandwiches and ale.

The Ship Inn, low-beamed and cosy, sits in a whitewashed square of eighteenth-century fishermen's cottages at Low Newton. Anchors and seafaring memorabilia adorn the houses and a little green runs straight down to the fine sands. The offshore rocky reef had given us an opportunity for some swimming, despite the big rollers. In calmer seas this bay is also very good for snorkelling. After our excellent lunch we walked up to Newton Point and swam again in the wonderful secret cove, Football Hole. No one could explain the origin of the name, but we were so taken with it we had an impromptu kick-about with some jetsam anyway.

Afterwards we lay in the meadows for a while, surrounded by pink sea thrift and giant daisies, watching black-backed gulls soar and dive in the wind and listening to the song of willow warblers. From this point Beadnell Bay lies to the north and Embleton Bay to the south; both are owned and protected by the National Trust. We cycled to Embleton and explored the fantastic fourteenth-century Dunstanburgh Castle – the largest ruin in Northumberland – a squat, impressive hulk with a huge gatehouse perched on an outcrop above the beach.

Wide grass downs link Dunstanburgh to Craster. We explored the rocks on the way, finding a large plunge pool, its water deep and purple-tinted. This is a good place for jumping. There are flat rocks for sunbathing and you can collect big, tasty mussels

147

231

232

228

from the low-tide rocks. Nearby Craster is said to produce the best kippers and oak-smoked salmon in the north, and connoisseurs recommend the seafood at the Jolly Fisherman. As evening fell, we pushed on and camped a few miles south under the trees at remote Sugar Sands. The moon rose over a calm sea as we made a small fire to bake our freshly caught shellfish, cooking them quickly among the embers. The next morning we washed in the brook before making for Warkworth, where a fabulous Plantagenet castle stands above the village. The castle mound is at the bend of the pretty River Coquet, which is a good size for swimming. Its clean, clear water meanders around an interesting outcrop where you'll find a hermitage with a series of rooms and a tiny chapel hewn by hand from solid rock. Here, a poor hermit prayed day and night for the Earl of Northumberland, for which he was paid £15 and a barrel of fish per year. You can swim over to the hermitage on the far side of the river or pay the ferryman to row you across and show you the interior.

We spent our last afternoon and evening exploring Druridge Bay, probably the loneliest of Northumberland's wild beaches and a stopping-off point for thousands of migrating birds. There we collected shiny black ingots of sea coal that had been washed up on the shore from the open coal beds that lie on the seabed. The distant chimneys of the Alcan aluminium works glowed on the horizon, the last vestiges of the region's once-thriving mining industry. Following the colliery closures of the 1980s the signs of deprivation are clear: vandalised housing estates that sit isolated among the fields, a nearby prison complex, and, more worryingly for us, a set of throwing knives lying on the sand, miles from anywhere.

Our driftwood and sea-coal fire kept our spirits up that night as we huddled under a star-filled sky. At one point a police helicopter buzzed down, its giant floodlight searching the desolate expanses and fixing on our camp. But the night passed without incident and the next morning, fire resurrected and sausages browning nicely, I sprinted down over dewy grass and soft sand flats to roll around in the bright white surf, the empty bay extending for miles into the bluest morning sky.

South Northumberland: Druridge to Embleton

226 DRURIDGE BAY, WIDDRINGTON
Remote beach, dunes and nature reserve.

→ 3 miles S of Amble (A1068), pass turn-off for Druridge Bay Country Park (NE61 5BX, good freshwater lake) and continue ¾ mile for next L (unsigned, opp Red Row turn-off). Park at the far end of lane. Path leads to the R through dunes on to the middle of Druridge Bay (500m) with a low dune hill to the R. 2 miles further S find **Cresswell beach** and 🍴 home-made ices (NE61 5LA)..

3 mins, 55.2800, -1.5717 🅰🅰🚶

227 WARKWORTH BEACH
Medieval castle with riverside hermitage upstream and good beach downstream.

→ From A1068 N of Amble (NE65 0XB), take narrow lane on N side of bridge to parking at end, ½ mile.

5 mins, 55.3516, -1.5945 🅱🅰🚶

228 NORTH ALNMOUTH, ALNWICK
Beach dunes near upmarket Alnwick.

→ From High Street, turn into The Wynd (NE66 2RB) and bear L to car park.

5 mins, 55.3894, -1.6040 🅱🚶

229 SUGAR SANDS, ALNWICK
Quiet wooded sands with stream pools.

→ From Longhoughton (B1339) turn for Low Stead Farm opp church, through farm to dunes, then bear L up coast ½ mile. A mile N is tiny **Rumbling Kern** cove and the Bathing House cottage of Howick Hall.

5 mins, 55.4376, -1.5896 🅰🐟🚶

230 CRASTER PLUNGE POOL
Large deep plunge pool on route to castle.

→ Head N, dir of the castle. 🍴 Robson's smoked fish (NE66 3TR, 01665 576223) and 🅸 Jolly Fisherman's crab sandwiches (NE66 3TR, 01665 576461).

10 mins, 55.4780, -1.5919 🅻🍴

231 EMBLETON BAY
Wide sandy Embleton Bay stretching beneath Dunstanburgh Castle ruins is the area's most spectacular beach.

→ In Embleton take B1399 S and turn L on last road opposite church (dir Craster) then L after 300m to Dunstan Steads and park at end near beach (NE66 3DT). Continue S a mile beyond Castle to reach Craster.

15 mins, 55.4972, -1.6102 🅰🚶

232 FOOTBALL HOLE, LOW NEWTON
Remote beach with traditional fishermen's cottages, now a pub. Hidden sandy cove to N.

→ Signed Newton by the Sea off the B1340/B1339 coast road, 2 miles N of Embleton. Bear R past Joiner's Arms. 🅸 Ship Inn (NE66 3EW, 01665 576262) offers crab sandwiches, real ales and live folk music. Swim from beach outside pub – several rocky reefs make for good snorkelling and also shelter the beach. Follow NT path in wooden fence just back up road, bearing L up over Newton Point headland ¾ mile NE to Football Cove. Or walk 2 miles S to Embleton Bay and Dunstanburgh Castle.

25 mins, 55.5241, -1.6171 🏊🅱

233 BEADNELL BAY, HIGH NEWTON
Beautiful Beadnell Bay, reached from High Newton or tiny Beadnell harbour.

→ Walk a mile N from Football Cove (above) or bear L in High Newton (NE66 3ED) to car park, signed Link House. For N end, continue 3 miles N on B1340 to Beadnell.

5 mins, 55.5326, -1.6286 🅰🅰🚶

Ross Back Sands

North Northumberland: Bamburgh to Holy Island

Our first experience of Northumberland was from the magnificent cycle route that snakes along much of this wild north coast. Equipped with just a lightweight tarpaulin we planned to bivouac in the dunes, gather driftwood and then cook our supper on the beach.

We were three lads – old school friends from way back – and were accompanied by Ciaran's little dog, travelling in a cycle trailer. Our first destination was Holy Island (Lindisfarne) and after hours of cycling across bog in an impenetrable wet mist, we only just managed to make it across the water before the tide enveloped the Island's causeway. The rising waters were lashing greedily at the road edge as we pedalled on, wet seaweed lay jettisoned on the tarmac and great barnacled waymarks loomed through the cloud. The sky was clearing to the west, though, and after a recuperative pint of ale at the Island's only pub we struck out across the hillocks of the interior to find little-known Coves Haven, a remote north-facing beach with red sandstone caves at its back, where we hoped to find shelter.

The rain had eased when we set up the bivouac on the bluff. Low rays of twilight started to break through the mauve-

238

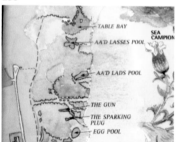

TABLE BAY

SEA CAMPION

AA'D LASSES POOL

AA'D LADS POOL

THE GUN

THE SPARKING PLUG

EGG POOL

236

234

grey clouds casting an auburn glow on to the beach below. Hot and tired, we dropped the bikes and tumbled down the sandhills on to the beach. Diving into the wildly rolling surf we were tossed about in the swell, shrieking with delight while the dog scampered about madly on the sand. Exhausted and bedraggled after that first night's fantastic swim on Britain's holiest island, we felt cleansed: this had been our ritual baptism into Northumberland.

Holy Island is the site of the ancient monastery, built entirely of wood, that St Aidan of Iona founded in the seventh century. The monastery became the centre of Christian learning in England and was the birthplace of the celebrated, exquisitely illuminated Lindisfarne Gospels. From here St Cuthbert set sail to the nearby Farne or 'retreat' islands to live in a cell and commune with the seals on the seashore.

The great king who helped the monks re-introduce Christianity to the region was King Oswald of Northumbria. His impressive castle, Bamburgh, lies just a few miles to the south, past the silvery glimmer of Ross Back Sands and Budle Bay. It sits on a high basalt bluff rising out of grassland and moor. The current superbly fortressed building, a predominantly Victorian rebuild, was constructed around Saxon and Norman ruins. Its chain rooms, from where wrecks were regularly hauled in to land, are a reminder of the vicious nature of the sea hereabouts.

The stunning beach below Bamburgh stretches for three miles. It's a great place to have fun in the breakers but there is also a string of more sedate natural swimming pools to the north among Harkess Rocks. A local map displayed on the cliff helps identify some of them: Half Moon is crescent-shaped and warms up quickly on a sunny day; Gun Pool and Spark Plug Pool are narrow channels into which the swell charges; Egg Pool – large, oval and deep depending on how much sand has been washed into it – was the best place to learn to swim, according to older residents. Look north to Holy Island Castle and south to Bamburgh Castle and marvel at the seemingly endless sand and dunes between. Come here to wallow in the breaking rollers and watch the storm clouds pass by.

235

North Northumberland: Bamburgh to Holy Island

234 ST AIDAN'S DUNES, SEAHOUSES
Good views of the Farne Islands.

➜ Head N out of Seahouses on B1340 dir
Bamburgh. After a mile park on R opp turn-
off for Shoreston. Wigwams, bunkhouse
and 1 mile after Shoreston at Springhill
Farm (NE68 7UR, 01665 721820). 🦺
Farne Island boat trips (NE68 7YT, 01665
720308). Well-loved 🍺 Olde Ship (NE68
7RD, 01665 720200) at Seahouses.
3 mins, 55.5885, -1.6676 🐚

235 BAMBURGH CASTLE SANDS
Sensational beach with iconic castle ruins
overlooking dunes. Never feels too busy.

➜ Signed Bamburgh from A1 near Belford.
Turn L for parking down The Wynding, dir
Golf Course (NE69 7DD). After houses on
R (300m) find two car parks for beach. The
🍺 Victoria, Castle and Lord Crewe Arms
are all recommended!
5 mins, 55.6130, -1.7131 🅱️ ⛺

236 HARKESS ROCK POOLS, BAMBURGH
Seven LT rockpools for plunging, with
their own information board and names.

➜ From Bamburgh parking (above)
continue along The Wynding ½ mile to find
pools below cottages, past clubhouse and
200m beyond. Depths vary according to
the amount of sand blown into the pools by
storms. Temperatures reach their warmest
during the afternoons LT. Continue on
500m to Budle Point sands.
5 mins, 55.6171, -1.7259 ⛺ 🐚

237 ROSS BACK SANDS, ELWICK
Perhaps Northumberland's wildest beach.
Spectacular, remote white sand beach
and dunes.

➜ Heading N on A1, turn R after Belford,
signed Warren Mill. L at T-junction (signed
Easington) then R signed Ross and park at
Ross Farm (NE70 7EN, 01668 213336),
which has self-catering cottages. Continue
a mile on foot, on road then dunes. Follow
beach a mile S to Budle Bay sands and
nature reserve.
20 mins, 55.6330, -1.7692 ⛺ 🚫 ⛺ ⛺

238 COVES HAVEN, HOLY ISLAND
Remote and little known sandy bay on N
side of Holy Island (Lindisfarne). Dunes,
crags and castles and place to seek
inspiration above roaring seas.

➜ Signed off A1. Continue 5 miles, across
the tidal causeway and to main car park
before Holy Island village . (The causeway
is not passable 2hrs either side of high
tide (northumberlandlife.org/holy-island).
Turn L and L again out of parking and
follow unsigned lane up to farm buildings
then farm track N, keeping straight for
a mile. At field end, head due N out on
to dunes to come to Coves Haven and N
shore. Best sand is at L end of beach. On
return, stop at the delightful churchyard
of St Mary and adjacent priory ruins. Visit
castle and admire upturned boat sheds
on the harbour bay. 🍺 Crown & Anchor
(TD15 2RX, 01289 389215). ⛺ Wigwam
glamping 10 miles up road on mainland,
at Pot-a-Doodle Do, Berwick-upon-Tweed
(TD15 2RJ, 01289 307107).
35 mins, 55.6878, -1.7993 🐚 ⛺

13 Grunta Beach

Cumbria and Lancashire

Cumbria may be celebrated for its mountainous interior but its vast coastline is well worth visiting. Moody and expansive, its beaches look out to the west and are truly glorious when sunsets fill the sky, outlining the dramatic peaks to the east.

Many love the silver, stone beaches and oak-clad shores of quaint Arnside on the estuary of the River Kent, a resort seemingly ignored by tourists heading lemming-like to the Lakes. The beach here is a mixture of sand and silt, and you'll see local people by the quay 'tickling' for flatfish with their bare feet or wallowing in the warm pools left by the outgoing tide. The peninsulas here border the sand and marsh flats of Morecambe Bay, so you need to beware of strong currents and shifting mud, especially if you venture far out on to the sands. The tide sweeps in so fast at Arnside that its arrival is heralded by a siren. The best place for a dip, however, is just below Grubbins Wood at high tide, or just under the trees at New Barns.

Heading north why not stop at Cartmel for some celebrated sticky-toffee pudding and a brief visit to the ancient priory before making for Walney Island? This 20-mile-long beach reef protects the port of Barrow-in-Furness. At the south end you'll find Piel Island, empty save for a pub and a ruined castle. The

155

247

243

246

publican is known as the 'King of Piel' and runs a small campsite and ferry service. I decided to swim across from the lighthouse and nature reserve at Walney's south end by crossing Bass Pool on a rising tide. It was a rather miserable day and the pub wasn't open when I arrived so I'd be inclined to recommend the north end of the island, North End Haws. There's no bar or local monarch but it is a truly remote isthmus of dune hills, freshwater ponds and smooth sands. The waters of the Scarth Channel snake in and around it, offering opportunities for a remote dip whatever the tide, and there are grand views out over the Duddon estuary to the whale-backed Black Combe mountain beyond.

Opposite is Sandscale Haws, another great swathe of estuarine dunes. The best route to the wide estuary is via Roanhead. You can swim in the Duddon Channel with care – preferably at low and incoming tides – but if you'd prefer to swim in the open sea then make for Silecroft, on the opposite shore, which is considered to be one of the region's very best beaches.

Seven miles up the coast you'll come to the attractive estuary of the Esk at Ravenglass. This is the terminus for a steam railway that will take you up to Eskdale, one of the best wild swimming rivers in Britain, with its legendary Tongue Pot pool beneath Scafell Pike. Take your bike on the train, explore, cycle back down, then enjoy a pint in the upmarket lounge bar at the Pennington Hotel as you watch the sun go down over the estuary. Or, if you are adventurous, wade across the channel at low tide and make for Drigg Point, where a thousand acres of untouched dune unfold and a white desert-island shoreline extends four miles up to the village of Drigg. This area is a nature reserve and an important breeding site for the rare natterjack toad, so the dunes are out of bounds. Otherwise, this is a perfect, wild-camping beach, a place to lie awake by the moonlit dunes, snug in your sleeping bag, waves lapping on the sands and toads croaking in the dunes. This is a place to contemplate the enormity and magnificence of the universe, the bright gossamer of its galaxies above you stretching out to infinity over the endless sea.

239

Cumbria and Lancashire

239 DRIGG, HOLMROOK
Miles of wild, remote sand beach and huge area of dunes, S of Sellafield.

→ From Drigg/B5344 turn off signed 'station and shore' (CA19 1XR) and continue 1 mile to beach. Walk L for 2 miles for huge dune system.

10 mins, 54.3604, -3.4548

240 RAVENGLASS CREEK & DUNES
Pretty estuary hamlet. Enjoy a drink on the shore at HT or wade the river Esk at LT to the wildest end of Drigg dunes.

→ From A595, head for ⬛ Pennington Hotel (CA18 1SD, 01229 717222) or arrive by Ravenglass and Eskdale Mountain Railway (01229 717171). Dunes to S are nature reserve and firing range, call to check when accessible (01229 71220).

20 mins, 54.3411, -3.4151

241 SILECROFT, MILLOM
Long stretch of sand under Black Combe.

→ Signed off A595/A5093. Head past ⬛ Miners Arms (LA18 5LP, 01229 772325) to park by beach golf club (LA18 4NY).

2 mins, 54.2172, -3.3502

242 HAVERIGG BANK DUNES
Golden sand flats and lagoons on the Duddon estuary. Watch for tidal currents.

→ Turn R at the Harbour Hotel, Haverigg (LA18 4EX) and continue beyond caravan park (LA18 4HB) to park at football club.

10 mins, 54.1898, -3.2958

243 SANDSCALE HAWS, DALTON
Tidal sandflats and nature reserve on Duddon Sands. Swim only on rising tides.

→ Turn L off A590 2 miles N of Barrow-in-Furness, signed Roanhead, just before roundabout. L again to car park.

5 mins, 54.1717, -3.2284

244 NORTH END HAWS, WALNEY ISLAND
Remote north end of island. Just dunes, lakes and the backdrop of Black Combe.

→ Cross on to Walney Island and turn R at lights by bridge. Turn L after ½ mile, then R, following signs for West Shore/Earnse Point to park at shore (LA14 3YR). Walk N up beach 1½ miles through dunes and lakes to reach the tidal Scarth Channel.

60 mins, 54.1498, -3.2661

245 BIGGAR BANK, W WALNEY ISLAND
Empty windswept beaches and sunsets.

→ Go straight at Walney bridge lights, then L at shore to car park on R after 1½ miles.

2 mins, 54.0858, -3.2496

246 PIEL ISLAND CASTLE BEACH
Ruined castle and pebble beach.

→ Ferry from Roa Island peninsula, off A5087, and ⬛ Ship Inn (LA13 0QN, 07516 453784) are both open summer only.

15 mins, 54.0620, -3.1732

247 FRITH WOOD, ARNSIDE
HT-only shingle swim under ancient oaks.

→ Follow B5282 through Arnside, bearing L up hill, then R. Continue to New Barns caravan site (LA5 0BN). Take footpath R.

2 mins, 54.1938, -2.8558

248 COVE WELL, SILVERDALE
Two ancient caves in cliffs. HT only swim.

→ On Silverdale to Arnside road turn first L after Elmslack. ⛺ Holgates Hollins at Far Arnside (LA5 0SL, 01524 701508).

5 mins, 54.1722, -2.8339

286 Near Abercastle

Wales

The Gower Peninsula and the Pembrokeshire Coast National Park offer some of the most spectacular coastal scenery, caves, islands and secret beaches in Britain. Cardiganshire is equally impressive but lesser known. In north Wales the beaches of Snowdonia, the Lleyn Peninsula and Anglesey – as dramatic as their high mountain backdrops – are punctuated by coves, rock arches and dunes.

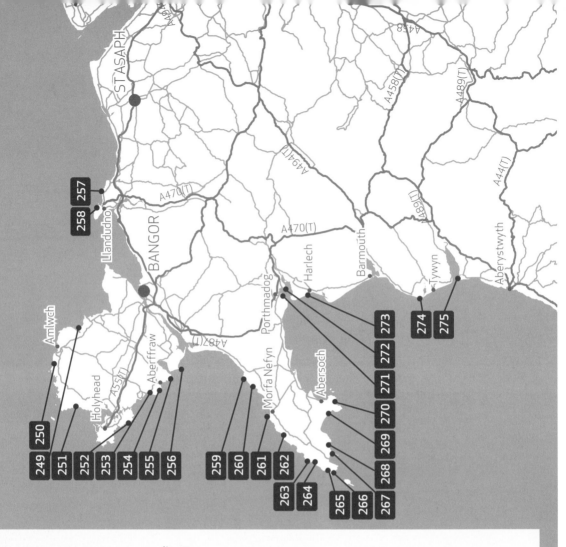

Highlights
Wales

Our favourites include:

250 Unmarked roads and tracks lead to the old ruined harbour, brick works and rock arch of Porth Wen on Anglesey.

266 Bardsey Island was considered one of the most sacred places in Britain. Visit the holy well at the old embarkation point.

273 Harlech Beach, with its backdrop of mountains and a ruined castle, is probably the wildest and most beautiful stretch of sand and dunes in Wales.

280 Historic, remote and beautiful, Mwnt is one of Wales' most perfect coves, sited beneath a tiny church with opportunities for snorkelling nearby.

281 The Witch's Cauldron is a dramatic inland lagoon and beach, formed when a massive sea cavern collapsed. You can swim in through the cave or waterfall.

286-287 Two islands on this stretch both have caves that pass through their centres. Close to the famous Sloop Inn.

289 Abereiddi Blue Lagoon is a drowned slate quarry, now breached by the sea, with jumping from the old engine house.

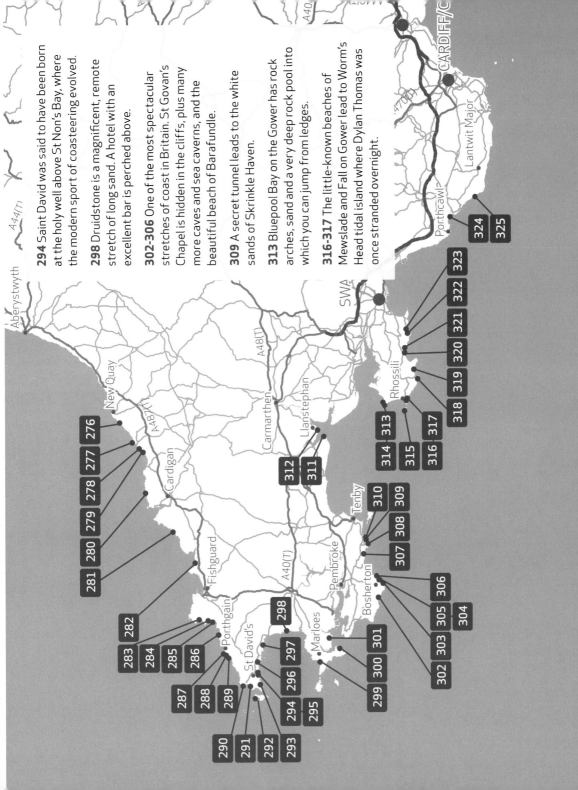

294 Saint David was said to have been born at the holy well above St Non's Bay, where the modern sport of coasteering evolved.

298 Druidstone is a magnificent, remote stretch of long sand. A hotel with an excellent bar is perched above.

302-306 One of the most spectacular stretches of coast in Britain. St Govan's Chapel is hidden in the cliffs, plus many more caves and sea caverns, and the beautiful beach of Barafundle.

309 A secret tunnel leads to the white sands of Skrinkle Haven.

313 Bluepool Bay on the Gower has rock arches, sand and a very deep rock pool into which you can jump from ledges.

316-317 The little-known beaches of Mewslade and Fall on Gower lead to Worm's Head tidal island where Dylan Thomas was once stranded overnight.

Anglesey

Ancient Anglesey, a land of burial cairns and neolithic sites, contains some of the finest sand coves on the north Wales coast, and some of its most dramatic coastal features, from caves and arches to volcanic lava flows.

About 570 million years ago during the Cambrian era much of Wales lay beneath the ancient Iapetus Ocean. Volcanic islands were common, with lava spilling out of vents on the sea floor. Some of this pillow lava, the oldest rock on earth, is still visible around the neck of Llanddwyn Island, a narrow isthmus studded with sandy inlets that is set against the vast tracts of Newborough Warren and forest.

The forests and dunes of the warren lie on much newer land, but were almost obliterated during the thirteenth century by sand storms. Three centuries later Elizabeth I forbade the cutting of the marram grass in order to protect the area and this ensured its long-term survival. The magic of the beach at Llanddwyn is due not only to its its eight miles of deserted shore but also to the spectacular backdrop of Snowdonia. Rising up from across the Menai Strait this mountainous region resembles an enchanted land with ever-changing cloud and light patterns played out on the sea.

The best swimming is among the tiny coves of Llanddywn Island. A whole community of pilots who helped to guide the ships in and over the notorious shifting sand bars of the Menai Strait once lived on this stunning outcrop. Go right to the end of the island where you will find coves by the lighthouse and beneath the old pilots' cottages. These have the best views and are fantastic for swimming.

251

249

252

Looking north from here you might be able to spy further coves up the coast to Aberffraw. There's no public access: the farmers are fiercely territorial and have refused all requests for a coast path. To reach these untouched gems you will need to walk for several miles along the shoreline, south from Aberffraw. Bring a picnic and make a day of it. The only other people who know about these coves are those with boats.

Two miles north of Aberffraw the popular surfing and swimming cove of Porth Trecastell (Cable Bay) has easier access direct from the roadside. The rock ledges along the right are good for jumping and there is a chambered cairn on the headland that you can explore with a torch if you collect the key from the local shop in nearby Llanfaelog.

Rhoscolyn and Borthwen (White Bay), another 10 miles north, are on the Holy Island separated from the rest of Anglesey at Four Mile Bridge. There's a gastro-pub here, the White Eagle and, as you would expect, a white sandy bay with several little islets, one with an iron bridge over a gulley. A dramatic walk from Rhoscolyn leads up to St Gwenfaen's Well, one of Wales' best-preserved holy wells where the water is said to cure mental illness, though you'll need to throw in a white quartz pebble first. From here you can descend past caves, chasms and blowholes to Bwa Gwyn and Bwa Du – the White and Black Arches – and after a steep scramble down to the water you can swim through them on calm days.

To the east of Holyhead Porth Trwyn and Porth Swtan (Church Bay) are idyllic sweeps of white sand with flower meadows behind. Set well back on the lane behind Church Bay, The Lobster Pot, a tiny local seafood restaurant, is worth a visit. Finally Porth Wen, near Amlwch up on the north coast, is one of the most interesting but spookiest of Anglesey's many coves. Down an unsigned, little-used path you come upon a ruined harbour and old brick works with a honeycomb of furnaces and chimney stacks to explore. Enjoy the perfect white shingle beach and rock arch as you think about the people who once lived and worked here and rejoice that nature has reclaimed this quiet place for herself.

250

Anglesey

249 TRAETH YR ORA, DULAS
Wonderful wide beach by river estuary.
→ Take footpath behind 🚩 Pilot Boat
(LL70 9EX, 01248 410205). Also lovely
🚩 Ship Inn, Red Wharf Bay, 01248 852568
30 mins, 53.3727, -4.2712

250 PORTH WEN, BULL BAY
**Eerie secret bay with old ruined harbour,
rock arch and white pebble beach.**
→ First R after 2 miles from Bull Bay/
A5025, past LL67 0NA). 800m, by L bend,
find 2 footpath signs on R. Take second
footpath (metal kissing gate) and descend
to bay (500m). A mile W on coast path leads
to ruins at tiny **Porth Llanlleiana**.
10 mins, 53.4245, -4.4061 🔄

251 PORTH SWTAN / CHURCH BAY
String of beautiful white sand coves.
→ Signed off A5025 at Llanrhyddlad.
R at T junction after a mile. Lobster Pot
🍴 (LL65 4EU, 01407 730241). Sea view ⛺
Gadlys (LL65 4ET, 07786547361) or ⛺ Ty
Newydd (01407 730060). Carry on 1 mile
for more selcuded **Porth Trwyn**.
3 mins, 53.3736, -4.5562 ⛺

252 BWA GWYN ARCH, RHOSCOLYN
**Coastal walk leads to holy well and giant
white rock arches for adventure swim.**
→ Walk up dead end lane up behind church
then footpath to coast. Bear R 400m for
arch. Use steep bank on opposite slope
for difficult scramble down to water. Bwa
Du/Black Arch is 300m beyond. Return
via coast path S and St Gwenfaen's Well
to pretty **Borthwen** beach (53.24409,
-4.58886) with islets, and back via 🚩
White Eagle gastro-pub (LL65 2NJ, 01407
860267). Or walk E along coast to wild,
sandy **Traeth Llydan /Silver Bay**, 1½ miles
(53.24611, -4.56199).
15 mins, 53.2539, -4.6110 ⛺🚶🚩

253 PORTH TRECASTELL / CABLE BAY
**Narrow sandy bay with rock jumps.
Chambered cairn on headland.**
→ By A4080, 2 miles S Rhosneigr
2 mins, 53.20719, -4.49803 🅱️🍴⛺

254 PORTH CWYFAN, ABERFFRAW
**Shingle sand bay with tiny island on which
stands an ancient chapel.**
→ From A4080 turn into Aberffraw village

centre and continue through 2 miles
(dir Eglwy Cwyfa church). Also explore
Abberffraw sands and dunes, 1 mile walk
(HT swim) from village along the beautiful
sandy creek. 🍴 Llys Llewelyn tearooms in
village (LL63 5AQ, 01407 840847).
5 mins, 53.1863, -4.4890 ⛺🚶⛺

255 PORTH TWYN-MAWR, ABERFFRAW
**Almost inaccessible without a boat, a
series of six perfect secret sand coves.
Known as Sixpenny to yachties.**
→ Explore the coast S for 2 miles from
Abberffraw, keeping close to the
foreshore. Popular with boats. No path.
60 mins, 53.1618, -4.4454 ⛺🚶

256 LLANDDWYN ISLAND, NEWBOROUGH
**Huge beach with forest behind. Stunning
Snowdonia backdrop. Island peninsula.**
→ From Menai Bridge (A4080) enter
Newborough, take L at post office (signed
Llys Rhosyr). Follow road 1 mile to toll
(LL61 6SG, £2) and then a mile to car park.
Follow beach/forest track R 1 mile and
cross to 'island'. Best coves on SE side.
30 mins, 53.1382, -4.4096 🚶

Porth Iago

North Lleyn and Llandudno

A tiny rocky headland looks out across two sweeping bays and the looming mountains of Yr Eifl. Picture-perfect seashore cottages huddle by the beach around the red-roofed inn.

Porth Dinllaen is a remote north Wales village set on the tip of the Lleyn Peninsula and has no road access. It was the site of one of the fiercest of Welsh contests: the battle to establish the official port for the proposed London to Dublin railway. Porth Dinllaen, a perfect natural harbour, had the backing of Isambard Kingdom Brunel, and the Porth Dinllaen Harbour Company was formed in 1808 to advance its cause. In 1810, however, Parliament rejected its plans and voted for Thomas Telford's more accessible road developments to Holyhead via the north Wales coast.

Anglesey's gain preserved the Lleyn Peninsula and it remains largely untouched by development. Porth Dinllaen, still a car-free hamlet, is now owned by the National Trust and can be reached only on foot. Ty Coch (the Red House) the old-established inn, is popular on summer evenings. Further round the harbour by the lifeboat ramp are two tiny sandy coves that are good for swimming, and you'll see seals basking on the rocks.

Across the bay to the north is the towering peak of Yr Eifl, with a beachside settlement of old quarrymen's cottages below it. This is now home to the National Welsh Language Centre (Nant Gwrtheyrn) and is reached by one of the most dramatic mountain roads in Wales that snakes down through alpine forest with stunning views out to sea. It's worth calling in just for the drive alone. There's an excellent café here too, and the long shingle foreshore is almost always deserted.

Along the peninsula's north-western coast mountain gives way to moorland and a string of pearly coves. Porth Oer (Whistling

259

261

264

'The Walrus and the Carpenter
Were walking close at hand;
They wept like anything to see
Such quantities of sand.'

Lewis Carroll,
Alice in Wonderland
(writing in Llandudno)

Sands) is perhaps the best known of these coves and the grains really do squeak underfoot, piping shrill notes when the wind blows in from the west. A small National Trust café provides sustenance after a morning of body surfing and swimming, and the cliff walk immediately south leads to the small island headlands of Dinas Bach and Dinas Fawr with sea caves for exploring.

Near Porth Oer, Traeth Penllech has a long stretch of sand reached across open fields and a small stream, while Porth Towyn further up the coast has two small coves with good rocks for scrambling. You can camp at nearby Towyn and Ysgaden farms and explore the tiny shingle inlets of Yslaig and Ysgaden where Irish sea salt and Welsh language almanacs were once smuggled in. Do make time to visit Porth Iago, my favourite among all these coves for wild swimming. The thick slice of white sand occupies a deep cleft between the cliffs and there are perfect rocks for diving, jumping and snorkelling – the archetypal swimmer's cove.

This rich scenery contrasts dramatically with the drab lines of caravan resorts along most of the north Wales coast, from Bangor to Chester. The notable exception is Llandudno. Named after sixth-century St Tudno and once a rich copper-mining town, Llandudno took full advantage of the Victorian sea-bathing craze and was one of Britain's most upmarket resorts with some of the finest shops outside London. It was here that Lewis Carroll wrote parts of *Alice in Wonderland* and created the Walrus and Carpenter characters.

The great carboniferous limestone hulk of the Orme – meaning 'worm' or 'serpent' – affords truly magnificent views of Snowdonia, Anglesey and the coast. Daredevils jump into the sea from some of the low cliffs to the right of the road and swim into Porth Helyg (Pigeon's Cave), but the best swimming is on Little Orme's Head at Porth Dyniewaid (Angel Bay), which is also popular with climbers. It's a short walk across gorse-covered headland to this tiny sand and pebble beach. There are good rocks for jumping and a sense of seclusion and ruggedness – a striking contrast to the faded grandeur of genteel Llandudno.

North Lleyn and Llandudno

257 PORTH DYNIEWAID, LITTLE ORME
Angel Bay. Shingle cove on the lesser-known Little Orme's Head set under cliffs and popular with climbers. Daredevil kids jump from Fisherman's Rock at HT.
→ Walk 1 mile around headland from far E end of Llandudno Bay. Or park in residential cul-de-sac at end of 'Penrhyn Beach East' (LL30 3RN, 3 miles E of Llandudno on B5115. First exit at roundabout, the first L at church, then first R until end). Walk up hill and bear R to end of headland (300m) and drop down to cove. Fisherman's Rock on R of cove. Don't swim out far, as there are currents at headland.
10 mins, 53.32784, -3.77631 ⛺ 🍴

258 PIGEON'S CAVE, GREAT ORME
Ogof Colomennod. Limestone ledges, pebble cove and sea cave at far E end of pebble bay. Popular with anglers.
→ 1 mile N of Grand Hotel/Llandudno pier (LL30 2LR), rough anglers path descends R down rocks. Or approach across pebble bay. Park to L under rock overhang, or continue ½ mile to hairpin bend.
10 mins, 53.3374, -3.8360 🏊 🤿

259 YNYS FAWR COVE, TREFOR
Pyramid rocks and mountain views.
→ A mile W from pier at Trefor (LL54 5LB). Nearby coastal ⛺ Aberafon, Gyrn Goch (LL54 5PN, 01286 660295). 🍴 Y Beuno, Clynnog Fawr, (LL54 5PB, 01286 660785)
20 mins, 52.9984, -4.4368 🧗 🛶

260 NANT GWRTHEYRN, LLITHFAEN
Long dramatic pebble strand in the shadow of Yr Eifl peaks and quarries.
→ Signed from Llithfaen on B4417, then 2 mile spectacular drive down to old mine village. 🍴 café, heritage centre, cottages (LL53 6NL 01758 750334).
5 mins, 52.9771, -4.4632

261 PORTH DINLLAEN, NEFYN
Peninsula with beaches, seals and pub.
→ From Morfa Nefyn on B4417 turn up to golf course (signed) and park at road end (LL53 6DA). Follow headland, exploring quiet shingle coves and islets of Borth Wen to L, before dropping down to 🍺 Ty Coch Inn (LL53 6DB, 01758 720498) and its busier beach on the R side.
15 mins, 52.9438, -4.5689 🛶

262 PORTH TOWYN, TUDWEILIOG
Little local beach with basic camping at farm and a tiny hut with refreshments.
→ Signed 'treath/beach' from Tudweiliog/B4417. Camp at farm or at cliff-side ⛺ Penrallt (LL53 8PB, 01758 770654) a mile down coast. Larger **Penllech Traeth** beach with stream and waterfall is a further 2 miles L (52.87843, -4.67064). Many informal ⛺ campsites.
5 mins, 52.9061, -4.6329 ⛺

263 PORTH IAGO, RHYDLIOS
Idyllic crescent cove with camping above.
→ Signed 1½ mile before Rhoshirwaun/B4413. Take second R after 2½ miles, then first L signed 'Iago' (LL53 8LP) then second track on L through old farm (£2) to ⛺ and grass parking in which you can also camp. Secret Widlin cove at 52.8596, -4.6960
3 mins, 52.8516, -4.7217 🛶

264 PORTH OER (WHISTLING SANDS)
Squeaky sands in little family bay
→ As above, but continue straight past 'Iago' sign (LL53 8LH). 🍴 NT café .
5 mins, 52.8349, -4.7242 🅱

Hell's Mouth

South Lleyn to Harlech

Bardsey Island sits at the distant tip of the Lleyn Peninsula and glimmers in the waters of Bardsey Sound. From here Cardigan Bay stretches out in a great arc to the remote and dramatic Rhinog mountains of Snowdonia.

There's been a church on this 'island in the tides' for 1,500 years and it was once considered as sacred as Iona in Scotland or Holy Island (Lindisfarne) in Northumberland. Devout Catholics considered three pilgrimages to Bardsey were worth one to Rome and to die here guaranteed a place in heaven. Many travelled here to spend their last days praying in the sea caves and holding vigils on the cliffs. It became known as 'the island of 20,000 saints'.

The journey across to the island has always been treacherous: on full spring tides currents flow like rivers. Pilgrims would embark from a narrow inlet near Aberdaron beneath the church of St Mary, now a ruin. A path still runs down to the embarkation point and here you'll come across St Mary's Well, a small natural trough near the low tide line. On a calm, bright day the water in this deep harbour cleft radiates light and rock ledges provide tempting places for jumping and snorkelling. However, you should only consider such antics on neap, turning tides when there is little tidal stream, and you should never venture out of the inlet into the main passage. Porth Felen further around the headland was also used as a harbour in stormy weather and offers a safer swimming option.

Exploring the lanes east, beyond Aberdaron and its 'Two Doors' cave, we came across a leafy path along a stream glade down to the hidden cove of Porth Ysgo. Here there are old mine workings and tunnels overgrown with ragwort and bindweed,

268

265

271

and on the grassy cliff-tops we found ruined engine houses and rusted turning wheels. Once at the beach I swam out to the old mooring rock that still has its iron ring. Larger boats would once have waited here for the smaller craft ferrying manganese ore from the shore, but today this podium makes an excellent place to jump and dive. It's also a great vantage point for admiring the bay's serpentine and gabbro rocks. Black, rough and crystalline, these started life in the heart of the Earth, where they were fiercely cooked and then slowly cooled.

Further up the coast Abersoch is the main resort. Photographer Martin Turtle, who runs the Turtle Gallery, took me from here to explore Porth Ceiriad, a remote beach with powerful surf that refracts off the golden sandstone, and where there is also a cliff-top campsite. On calmer days it's good for snorkelling and you might see thornback rays, skate, mackerel, flounders and whiting. A rare Kemp's Ridley turtle was washed up on this beach not so long ago.

East from here, the coast passes the castle towns of Pwllheli and Criccieth before reaching Porthmadog, from where Prince Madog is said to have set sail to discover America almost 300 years before Christopher Columbus. The town stands at the head of the great Glaslyn Estuary, a dramatic plain that drains the Snowdon massif. One of the best views is from Borth-y-Gest where there are deep sandy pools and lagoons at low tide. It's also possible to bathe in the river in front of the village of Portmeirion – which has an eccentric mix of architectural styles – on the adjacent Dwyryd Estuary, but take great care when the tide is flowing seaward.

Cross on the toll bridge and continue seven miles to the foreboding ruins of fourteenth-century Harlech Castle, built when the sea still lapped at its massive crag. The stunning beach below is one of the few dune systems in the country that is accreting, extending ever further into Cardigan Bay. You might also catch a glimpse of dolphins offshore. In the distance the Rhinog summits rise up, their slopes studded with Bronze-Age tracks and stone circles. This is ancient Wales, a land of mountains, islands and sea.

South Lleyn to Harlech

265 OGOF GÔCH, UWCHMYNYDD
Narrow pebble cove with great jumps and huge sea caves in cliffs a swim to the R.
→ From Aberdaron bridge follow signs for Porth Oer, then St Mary's Well then L for Uwchmynydd. After a mile find footpath on R opp Pen-y-Bryn (LL53 8BY) and follow this a mile to creek bottom at coast. ⚠ Llanllawen Fawr (01758 760223)
20 mins, 52.8054, -4.7518 🄻🄯🄼🄳

266 ST MARY'S WELL, UWCHMYNYDD
Steep, deep rocky inlet where pilgrims embarked for Bardsey Island. St Mary's Well appears as a pool at low tide.
→ As above, but continue ½ mile, past Penbryn Bach Seafood 🍴 (01758 760216) and final house, ⚠ Mynydd Mawr (01758 760223) to find footpaths on L, as road bends R up to parking. Bear down to R of hill or bear down to L of hill for rocky Porth Felen (52.790, -4.754). Offshore currents.
10 mins, 52.7921, -4.7602 🄰🄥🄯🄳

267 OGOF DDEUDDRWS, ABERDARON
Two Doors cave, far E end of beach.
15 mins, 52.7966, -4.6922 🄳🄯

268 PORTH YSGO, LLANFAELRHYS
Remote sand shingle cove beneath mine ruins in secret valley. Beautiful views.
→ Signed, R at second cross roads, 2½ miles E from Aberdaron (LL53 8AN). Park where road bends R, after 500m, and follow footpath. Return loop via Ysgo Farm.
15 mins, 52.8054, -4.6610 🄯🄳

269 HELL'S MOUTH, ABERSOCH
Wonderfully long, wild bay behind dunes.
→ Exit Abersoch dir Pwllheli, but turn L up hill past Harbour Hotel and follow Llanengan Rd 2 miles, beyond LL53 7LG, for car park. ⚠ Treheli Farm, Rhiw on far W end (LL53 8AA, 01758 780281).
5 mins, 52.8078, -4.5503 🄰

270 PORTH CEIRIAD, ABERSOCH
Quiet beach with good surf and campsite.
→ Exit Abersoch dir Sarn Bach, taking second L down tiny lane a mile after Sarn Bach, through ⚠ Nant-y-Big (LL53 7DB, 01758 712686) to parking.
5 mins, 52.7942, -4.5064 🄰

271 PEN-Y-BANC, BORTH-Y-GEST
LT sand and pools on estuary under mountain backdrop. Tidal currents so best at turning tide.
→ Borth-y-Gest is signed from Porthmadog. Park at main bay on cove (LL49 9TY) and follow road then path down shore ½ mile. Connects to Black Rock Sands/Morfa Bychan.
10 mins, 52.9110, -4.1414 🄰🄯🄳

272 WHITESANDS, PORTMEIRION
Estuary sands beneath wooded headland.
→ Locals access from end of unsigned lane (LL48 6HY). Or better via Portmeirion (£10) then head along shore path to white lighthouse, from beneath the hotel.
20 mins, 52.9092, -4.1053 🄰🄳

273 HARLECH BEACH
Vast beach with dunes beneath Harlech castle. Dolphins and mountain sunsets.
→ Signed from station, Lower Harlech/ A496 (LL46 2UG). ⚠ Shell Island (LL45 2PJ, 01341 24145) in nearby Llanbedr.
5 mins, 52.8623, -4.1278 🄳🄱

Cardiganshire

It was early evening as I followed the lanes down through twisted woodland and along a stream glade to emerge at the cove of Cwmtydu, its walls lined with caves.

The sun was sinking rapidly in a cloudy pink haze and I rushed to set up camp on the headland. It was a warm night and after a deep sleep I woke early, already too hot in my sleeping bag, and scrambled down to the beach to plunge into a clear sea. After a few lengths I clambered out on to some black rock ledges near a cave and explored tentatively inside, keeping an eye on a seal that bobbed about in the middle distance watching me.

A short walk on the coast path north from Cwmtydu, just before the faint hillside remains of Castell Bach, brings you to another cove and you can swim from one side around a mini-island to the other. Flower meadows bloom here and cliffs drop dramatically to the sea. When I arrived, a couple from a seal-watch charity were already in residence, warning walkers to stay away. Down below a tiny white seal pup was flopping about on the beach and the couple were concerned it would be disturbed (walkers' dogs can be particularly worrying) and that the mother might then abandon it.

Cwmtydu is a pleasant, low-key place with a little shop, a campsite and a stream leading down to the shingle beach. Even more picturesque is Llangranog, a few miles down the coast, with excellent sea-facing pubs and a jumble of cottages clustered on the steep lanes above. This is the kind of village

175

281

280

276

that you imagine Dylan Thomas had in mind when he wrote *Under Milk Wood* in nearby New Quay.

There are caves here, too, and rock stacks known as the Giant's Teeth. At low tide you can follow the sands along to Cilborth Cove or gain access via wooden steps from the cliff path above. The sandy inlets continue all the way along the cliff base to the dramatic pointed finger of Ynys-Lochtyn headland. Here a precarious cliff promontory leads to an island with ledges, a rock arch, a hidden beach and a low-tide causeway.

Two miles south you'll find longer beaches at Penbryn and Tresaith but I continued 10 miles west to Mwnt and arrived at the most perfect sandy cove sheltered by sandstone cliffs, which is great for snorkelling and exploring and is watched over by an ancient church. As you approach the coast through empty countryside and down miles of tiny lanes it's difficult to imagine that this area was the scene of a major twelfth-century battle. Whole skeletons are still unearthed periodically from the fields around.

Mwnt, though remote, is far from secret and popular with families, so if you're yearning for a wilder adventure, explore a few hundred yards along the coast path to the east. Here you'll find great slabs of rock that shelve into perfect pellucid seas, ideal for sea-caving and snorkelling. If you want a really big cave adventure though, head for the extraordinary landscape of Ceibwr Bay and the Witch's Cauldron. Twisted, contorted layers of black rock make up this remote and forbidding coastline. Deep caves and sea tunnels punctuate the headlands and 20 minutes from the main bay you'll find an open lagoon with a beach in a chasm behind the cliffs. On hot days the water is clear, green and iridescent. According to local legend the Cauldron was a sea-witch's lair and she would consume anyone who ventured in alone. Indeed, it's remarkably easy to imagine mythical creatures floating out from the catacombs and shimmering in the air. The Witch's Cauldron has three separate entrance tunnels leading you in from a rocky cove: one is a scramble down a waterfall and underground stream bed; the other two are sea caves that meet in an underground cavern. If you plan to explore, bring waterproof torches and plenty of courage.

Cardiganshire

274 TON FANAU STATION, TYWYN
Endless LT sands and eerie army remains.
→ LL36 9LP. Wild rocky beachside △. Cae
Du is 3 miles N (LL36 9ND, 01654 711234).
3 mins, 52.6128, -4.1285 △ △

275 DYFI / YNYSLAS, BORTH
Popular estuary beach with dunes.
→ 3 miles N of Borth/B4353. SY24 5JZ
10 mins, 52.5291, -4.0526 🅱

276 CASTELL BACH, CWMTYDU
Cwmtydu beach with car park and caves
leads to two secret coves with seals.
→ From parking (SA44 6LQ) follow coast
path N 500m to cove with tiny island
(Castell Bach) or another 500m to second
cove at bottom of pretty stream valley.
Excellent 🍴 Crown Inn (Llwyndafydd,
SA44 6BU, 01545 560396).
20 mins, 52.1985, -4.3977 △

277 YNYS-LOCHTYN, LLANGRANOG
Stunning headland with island, arch and
secret beaches by charming Llangranog.
→ From Ship Inn (SA44 6SL) climb steps

to follow coastal path N. Pass steps to
tiny Cilborth cove L (300m) and continue
to headland. Drop down on R of headland
to find steps to **Traeth-yr-yynys** beach
(shaded in afternoon). Explore sea ledges
and rock arches around headland. 🍴
Pentre Arms (SA44 6SP, 01239 654345)
15 mins, 52.1687, -4.4647 🟦 🏊 🍴 🚻 △

278 CARREG-Y-TY, LLANGRANOG
Remote sandy cove with tiny island
pierced by a long sea cave.
→ Coast path 1 mile S of Llangranog or N
of Penbryn. At footbridge drop down via
stream through woods then scramble. Also
faint path on SW side.
20 mins, 52.1533, -4.4855 🟦 🏊 △ 🅻

279 PENBRYN SANDS, ABERPORTH
Long, wild, beautiful with glamping above
→ Traeth Penbryn. Signed off A487
near Tan-y-groes. 1½ mile, past free car
park and white chapel, then L to tea shop
and pay parking (SA44 6QL). Fabulous
glamping at △ Fforest (SA44 6QH, 01239
623633) up lane.
5 mins, 52.1445, -4.4972 🅱 ✈

280 MWNT, PENPARC, CARDIGAN
Perfect sandy cove beneath tiny chapel.
→ Signed from Penparc/A487 (Cardigan).
Straight across dog-leg junction after 2
miles, then second on L, to adjacent △ Ty-
Gwyn (SA43 1QH, 01239 614518). Follow
path beyond church E, 500m, to find large
slab rocks with stacks and caves.
5 mins, 52.1360, -4.6405 🅱 🟦 ✈

281 WITCH'S CAULDRON, CEIBWR BAY
Mysterious inland lagoon beach reached
by swimming in through sea cave.
→ From Newport follows signs all the way
to Moylegrove (5 miles). Then at chapel
turn L signed Ceibwr (SA43 3BU). Follow
coast path W 15 mins to find lagoon. At
footbridge descend into stream passage
by waterfall (if you can climb back out!) or
at LT 100m swim leads in via sea cave on R.
Or at MT swim out of cove 30m and back in
via inlet and arch. From Ceibwr Bay itself
a 200m swim SW leads to the giant **Careg
Wylan/Gull Rock**, with sea cave through
connected headland. A very long tunnel
pierces next headland too. Torch & wetsuit!
15 mins, 52.0715, -4.7715 🟦 △ △

Abereiddi Blue Lagoon

North Pembrokeshire: Abereiddi to Strumble Head

After a bumpy ride along twisting lanes through a landscape of scattered Neolithic remains, catching glimpses of sea through the hedgerows, we arrived at remote Pwll Deri Youth Hostel on Strumble Head. A great silvery lagoon glimmered below in the afternoon sun and we imagined Jason and the Argonauts setting sail across the Ionian Sea.

There are dramatic steps leading diagonally down the cliff-face at Porth Maenmelyn, half a mile up the coast path, but the rusty railings hang off at right angles and many of the steps have crumbled away. So we spent much of the afternoon searching for a safer way down to the water's edge. Scrambling to the top of the grassy headland lookout of Ynys Melyn, the hot afternoon sun beating down, we saw seals bobbing and kittiwakes squawking around their cliff nests. Melyn was an Iron Age fort and the remains of earthworks survive at the narrow neck leading to the summit. From there a rough goat path descends through gorse to a rocky spur and an old fishermen's ladder. The deep, silky water shifted slowly in lazy ripples and kelps in shades of purple and indigo waved below the surface. There was only the gentlest of splashes as we dived in and began exploring the caves. Once we were alongside, water gurgled through fissures along the rock base and the cliffs rose vertically from the sea.

The grandeur and remoteness of the cliffs along Strumble Head make this stretch feel like a final frontier. By complete chance

286

283

283

this is indeed the site of the last invasion of Britain: in 1797 a motley band of French revolutionaries, intent on taking England at Bristol, were blown off course by a storm and landed at this headland some days later. Jubilant, they looted the first farm they found and couldn't believe their luck when they came upon several hundred gallons of wine stored there in readiness for a wedding party. The soldiers quickly became exceptionally drunk and incoherent and were all too easily rounded up by a group of angry farmers' wives with pitchforks.

From Strumble Head 20 miles of perfect coastline unfold to the south. The first stop is Pwllcrochan, a wonderfully remote and dramatic cove with low-tide sands, rock formations and a difficult climb down via a rope and waterfall. Aber Bach, the next inlet, at the bottom of bumpy lanes and woods filled with bluebells in spring, gives access to a set of large sea caves with walls of pink and purple rock and dark pebble coves inside. At the tiny fishing village of Abercastle we waded over to an island with a cave that runs right through its centre and makes a fantastic swim or scramble. The village is overlooked by the ancient Careg Sampson 'cromlech' or burial chamber.

West of Porthgain – a pretty harbour village with a restaurant, gallery and pub – there are more treats, including a swim through a giant arch at Porth Dwfn, the wide sands of Traeth Llyfn and finally Abereiddi's famous 'Blue Lagoon', a disused quarry long since breached by the sea to become an inland lake. The quarry's old wheelhouse provides three platforms for leaping into the deep blue abyss below – a famous rite of passage for local swimmers and visitors alike. But after a few leaps and lunch at the Sloop Inn at Porthgain, we decided to set out to explore Ynys-fach, a small islet just a mile to the north-east. From the coast path we climbed over a fence and down a steep overgrown path to a double shingle cove. A swim led round to a deep cave that extended all the way through the islet, as at Abercastle, and a path with ropes led up to the island's flat top, which was carpeted in sea thrift. Here we found the remains of a campfire and decided to sleep wild, high above the sea, the sparks from our fire flying into the dark night as we watched the stars moving gently across the sky.

288

North Pembrokeshire: Abereiddi to Strumble Head

282 ABER RHIGIAN, NEWPORT
Shingle cove with woods and waterfalls.
→ 1 mile W of Newport on A487, park by track/footpath on R (SA42 0UF), 200m after ▲ Ty Canol (SA42 0ST, 01239 820264). Also Aber Fforest 1 mile E. Tiny beachside 🍴 Old Sailor's at Pwllgwaelod beach signed from Dinas/A487 (Bryn-henllan, SA42 0SE, 01348 811491).
10 mins, 52.0192, -4.8788 🚶🚻

283 PWLL DERI, STRUMBLE HEAD
Rocky ledges and caves below ancient headland fort. Caves and seals.
→ 4 miles SW of Fishguard/A487, turn off to and through St Nicholas, 5 miles to Pwll Deri Youth Hostel (SA64 0LR, 0845 371 9536). Take coast path down hill 500m. Continue on to view Porth Maenmelyn with hazardous ancient stairway in cliffs, or bear off L on faint path to headland (Dinas Mawr) and after 400m, at bottom, bear L down gorse path, to iron ladder to sea. NB Carreg Onnen Bay at Strumble Head lighthouse (SA64 0JL) is popular for coasteering, seals and dolphins.
15 mins, 52.0058, -5.0778 🏖🤿🏊🤿

284 PWLLCROCHAN
Difficult descent to dramatic LT beach via path and rope. Waterfall.
→ 1 miles on coast N of Aber Bach (below).
25 mins, 51.9863, -5.0807 ▲🏖▲🚩

285 ABER BACH CAVES, ABERMAWR
Pretty shingle cove with sea caves to N.
→ 4 miles SW of Fishguard/A487, turn off to Abermawr/Woollen Mill (good 🍴 SA62 5UX, 01348 891225). Over cross roads and L at bridge. Continue to long pebble Aber Mawr at road end or take footpath on R to little Aber Bach. Secret Porth Dwgan cove and huge sea cave are 300m beyond (scramble down into gulley form coast path above). Preseli Venture (01348 837709) run coasteering courses here.
15 mins, 51.9761, -5.0845 🏖🤿🚣🏄

286 ABERCASTLE CAVE.
Little island with sea cave that passes through middle. Careg Sampson on hill R.
→ 300m swim from harbour beach (SA62 5HJ) at HT or walk it at LT.
5 mins, 51.9619, -5.1288 🏄🏖

287 PENCLEGYR, PORTHGAIN
Headland with arch and chasm. Descend on ledge and you can swim around it.
→ 1 miles W of Porthgain (Superb 🍴 The Shed SA62 5BN, 01348 831518, 🍺 Sloop Inn 01348 831449) on coast path. Far end of old quarries. NB 1 mile E to secret island (Ynys-fach) with cave tunnel and camp above but no path (51.9503, -5.1704).
20 mins, 51.9498, -5.1946 🏖▲🏄

288 TRAETH LLYFN, ABEREIDDI
Superb wild beach with beautiful sand.
→ Continue ½ mile W, or 1 mile E from Abereiddi Bay. Rips in surf conditions.
20 mins, 51.9435, -5.1992 ▲▲

289 ABEREIDDI BLUE LAGOON
Popular inland lagoon in breached quarry with mine tower ruins for jumping.
→ Signed Abereiddi, 9 miles from Fishguard/6 miles from St Davids (SA62 6DT). Follow coast path 300m N to find lagoon. Do not jump from top tower at LT. Bottom platform safe at all tides. ▲ Pwll Caerog Farm (SA62 6DG, 01348 837405)
5 mins, 51.9377, -5.2088 🍴

St Non's Bay

Mid-Pembrokeshire: St David's

The coast of St David's is home to Wales' patron saint and the location of some of its most savagely beautiful scenery. The combination of sandy coves and dramatic coastal formations is perfect for wild swimming.

David or Dewi was originally the name of a Welsh sea god. His totem, a great red serpent, was transformed over time into the Welsh national symbol, the red dragon. Up on the bare wind-blown moor of St David's Head, where fallen rocks and burial cairns lie among heather and gorse, it's easy to imagine that huge serpents may once have roamed the sea.

Below cliffs cloaked in buttercups and sea-lavender, Porthmelgan cove lies tucked into the rocks. There are sea caves in the left-hand wall but big swells here can generate rip tides along the cove edges so leave any explorations for a calm day. Neighbouring Whitesands Bay is a long sweep and a popular surfing beach. It leads down to Porthselau in the south, an excellent swimming cove with a campsite on the fields above.

The rocky promontory at the north end of Whitesands is called Trwynhwrddyn (Ram's Nose) and has a cave that passes through from one side of the nose to the other that's fun to swim through at mid-tide. It's also a good introduction to 'coasteering', a term coined back in the 1990s by TYF Adventures, a centre in St David's that runs such courses.

This outdoor pursuit is becoming increasingly popular all around Britain and is not dissimilar to coastal wild swimming. Put simply, it's a combination of scrambling along the

292

291

296

foreshore and swimming the bits in between, but with plenty of jumps thrown in. Decked out in wetsuits, trainers, helmets and buoyancy aids, groups can go further, jump from higher up and enjoy heavier swells in locations such as the famous 'toilet bowl' at St Non's Bay, a classic coasteering venue, where large waves flush you out from between the rocks.

St Non's Bay is immediately south of St David's. I first explored this coastline in early May when primroses were growing in clumps around the delightful remains of St Non's chapel and holy well. The well water was considered particularly beneficial for women in childbirth and Saint Non, the royal princess, was said to have given birth to Saint David beside this bay in AD 500. To the far east of the bay is a sea cave with a towering, vaulted roof and a sandy floor. There are several entrances and a great skylight casts sunbeams down through the water. To the west you'll find Chanters' Seat, a series of stratified ledges dropping steeply to the sea with a deep inlet for swimming and diving. If you try, you can almost imagine a whole choir singing in praise of the ocean.

Further east at Porth Ffynnon, the purple and black triangular stacks were formed from red sandstone strata set on end. These are popular for jumping and climbing and can be accessed from below the campsite at Porth Clais. On the eastern side of Porthclais harbour, you'll find another popular rocky swimming spot at Ogof Golchfa, a deep inlet with large shallow rock pools on either side, perfect for warming up afterwards.

The characteristic red and purple rocks of this coastline are most intense at Caer Bwdy Cove where the stone for St David's magnificent cathedral was quarried. Continue on to Porth y Rhaw, another remote shingle cove with islands for snorkelling, a waterfall and cave, a freshwater quarry lake, and scope for even more coasteering. There's an eight-foot-deep plunge pool here at low tide, but watch out for the keen claws of spider crabs lurking in the bottom when you jump in. If you survive all this then make for the Druidston Hotel, 10 miles to the south. Set high above the beach facing west, it's the perfect location to watch the sun go down.

290

Mid-Pembrokeshire: St David's to Druidstone

290 PORTHMELGAN, WHITESANDS BAY
Sandy cove near popular Whitesands Bay
→ Leaving St David's, dir Fishguard,
Whitesands is soon signed. From beach
car park (SA62 6PS) follow coast path 1
mile N, passing Porth Lleuog on way. Path
continues to burial chambers of St David's
Head. 🍴 Cwtch, St Davids (SA62 6SD,
01437 720491) and 🍺 Farmers Arms
(01437 721666).
15 mins, 51.9033, -5.3044 ⛺

291 PORTHSELAU, WHITESANDS BAY
Beautiful beach for sunset and rockpools
→ From St David's cathedral car park
follow road 1¼ miles (signed St Justinian).
Turn R for ⛺ Pencarnan (SA62 6PY, 01437
720580) where you can park. Walk to
bottom camping field to reach beach.
5 mins, 51.8866, -5.3049 ⛺

292 OGOF ORGAN, RAMSEY ISLAND
Swim into LT beach in double sea cave.
→ Extreme NW corner of island, 1 mile
from quay. Descend rocky ledges. Swim L,
inside of inlet. Fierce currents seaward side
30 mins, 51.8753, -5.3472 🏊🤿⛺⛺

293 PORTHLYSGI BAY, PORTHCLAIS
Large secluded pebble bay, a lovely walk
from Porthclais. Giant rockpool enroute.
→ Bear R/W from Porthclais harbour (St
David's, SA62 6RR). 200m from harbour
mouth **Ogof Golchfa** below is popular
for jumps at HT with huge rockpool at LT
(51.8656, -5.2827). Continue 1 mile to bay.
30 mins, 51.8653, -5.2967 🍴🤿📷⛺

294 ST NON'S BAY CAVE, ST DAVID'S
Dramatic bay, birthplace of St David and
coasteering, with spectacular sea cave/
arch to E end. Many other features, but
for advanced swimmers – with wetsuits
and in calm seas only.
→ St Non's is signed off the Porthclais
road (SA62 6BN). Park at end and walk R
across field past chapel ruins, L onto coast
path. Cave can be seen ahead but drop
down on far side via steep gulley after
500m (also from Caerfai Bay). Bear L for
Chanter's Seat jumping ledges (51.8690,
-5.2725) and gaint slabs in Porth y Ffynnon
(difficult access). Cliff-side ⛺ Porthclais
(SA62 6RR, 01437 720616).
15 mins, 51.8706, -5.2628 🏊🤿📷

295 CAERFAI BAY, ST DAVID'S
Popular sandy cove with camping. Carry
on a mile on coast to shingle Caer Bwdy.
→ Signed on E outskirts of city (SA62
6QT). ⛺ Caerfai Farm (01437 720548).
5 mins, 51.8719, -5.2541 🐶

296 PORTH Y RHAW
Beautiful woodland stream leads past
freshwater lake to LT cove with giant
rockpool on L, waterfall and cave.
→ From St David's take Solva road (A487).
Turn R onto track for Nine Wells (SA62
6UH), in road dip a mile before Solva. Park
on L and follow woodland track. 🍴 Old
Chapel, Solva (SA62 6UU, 01437 721907).
10 mins, 51.8733, -5.2174 📷⛺🚶

297 PORTHMYNAWYD, NEWGALE
Shingle and LT sand cove with large sea
arch to L and islets for snorkelling to R.
→ 2 miles from Solva (A487 to Newgale)
take first R. Go through farm and find
wooden gate and footpath through hedges
immediately on L. Bear R then L down to
valley bottom.
15 mins, 51.8631, -5.1576 🏊🤿📷⛺

305 Sandy Bay, Broad Haven

South Pembrokeshire: Marloes and Manorbier

Volcanic black basalts and rich red marls give way to silver and gold limestone as you enter south Pembrokeshire. This rock is the remains of reefs, corals and plankton that once flourished in a shallow tropical sea. Clefts and cracks in the rock make this coastline rich in caves, great arches and white sandy coves.

One such cleft on St Govan's Head hides the tiny chapel of St Govan (Gawain), a place of contemplation and pilgrimage for many centuries. A flight of worn stone steps – allegedly uncountable by mortals – leads down through the rocks to a small doorway. According to Arthurian legend Sir Gawain was being chased by pirates when a chasm in the cliffs suddenly opened up to give him an escape route. Once Gawain was safely inside, the rock face sealed itself, concealing the knight until his pursuers had given up and departed. Gawain is said to have established a hermitage here. The dim stone cell has a view of the ocean and its sixth-century altar is hewn from the cliff-face. Below, more steps lead down to the foot of the cliffs where giant boulders have fallen into the sea and sit draped in bladderwrack among jade rock pools. A holy spring reputed to cure leprosy once bubbled up from beneath the chapel.

Continuing up the coast to the east is New Quay, a deep snaking inlet that was once a narrow harbour and smuggling cove. From here it's possible to swim out to the left and around to impressive caves. A little further along is Broad Haven, a popular and beautiful National Trust beach with Church and

302

306

306

Star rocks out in the bay. Fields stretch right down to a couple of tiny coves just to the south of the beach and the farmer is happy for tents to be pitched here if you don't mind fairly basic facilities.

The tide ran a quarter of a mile inland from Broad Haven until the first Baron Cawdor dammed the tidal creeks during the eighteenth century and created a large freshwater lake system, the Bosherston Lily Ponds, which are covered in white lilies in early summer. Keep still and silent and you may catch sight of an otter in the pools along the banks.

If you are feeling adventurous, there are several dramatic swims between Broad Haven and Barafundle Bay. One of the best is at Confucius Hole, a huge crater that fills up into a great blue lagoon with each tide. In calm seas you can enter via a sea cave in the sea cliffs, though this is only accessible at low tide. Just to the left is the narrow chimney cave of Confucius Hole – a name bestowed on it by 'deep-water solo' climbers who love to scale its interior without ropes, knowing that if they fall there is deep water below them. It makes an exciting swim, too.

Further along is Sandy Cove, a totally inaccessible beach with caves and sand but no route down. Behind it is Sandy Pit, another great crater, filled with sand not water, which was once connected to the beach. The passageway is now blocked so we swam into Sandy Cove from a rock ledge on the inside of the south headland. It was a tricky scramble down followed by a 150-yard swim through beautiful crystal waters. Landing on this fabulous deserted beach and wading ashore in the bright sun was like being Robinson Crusoe for a day, washed up on a desert island.

Continue walking and beautiful Barafundle Bay comes into view, with its lovely dunes and woodland. Clamber down to the end of the headland to find three fantastic natural arches with Gaudi-esque spires supporting them. Rutted and puckered, the extraordinary formations continue underwater and the effect is like a sunken gargoyle-covered cathedral. Barafundle was once voted the most beautiful beach in Britain and from here the intrepid might like to try coasteering around to the north and east to Stackpole Quay, checking out the massive Lorts Cave on the way. If you've managed all this, a well-earned cup of tea awaits at the National Trust café, or you may be in need of something stronger at the recommended Stackpole Inn.

Just a few miles to the east, at deserted Swanlake beach, we enter red sandstone country. Thousands of foxgloves cover the headland in June, creating a sheet of purple that moves in the warm breeze. There are deep crimson grooves in the rock here and a remote, basic campsite in the field above the bay. It's only a mile to medieval Manorbier, where you'll find a Norman castle with a warren of corridors and cells, a church and an ancient dovecote. You might even agree with Gerald of Wales – whose famous twelfth-century book The Journey Through Wales is still in print – who describes this village as 'the pleasantist place in Wales'.

Follow the coast path on past King's Quoit, a Neolithic burial chamber dating from around 3000 BC, to Presipe Bay. Steep steps lead down to this dramatic tidal beach, with shallow sandy pools in the hollows beneath the chine. Further on, the scenery reverts to rocky limestone at the adjacent coves of Skrinkle Haven and Church Doors, where striated pillars have created an abbey-sized archway. The steps to Skrinkle collapsed in 2008 but you can still access this superb beach via a tunnel from Church Doors at low tide. You can also swim around the dividing rock buttress, though it's further than it seems as Skrinkle's beach is lower and the waterline is further back.

More dramatic scenery awaits you at the last beach on this stretch: the multiple coves and caves of Draught. At low tide a wide sweep of sand allows you to paddle around immediately to the right into various arched caverns with dramatic ceilings and rutted floor formations. Immediately to the left is a narrow cave with a long chamber leading to a skylight opening at the end. If the tide is up and the sea is calm, these make wonderful snorkel routes. But take care if there is any swell because the beach is very rocky. At low tide there's a chance to explore on foot or swim from the pure shore sands, laid out like fresh snow with a dramatic backdrop of caves.

303

310

308

304

South Pembrokeshire: Marloes to Broad Haven

298 DRUIDSTON HAVEN
Long expanse of wild sands with caves. Hotel perched above with great views.
→ 7 miles S of Newgale on coast lanes. The Druidstone Hotel 🛏 (SA62 3NE, 01437 781221).
5 mins, 51.8120, -5.1048 🅱

299 MUSSELWICK SANDS, MARLOES
Beautiful LT sands hidden beneath cliff.
→ Pass through Marloes (dir St Martins) and find the footpath on R 300m after final house (SA62 3BE). Continue for cliff-top 🔺 West Hook (SA62 3BJ, 01646 636424). Also popular Marloes Sands with Albion Sands at far NW end (51.7219, -5.2288).
5 mins, 51.7350, -5.2093

300 WATWICK BAY, DALE
Remote LT sand cove on Milford Haven.
→ Park in the village and walk down lane past 🛏 Griffin Inn (SA62 3RB, 01646 636227) to find a footpath on R after 10 mins. Follow the path past pretty Castlebeach Bay and go on another mile to Watwick.
20 mins, 51.6924, -5.1597 🚶

301 LINDSWAY BAY, ST ISHMAEL'S
Quiet LT orange sand beach. Pretty church in woodland beyond.
→ Park by recreation ground clubhouse just E of St Ishmael's (SA62 3TB). Follow footpath between toilets and playground ½ mile, bearing L at coast path.
10 mins, 51.7165, -5.1240

302 BULLSLAUGHTER BAY, MERRION
LT sand cove and huge limestone caves beneath the 'Green Bridge of Wales'.
→ 2 miles beyond the turn off for Bosherton (B4319 dir Castlemartin) turn L for Stack Rocks viewing platform and parking (SA71 5HT). Bear L on coast path ¼ mile to inspect the amazing Cauldron and Flimston Bay (descend on headland between them for access/amazing coasteering). Continue 1 mile to much easier path down to Bullslaughter, far side.
25 mins, 51.6101, -4.9752 📷🥽⛏

303 NEW QUAY, BROAD HAVEN
Narrow sandy inlet with caves close to famous St Govan's chapel in cliffs.
→ Continue past 🛏 St. Govan's through

Bosherston (SA71 5DN, 01646 661311) and take first L for Broad Haven parking (basic, amazing 🔺 Trefalen, SA71 5DR, 01646 661643). Follow coast path ¾ mile to the sandy snaking inlet. Continue ½ mile further R to St Govan's Chapel.
15 mins, 51.6005, -4.9261 🚶

304 CONFUCIUS HOLE AND CAVES
Huge lagoon crater and smaller caves
→ 100m SE from Broad Haven on cliff path. Its smaller cousin is 30m beyond. Feasible to swim in via sea cave (at LT) by swimming off steep rocks below.
15 mins, 51.6105, -4.9139 🥽🐟🅥

305 SANDY BAY, BROAD HAVEN
Box Bay. Swimmers only to exciting Sandy Bay with secret tunnels beyond giant crater lagoon.
→ Head L/NE from wonderful Broad Haven (above) following the cliff edge path past Confucius Hole Continue 200m to see Sandy Bay. To access, scramble down on the small promontory between the cove and Saddle Point headland and swim.
15 mins, 51.6113, -4.9147 🥽📷🥽🍴

South Pembrokeshire: Barafundle to Manorbier

306 BARAFUNDLE BEACH ARCHES

HT triple rock arches make for great snorkelling. Leading onto beautiful beach.

→ Continue from Sandy Bay ¾ mile, cutting off Stackpole Head, to see arches on headland S of Barafundle (Griffith Lorts Hole). Descend on far side. Or access from Stackpole Quay ¾ mile (🅟 Stackpole Inn, SA71 5DF, 01646 672324). 🍴 café Boathouse Tearoom (01646 672672).

20 mins, 51.6160, -4.9004 🔵🔵🔵

307 SWANLAKE BAY, MANORBIER

Remote sandy bay, near pretty village

→ Descend towards beach from village and park in layby just beyond (SA70 8QR). Join coast path bearing W for a mile.

20 mins, 51.6466, -4.8262 🔵🔵

308 PRESIPE BAY, MANORBIER

Tidal beach with beautiful crimson rock stacks and deep sand pools and lagoons.

→ Follow coast path E from Manorbier 1½ miles to find steps on near/W side. Or slightly quicker from behind army camp (SA70 7TT), see Skrinkle Haven below. 🅟 Castle Inn, SA70 7TE, 01834 871268. 🔵

Skrinkle Bay, Windy Ridge Farm (SA70 7TX, 01834 871005).

30 mins, 51.6377, -4.7896 🔵🔵

309 SKRINKLE HAVEN, MANORBIER

Small cove with dramatic Church Doors arch and secret cave tunnel through to spectacular Skrinkle Haven beach with further impressive caverns.

→ Head W out of Tenby/A4139 and turn L to army camp (dir Skrinkle Haven/youth hostel) after ½ mile (SA70 7TT). Proceed straight, then L, past youth hostel (0845 371 9031) at army gates to curve round on to large concrete picnic/parking area. Walk back (W) along coast path 400m to find metal staircase down to pretty Church Doors cove. At LT small cave tunnel on R allows access to Skrinkle Haven, via gulley scramble. Find huge vaulted cavern with skylight. At HT access via 200m swim.

5 mins, 51.6423, -4.7747 🔵🔵🔵🔵

310 DRAUGHT SANDS, MANORBIER

Part-sandy LT beach with spectacular rock arches and hidden cavern to L.

→ As for Skrinkle Haven (above) but head

E on coast path for 500m, dropping down into steep valley leading to narrow rock and sand cove on R. To immediate L is narrow but long tidal cave with skylight at far end. To R are two large rock arches with caverns.

10 mins, 51.6438, -4.7673 🔵

311 PENDINE SANDS, GINST POINT

Shimmering estuarine shell sands. MoD so closed until 4pm everyday. Currents.

→ Turn R off A4066 2 miles W of Laugharne (SA33 4RS, signed Hurst House/B&B). Follow road straight all the way to the range gates. Turn L and continue 2 miles to end of the road car parks. Powerful estuary currents, so only swim on a turning neap tide, preferably inbound.

5 mins, 51.7442, -4.4238 🔵🔵

312 SCOTTS BAY, LLANSTEFAN

→ Estuarine beach beneath castle ruins. Follow Church Road (SA33 5JP) to L of castle then shore path ½ mile. Or visit Wharely Point via parking at 51.7624, -4.4138 (first L, W of Llanstefan). Currents

20 mins, 51.7578, -4.4019 🔵🔵

313 Blue Pool Corner

Gower and Glamorgan

We reached Gower's Bluepool late that afternoon, the cliffs bronze-tinted in the summer sun and a glinting sea pulling at the sand as the tide began its ebb. The great rock pool stood like a perfect tub beneath us while the Three Chimneys cave arches marked the furthest reach of the bay.

This is one of the best plunge pools in Britain, scoured out of the rocks by wave-driven eddies that tumbled giant cobbles in its depths. A friend and I had been given a tip-off about its location. We arrived on mountain bikes, threw them into the long grass and scampered down the rocky path to join a group of teenagers who were practising somersaults into the dark purple waters. I eased myself in and swam around for a while, 'plumb lining' to try to calculate the depth. But I couldn't touch the bottom so I joined the others and they showed me how to do a back flip.

If you make it to this lesser-known beach, tucked away at the top end of Rhossili Bay, you can also enjoy a swim in the surf and explore the Three Chimneys rock arch and caves, in which gold moidores and doubloons – Portuguese and Brazilian gold coins from an eighteenth-century shipwreck – can still be found. Adjacent is one of Gower's two ancient Culver Holes; when this one was excavated the remains of 30 bodies dating from the middle of the Bronze Age were found inside.

You soon realise that Gower is an ancient region, riddled with sacred monuments, standing stones and caves. It even boasts King Arthur's stone, a 6,000-year-old dolmen sited above a holy well. This limestone peninsula, extending out into the sea

321

323

325

'I stayed on that Worm from dusk to midnight, sitting on that top grass, frightened to go further in because of the rats and because of things I am ashamed to be frightened of. Then the tips of the reef began to poke out of the water and, perilously, I climbed along them to the shore.'

Dylan Thomas

from the valleys of Wales, has remained a world apart and is steeped in its own legends and curses. Indeed Rhossili Bay is the site of what many consider to be the most haunted house in Britain, the Old Rectory, built in a desolate spot equidistant between the two churches it served, and surrounded by the sea and dunes. Even respected broadcaster Wynford Vaughan Thomas remarked that in the depths of winter, 'something very unpleasant comes out of the sea and into the house'.

The day was drawing to a close as we left Bluepool with our bikes. We needed to find somewhere to wild camp for the night, so we headed south down the bay, pausing at the Old Rectory but moving rapidly on. We had considered Burry Holms, a tidal island with the ruins of a medieval monastic settlement where Gower's patron saint, St Cenydd, came to pray, but the tide hadn't been low enough to cross. So we pushed on to the famous Worm's Head, a giant serpent-shaped tidal promontory that marks the most westerly tip of Gower. Its name is derived from wurm, the Norse word for dragon.

By the time we arrived the tide was low enough to cross and we made the half-mile clamber through seaweed and jagged rocks to reach the steep grass slopes of the Inner Head, just before Devil's Bridge rock arch and blowhole. This was a favourite retreat of Dylan Thomas who came here to write poetry and explore. On one occasion he fell asleep, became stranded by the tides and spent a night alone on the Worm, consumed with fear, his imagination conjuring up all sorts of terrors. We, at least, were not alone, but sleep was fitful and we spent a rather uncomfortable night propped up against boulders to stop us rolling down the hill and into the sea. I woke periodically to listen to the waves in the blowholes and watch the gossamer-like Milky Way pass across the clear sky of a midsummer night.

By seven o'clock the sun was up and we roused ourselves with a dip before clambering back to the mainland to retrieve our bikes. The day was heating up nicely so we headed for Fall and Mewslade Bays, perfect sands beneath craggy golden cliffs encrusted with pinnacles and tiny tors. The approach to these little-known beaches is via a hidden valley near Pitton. From here the south coast unfolds: miles of great rock slabs appear to be piled on top of each other and thrusting upwards at an angle of forty degrees. The rock crevices are pitted with neolithic caves, forts and chambers; in Paviland Cave the body of a 24,000-year-old Stone-Age hunter was discovered in 1823. South of Port Eynon you'll find another Culver Hole, a smuggler's retreat fortified with walls, windows, floors and staircases. At one stage it was owned by the notorious John Lucas, head of the local smuggling dynasty. These remote coves – and others nearby such as Pwlldu Bay and Brandy Cove – were used to store contraband destined for the markets of Swansea. Salt House was another old smugglers' retreat. Salt was indeed produced there but it served principally as an armoury and lookout to warn against approaching customs officers.

303

Pennard Castle, a legitimate military defence, is now a spectacular ruin above the famously scenic Three Cliffs Bay. A small settlement with a church grew up around the castle but was abandoned in 1532 when the inhabitants were overwhelmed by sandstorms. The Pill meanders below, a beautiful river that opens out in a wide arc through the sand before running into the sea. The headland has three peaks above a natural sea arch. To the left is Pobbles Beach and to the right Tor Bay, both good swimming beaches.

320

Gower is without doubt the jewel in the crown of the south Wales coast but there are many other places worth exploring too, especially during the summer holiday period when the lanes and approaches to Gower can become heavily congested. If you have enough time, make a detour to visit the majestic Glamorgan heritage coastline south of Bridgend, where the cliffs are composed of stacked limestone strata, and flat limestone pavements stretch into the sea. Monknash makes a perfect base: from here a stream with a ruined mill leads to the vast beach of Traeth Mawr while, back in the village the atmospheric Plough and Harrow Inn, built from the ruins of the adjacent monastery, specialises in real ales and ciders from the West Country. With a fire roaring in the inglenook, this is the ideal spot to dry wet socks and towels and warm up after a very long day of swimming.

318

North and West Gower

313 BLUEPOOL CORNER, LLANGENNITH

Huge deep rock pool in corner of beautiful LT sand bay. Popular for jumping. Difficult descent. Rock arch at far end of beach.

→ Llangennith is at far NW corner of the Gower (A4118, then first R after Oxwich). Carry on through the village, pass the King's Head pub, over mini roundabout (signed Broughton) to park after a mile at the entrance to Broughton Farm Caravan Park (SA3 1JD). Walk into and through park, bearing L and on to coast path. After ¾ mile Bluepool Corner bay is directly below with pool at the near (E) end about 3m deep for jumping. Tricky scramble down. Massive beach-side ◭ Hillend, from Llangennith (SA3 1JD, 01792 386204).

20 mins, 51.6141, -4.2986 ⬛ 🍴

314 BURRY HOLMS, LANGENNITH

Beautiful remote N section of Rhossili Bay with island and ruined hermitage, connected by LT sand bar.

→ Continue on path from Bluepool (above). Culver Hole and Three Chimneys rock arch/ caves accessible to R (W) at LT.

35 mins, 51.6103, -4.3095 ◭ ◭ ◭ 🏃

315 DEVIL'S BRIDGE, WORMS HEAD

No beaches, but you can swim and snorkel amongst the rocks under the impressive rock arch. Dangerous tidal currents at tip.

→ Head across causeway 2 hours before LT. Strong N–S tidal currents at headland.

45 mins, 51.5656, -4.3268 ⬛ ↻ ⬛ 🏃

316 FALL BAY, RHOSSILI

Quiet LT sand with Giant's Cave and good bouldering for climbers.

→ Take footpath next to the bunkhouse in Middleton, ½ mile before Rhossili (SA3 1PL, 01792 391509) and bear L. Or access from Mewslade Bay (see below). 🍴 Bay Bistro, (SA3 1PL, 01792 390519) with great views of Rhossili.

15 mins, 51.5620, -4.2907

317 MEWSLADE BAY, RHOSSILI

Pretty valley walk to LT sandy cove. Cave enroute. Continue over cliffs to Fall Bay.

→ A4118 then B4247 from Swansea. In Pitton, a mile before Rhossili, turn L (signed Mewslade car park) and take footpath on R.

10 mins, 51.5604, -4.2823

318 CULVER HOLE, PORT EYNON

Fortified cave in cliff, accessible at LT. Rocky but swimming possible when calm. Good rock-pooling.

→ Park at final beach car park in Port Eynon. Follow signs to youth hostel along coast path, past huge campsite (◭ SA3 1NN, 01792 390795) to reach Salt House ruins and the headland. Continue around, keeping low, and drop down to gulley after about 300m. Rope climb leads to entrance. Bring jelly shoes if you plan on swimming from the rocks.

20 mins, 51.5389, -4.2142 ⬛ ↻

319 SLADE SANDS, PORT EYNON

The Sands. A little slice of secluded sand beach in the rocky foreshore, a mile to the E of Horton on busy Port Eynon.

→ 1 miles E on coast path from Horton. Or drop down on footpath from basic ◭ Eastern Slade (SA3 1NA, 01792 391374) beyond Oxwich Green, Oxwich.

20 mins, 51.5480, -4.1825

South Gower to Glamorgan

320 TOR BAY, PENMAEN

Wild, sheltered stretch of long sands beneath dunes and dramatic Great Tor. Between Oxwich and Three Cliffs Bay.

→ Parking area by bus stop/post box W edge of Penmaen (SA3 2HJ, A4118). Take path SE down through fields to headland then bear R after ½ mile, as path opens out, bear R down through Nicholaston dunes. L is a quick route down to Three Cliffs. ( Nicholaston Farm, Penmaen, SA3 2HL. 01792 371209).

20 mins, 51.5688, -4.1254

321 POBBLES, THREE CLIFFS BAY

Beautiful bay with three-peaked cliff and tidal sea arch. River and stepping stones. Rip currents develop by river channel.

→ From Pennard/Southgate (B4436) park by Three Cliffs Coffee Shop (SA3 2DH, 01792 233230) and follow main coast path W 1¼ miles to Three Cliffs, dropping down on broad walk through dunes to Pobbles Beach in front of cliffs to find arch. From Parkmill (A4118, near Penmaen) park by shop (SA3 2EQ, Shepherds), cross road and stream, bear R then climb up through

wood. Head to dramatic Pennard Castle and descend down to stepping stones (1½ miles). Excellent views Three Cliffs Bay (SA3 2HB, 01792 371218).

30 mins, 51.5687, -4.1082

322 PWLLDU BAY, PENNARD

Magical stream and woodland approach to remote sand and shingle bay.

→ Simplest approach is along coast path a mile W from Brandy Cove (below). A very beautiful approach is from the bottom of the very narrow lane at Widegate (turn off B4436 from The Mumbles by Pennard church, SA3 2AA), entering forest through wooden gates to follow stream 1 mile.

25 mins, 51.5639, -4.0565

323 BRANDY COVE, CASWELL BAY

Tiny smuggler's cove. Rocks for jumping at HT. Sand at LT.

→ From White Rose on Mumbles seafront, follow signs Langlands/Caswell (B5493). ½ mile beyond Caswell Bay see footpath on L as the road bends sharply R at top of steep hill. Difficult parking here.

10 mins, 51.5673, -4.0419

324 MERTHYR MAWR WARREN

Huge area of sand dunes leads to beach.

→ 1½ miles Park at Candleston Castle car park (CF32 0LS, signed off A48, S Bridgend). Or by Ogmore Castle stepping stones (CF32 0QP, B4524 / B4265).

30 mins, 51.4739, -3.6481

325 TRAETH MAWR, MONKNASH

Woodland stream leads to tidal sands beneath remote cliffs with limestone pavements. Part naturist. Also good cliff walks S to St Donat's and Marcross.

→ B4265 (dir Llantwit Major) from A48 Brigdend. After 4 miles Monknash is signed R. Continue 2 miles to find Plough and Harrow (CF71 7QQ, 01656 890209), once part of medieval monastery with inglenook and good beer. Park near end of lane by farm. Continue on lane, bear L over stile and follow woodland path ¾ mile to beach. Bear R (N) ½ mile to find best LT sands and, if enough LT time, continue another ½ mile on for Whitmore Stairs back up to cliffs. Traeth Bach is just beyond.

15 mins, 51.4185, -3.5767

333 Tràigh a' Mhill near Fidden

Scotland

The beaches of many of the Hebridean Isles wouldn't look out of place in the Seychelles, so fine and white are their sands. The west coast sports spectacular mountain and island backdrops, from Wester Ross right up to Cape Wrath in the far north. On Skye and along parts of the Aberdeenshire coast, volcanic rock has formed caves, rock pools and arches that are absolutely perfect for adventure swims.

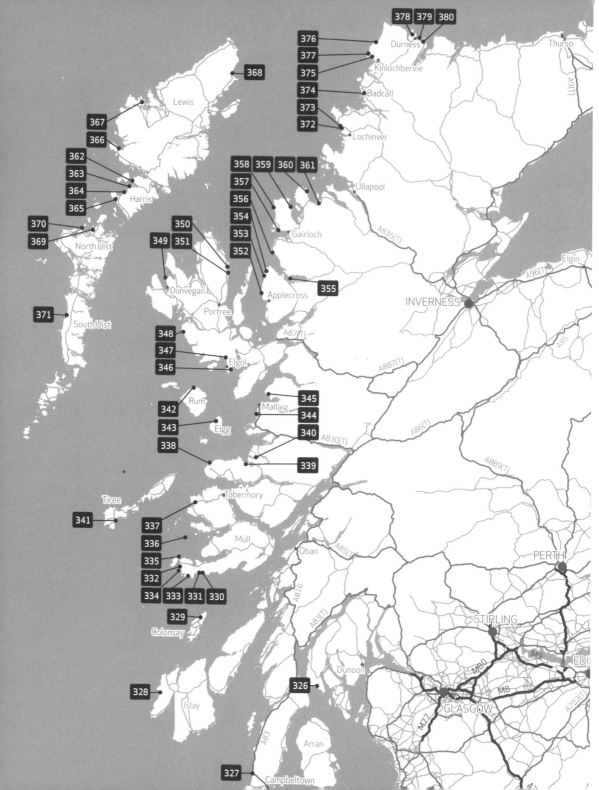

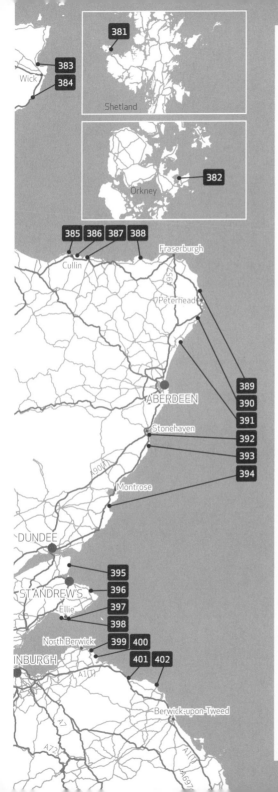

Highlights Scotland

Our favourites include:

330-334 The south-west coast of Mull has some of the best icing-sugar coves in Britain, yet few people know about them.

336 Giant Fingal's Cave on Staffa island is an awe-inspiring amphitheatre of towering basalt columns into which you can jump and dive.

338 Sanna Bay is the westernmost point of the British mainland and its white-sand beach overlooks the isles of Eigg and Rum.

344 The famous beach scenes in the film, Local Hero were shot here, at Morar.

346 Delve into Spar Cave on Skye's coast to find the deep Mermaid Pool.

349 The coral beaches near the Isle of Skye's fairy castle are made from the twisted shapes of petrified algae.

353 This waterfall at remote Applecross cascades through plunge pools into the sea.

361 Swim overlooking 'Anthrax Island' – Gruinard Island – now safe and decontaminated.

362 At Luskentyre, the Outer Hebrides' most famous stretch of white sands, the water glows azure blue even on overcast days.

376 A four-mile walk leads to Sandwood Bay with its giant stack. Many make the pilgrimage to this, Scotland's wildest beach, though other stunning beaches lie nearer.

379 Looking out towards the arctic on the far north coast, Smoo Cave is a large sea cavern with a range of dramatic coastal arches and pools.

381 Papa Stour off Shetland has sea-cave tunnels that stretch under the island, from one side to the other.

391 Visit the ruined church in the Sands of Forvie – all that remains of this 'cursed' village. The rest still lies buried after a nine-day sandstorm.

Near Knockvologan

Argyll, Mull and Iona

Mystical Mull has perfect white sand and swimming coves galore, yet few people ever find them. You can also snorkel into the cathedral-like vaults of Fingal's Cave and visit tranquil, sacred Iona – one of the sunniest places in Scotland.

My first experience of wild swimming was at Fidden campsite. Tufted grass ran down to an islet-studded bay and the dying sun seemed to be setting the distant archipelago on fire. I took a shallow dive into this great iced cocktail and swam down to touch the rippled grooves of sand along the shallow seabed. That night we made a fire in the dwindling half-light and sang songs under the stars on the beach.

Fidden is a perfect base for exploring the best beaches of the Ross of Mull. The uninhabited island of Erraid is accessible at low tide by a sandy causeway and has a beautiful cove on its south side. It was used as the shore station and stone quarry for the building of one of Scotland's most impressive lighthouses, Dubh Artach, 16 miles offshore. Life for the lighthouse keepers was harsh: living conditions were cramped and the sea was fierce, with 100-foot waves a regular occurrence, even in summer. One keeper became so desperate to escape that he even attempted to swim ashore. Robert Louis Stevenson, Scottish author and son of the famous lighthouse-building brothers who engineered Dubh Artach, visited Erraid several times and his heroic Scottish novel Kidnapped is set here.

To the east of Fidden an old road leads through birch and willow scrub, and past one of Mull's oldest oak trees to Tireragan, an abandoned settlement where crofters collected seaweed, and

335

334

336

where you'll find several very remote white beaches. This is a perfect place for wild camping. There are many more coves along this multi-coloured shore where the granite is pink, the sand looks like white icing-sugar and the water is duck-egg blue. Uisken's steep crimson outcrops provide diving platforms for plunging into sandy-floored channels of luminescent turquoise water, while Garbh Eilean, the 'rough isle', is a beautiful dome on a perfect arc of sand.

For many, though, Iona is the main attraction. From this sacred island settled by St Columba in AD 563, Christianity spread throughout much of Scotland and northern England. Its ancient abbey, destroyed by Vikings in 794, was rebuilt as a Benedictine Monastery in 1203 and pillaged again during the reformation. It is the burial place of many early Scottish kings. Iona is a place for quiet reflection, with sweeping views of the ocean and the great Ardmeannach escarpment.

From Iona there are regular boat trips to Staffa, an uninhabited island composed of giant basalt columns similar to those at the Giant's Causeway in Ireland. It is the site of the famous sea cave, Fingal's Cave, or Uamh-Binn – 'the melodious cave' – in Gaelic. Inside, the hexagonal stones rise up like organ pipes to the ceiling and plunge down into incredibly clear depths. The acoustics in this natural sound chamber inspired one of Mendelssohn's overtures and the cave attracted visitors from Wordsworth and Turner to Queen Victoria.

After several days on the Ross of Mull and Iona we followed the spectacular mountain coast north, skirting Loch Scridain, rising over Ben More and dropping perilously into Loch Na'keal. We stopped to bathe and swim at Eas Fors, a series of plunge pools that cascades down through rowan-clad glades over a dramatic waterfall to the sea loch below. Finally we arrived at Calgary, a great bay by a tiny settlement with a superb farmhouse restaurant and hotel. The sands here are white and the water is shallow. It's a place where, on sunny days, children can learn to swim in safety among shoals of tiny fish. A little further round on the coast path you'll find the abandoned quay, constructed from giant pink granite blocks and a good place for jumping as long as you check the depth of the water.

330

Argyll, Mull and Iona

326 KILBRIDE BAY, BUTE
Warm shallow bay with views over Arran.
➔ From Millhouse/B8000 take Ardlamont road S (PA21 2BW). After 2 miles, before gabled house, park and take track on R. Turn L after lake, ¾ mile.
20 mins, 55.8525, -5.2619 🧍‍♂️ ⛺

327 MACHRIHANISH BAY, KINTYRE
Miles and miles of wild sand and dune.
➔ Parking by A83 as it turns inland 5 miles before Campbelltown, signed Westport Beach,. ⛺ Point Sands (PA29 6XG, 01583 441263) 2 miles N of Tayinloan (A83).
5 mins, 55.4715, -5.7124 ⛺ ⛺

328 MHACHIR BAY, KILCHOMAN, ISLAY
Islay's best beach with many wild flowers.
➔ Off B8018 in NW (PA49 7UT). Wild ⛺
5 mins, 55.7781, -6.4562 ⛺ ⛺

329 KILORAN BAY, COLONSAY
Colonsay's best, but also try behind the golf course, and E side of Oronsay
➔ Off far N end of B8086 (PA61 7YT).
5 mins, 56.1045, -6.1816 ⛺ ⛺ ⛺

330 GARBH EILEAN, BUNESSAN, MULL
Sublime double white cove and island.
➔ ½ mile before Bunessan/A489 turn L (dir Scoor House) 2 miles. Pass loch, bear R up track, park beyond ruined church. Track on R descends to Garbh Eilean.
15 mins, 56.2902, -6.1862 ⛺ 🏊 🧍‍♂️

331 UISKEN BAY, BUNESSAN, MULL
Sleepy bay with informal camping.
➔ L in Bunessan, signed Ardachy Hotel (PA67 6DT). Bushwhack E for more coves.
5 mins, 56.2902, -6.2144

332 FIDDEN, FIONNPHORT, MULL
W-facing bay overlooking islets of Iona.
➔ Turn L in Fionnphort before ferry and ⛺ Keel Row (PA66 6BL, 01681 700458) and find simple beachside ⛺ (PA66 6BN, 01681 700427) at farm after 2 miles.
1 min, 56.3085, -6.3672

333 TRÀIGH GHEAL, KNOCKVOLOGAN
Follow trail through ruined Tìr Fhearagain village to remote wooded coves.
➔ Continue down lane from Fidden 2 miles to Knockvologan to find small 'walks' sign/ leaflets at barns on L. Or bushwhack S, via headland 1 mile to tiny Tràigh a' Mhill.
60 mins, 56.2729, -6.2985 ⛺ ⛺ 🧍‍♂️

334 TRÀIGH GHEAL, ERRAID
LT crossing to Erraid beautiful cove.
➔ Walk past Knockvologan farm, down track 500m and cross Erraid Sound to R.
60 mins, 56.2902, -6.3744 ⛺ ⛺ ⛺

335 TRÀIGH BHÀN, IONA
White sand beach on northern tip of Iona.
➔ N on road past abbey to field below Iona Hostel (PA76 6SW, 01681 700 781).
30 mins, 56.3493, -6.3815 ⛺

336 FINGAL'S CAVE, STAFFA, MULL
Great jumps from basalt columns.
➔ 3hr trips, Fionnphort (01681 700358).
10 mins, 56.4314, -6.3415 🍽 🚢

337 CALGARY BAY, NORTH MULL
White sands and old granite jetty.
➔ Wild camping and toilet (PA75 6QU)
2 mins, 56.5793, -6.2805 🚻 🅱

Sanna Sands

Ardnamurchan, Morar and Inner Hebrides

The breeze whistled through acres of dune grass as we followed the stream to the beach. We stripped off and swam in the gently lapping water, giving thanks for the sunshine and blue skies, and then scampered around on the sand like excited dogs as we shook the salty water off our skin.

Sanna Bay, the most westerly point of the British mainland, was bathed in bright morning light. Shells were strewn along the sand, and rocks covered with yellow lichen linked shallow blue pools. Most of the Ardnamurchan Peninsula shoreline is fringed by stony coves, but here it is as if the rocky claws of this far-western promontory have sifted out the seaweed and gathered in the pure white-shell sand, creating inlets with beautiful views to the Small Isles of Eigg, Muck and Rum.

We had crossed from northern Mull by ferry and after detouring to Sanna, we were heading inland via the single track road to Acharacle. Following a visit to the legendary Bakehouse for some of Helen MacGillvray's fantastic pasties, we swam at the ruins of Castle Tioram, situated on its own island with a shingle swimming cove. There's also an ancient stone shelter near the shore with a fireplace and a hole in the roof; you can change here or make a small fire and brew up some tea. Nearby Ardtoe is also worth a visit on a hot day – its pink basalt rocks form swimming ledges and small islands in the wide, shallow bay.

If you are looking for a really wild beach and don't mind a good hour's walk (it's much quicker by bike), head for Camas an Lighe and its 'singing sands'. You hike past the flats of Kentra Bay and

344

340

341

emerge through woodland to find a remote heather and birch-lined beach with grand views to the Small Isles (and there are further adventures to be had if you go east to the bays of Cul na Croise). To make the sands sing, shuffle across them with bare feet. Singing sands occur when sand grains are completely round and between 0.1 and 0.5mm in diameter. To generate the low frequency sound of about 450Hz they must also contain silica and have the right level of humidity. In dune systems they can be heard to roar or boom at certain wind speeds.

The most famous singing sands are those of Camas Sgiotaig, just 20 miles to the north. These are on the beautiful Isle of Eigg, purchased and saved by its community in 1997. It can be reached by day trip from Arisaig and there are spectacular views across to the towering 8,000-foot peaks of Rum, just 10 miles away. The island consists of the ancient remains of one of many volcanoes that erupted along this coast when the landmasses of Scotland and America were breaking apart. Arisaig is also the first stop for exploring the famous 'Sands of Morar', a string of beaches made famous in the widely acclaimed 1983 film, Local Hero. The plot centres on the frustrations experienced by a Texan oil giant (Burt Lancaster), who is negotiating to buy a small west coast village for development. Meanwhile, Marina, a wild-swimming marine biologist is under the impression that the beach is to become a nature reserve.

Despite recent tourist developments south of Arisaig along this short coastline, and the new A830 road bridge to the north at Morar itself, the original Local Hero beach location remains undeveloped. You can watch the sun setting over Rum and Skye and experience the magical Northern Lights here on summer nights. Camusdarach is the actual location of the chapel and beach-shack scenes from the film, but my favourite swimming cove is the little-known bay to the north, Rubh' An Achaidh Mhoir. Here the headland forms a smooth peninsula with perfect diving ledges. You can also keep walking around and up the magical river estuary of Morar, the shortest river in Britain, to find more white sand, oak groves and caves reaching right down to the water's edge.

343

Ardnamurchan, Morar and Inner Hebrides

338 SANNA SANDS, ARDNAMURCHAN

Most westerly headland on the British mainland. Stunning bay of coves and rocky islets, with views to the Small Isles.

→ From Kilchoan (community tourist centre with 🍴 PH36 4LJ, 01972 510222) follow dir Portuairk but turn R after a mile for Sanna (PH36 4LW). Good sand and coves at Portuairk, too. ⛺ Ardnamurchan, Kilchoan, (PH36 4LL, 01972 510766.)

10 mins, 56.7479, -6.1859 ⛺ 🅱

339 SINGING SANDS, ARDNAMURCHAN

Whistling sands of remote Camas an Lighe are set in a bay lined with birch trees, with further coves to E and views of Eigg and Rum.

→ Take A861 from Salen, pass through Acharacle (🍴 pasties at The Bakehouse PH36 4JL, 01967 431484), turn L B8044 dir Kentra, Ardtoe, and L again after ½ mile to Arivegaig (PH36 4LE). From car park go through gate and follow clear track a mile, hugging shore, bearing R past Gorteneorn House, then into forest. After further 1½, miles, bear R at sign for beach.

60 mins, 56.7527, -5.9045 🅿 ⛺ 🍴

340 CASTEAL TIORAM, SHIELFOOT

Dramatic castle ruin on tidal island.

→ Signed Castle Tioram from A861 (PH36 4JY). NB Great river swim by footbridge on route. Head around to far side of castle to find beach with bothy hut.

10 mins, 56.7851, -5.8285 🏊 🏃

341 SOROBAIDH/SORBY BAY, TIREE

Legendary sunshine, endless beaches.

→ Next to fab 🍴 café Balemartine Farm.

5 mins, 56.4756, -6.8930 🍴

342 KILLMORY BAY, RUM

Red deer and views of the Skye Cuillins

→ 5 miles N via bumpy landrover or bike.

120 mins, 57.0527, -6.3499 🅿 ⛺

343 SINGING SANDS, EIGG

Great views of Rum. from brilliant Eigg

→ Day trips from Arisaig (01687 450224). Hire bikes from the pier (01687 482432), take the minibus (01687 482494, £2) or walk the 4 miles to Camas Sgiotaig on N of island. ⛺ Cleadale (01687 482480).

80 mins, 56.9315, -6.1580 ⛺ 🅿

344 ACHAIDH MHOIR, MORAR BAY

Wild beach next to sands of Morar (made famous by Local Hero). Great campsite.

→ From Arisaig follow old coast road (B8008) past beaches and caravan parks. After golf club (2 miles) find good swimming at next car park (500m) or continue on a mile, past ⛺ Camusdarach on L (PH39 4NT, 01687 4502210) and turn L into small car park. Walk down path by stream 500m. Sands of Morar are to the L with further coves beyond, but continue on R side of stream and go round headland (NE) to find Rubh' an Achaidh Mhoir with diving rocks and empty beach. At LT continue on N around into the Morar estuary to find tiny coves and caves.

10 mins, 56.9627, -5.8472 🏊 🍴 🅱

345 AM PORT, SANDAIG, KNOYDART

A string of lost white sand coves behind Rubba Raonuill on wildest Knoydart.

→ Rent Sandaig House (01732 781170) and walk S a mile. Or walk W a mile from road past Glaschoille House from Inverie.

60 mins, 57.0425, -5.7568 🅿 ⛺

Coral Beaches north tip

Isle of Skye

Many would say that Loch Coruisk, in the heart of Skye's highest mountains and at least a day's walk from the nearest road, is one of the wildest places in Britain. The peaks of the Black and Red Cuillins tower above it into the mist and gabbro slabs plunge into crystal-clear, jade-green water.

Here, among all the natural wonder, is a tiny shell-white beach at the head of Loch nan Leachd, one of the only sand beaches on Skye. You can reach Coruisk by taking one of the regular boat trips from Elgol and, if you're having difficulty finding the beach, just ask for the 'Bad Step' – the notorious slab of rock that hangs over the sea and is traversable only via the deep fissure across its face.

From Elgol you can also enjoy another very different wild-swimming experience in the deep Mermaid Pool within the Spar Cave. When Skye was one of the stops on the 'grand tour' of Britain, many artists of the Romantic school visited this cave, including Sir Walter Scott, who alluded to it in *The Lord of the Isles*, published in 1815 to raise money for a new house he was building. The huge vaulted structure is 50 yards long with a flowstone staircase and columns that look like marble. In places the roof has been discoloured by the candles and

351

347

351

torches of the visiting Victorians, who also removed most of the stalagmites and stalactites. A door once blocked the entrance so that an admission charge could be levied, but it was blown out by a yacht's cannon following a dispute. Few people come here today. On the north side of the Cuillins you can find Talisker Bay. The beach is made up of strata of silver and black sand that alternate in bands down to the shoreline. There's a great waterfall cascading down the cliffs to the right and a giant rock stack to the left, surrounded by dark, shallow rock pools that are decorated with jet-black pinnacles and grotesquely contorted volcanic shapes.

No trip to Skye is complete without visiting the Quiraing and the Old Man of Storr, but few know about the dramatic coast that lies just below. There are great waterfall plunge pools at the shingle cove of Inver Tote, but the real local treasures are the caves, natural arches and natural harbour at Leac Tressirnish, a dramatic shoreline far below the cliffs accessible only by a scramble down a steep grassy slope. The harbour is a strange hook-shaped formation that forms a great platform of rock and is a perfect place for diving and jumping into deep water. You can also scramble round it and swim into several sea caves, some with roof openings.

The famous coral beaches of Skye are at its north end, just beyond Dunvegan where the castle displays the famous Macleod 'faerie flag'. This is no tropical coral, of course, but Scottish coral composed of the large fragments of billions of bleached skeletons of the red algae, Lithothamnium calcareum, that grow at the bottom of the ocean nearby. We arrived on the day of a wedding ceremony and the bridegroom explained that this was the couple's favourite place in the world. Thankfully, for them and us, the afternoon sun broke through the haze to illuminate the coral's milky glow. Cows lolled about on the beach sniffing at the seaweed and chewing the cud while we explored to the north to find a fabulous set of basalt columns that formed steps down into the sea. The island of Islay shimmered offshore like a backdrop to a Greek play as we dived, swam and snorkelled in the clearest waters I have ever experienced.

Isle of Skye

346 MERMAID POOL, SPAR CAVE, ELGOL

Cathedral-like sea cave popular with Victorian explorers. 1 hour from LT only.

→ As you drop down to Elgol on B8083, turn L signed Glasnakille as road bends R. At T junction park by telephone box (IV49 9BQ) and enter field down hill 100m on L, by ruined barn. Bear L down to inlet and boulder hop L along LT foreshore rocks 100m, passing another inlet, then traverse around into Spar Cave canyon. Inside, R passage diminishes but L one bears R and rises in flowstone staircase, descending to deep Mermaid Pool. Bring torches!

15 mins, 57.1401, -6.0685

347 LOCH NAN LEACHD, CORUISK

Tiny white beach overshadowed by Cuillin Hills. Reached by boat or long walk.

→ The Misty Isle (01471 866288) and Bella Jane (0800 7313089) both make the 30 min boat trip from Elgol quay (IV49 9BJ). On landing take path along Scavaig River to cross at Stepping Stones (300m) then main coast path E 300m. 5 mile coastal walk E via the Bad Step leads back to Elgol.

20 mins, 57.1958, -6.1514

348 TALISKER BAY, CARBOST

Dramatic silver bay with waterfall and huge purple rockpools on far L.

→ As you enter Carbost from E on B8009, bear L up hill, signed Talisker, then first R (signed, carry on L for Faerie Pools) and 3 miles to parking and track 'to beach'. In Carbost ☐ Old Inn (IV47 8SR, 01478 640205) and visit Talisker Distillery.

30 mins, 57.2811, -6.4625

349 CORAL BEACHES, DUNVEGAN

Made entirely of white coral pieces. Best swimming at HT. Beautiful rocks at N end for swimming too and diving.

→ Pass Dunvegan Castle car park on A850 (IV55 8WF) and continue 3½ miles to T-junction. Park on L in 'Coral Beaches' car park. Walk down track and along coast a mile. Behind hill at N end of beach find basalt column rocks on water's edge. ☐ Loch Bay seafood (Stein, IV55 8GA, 01470 592235) is well worth the 7 miles drive.

40 mins, 57.500, -6.6372

350 INVER TOTE WATERFALLS, LEALT

Coastal waterfall with pebble beach.

→ Inver Tote and Lealt are about 4 miles N of the Old Man of Storr (A855 E coast). From the large layby car park (IV51 9JW) take the path to the waterfall viewpoint and then descend to the pebble beach for a swim in the sea, or in the waterfall itself.

15 mins, 57.5659, -6.1480

351 LEAC TRESSIRNISH, THE STORR

Hook-shaped, natural harbour rock formation for snorkelling and jumps plus two sea caves. Calm seas only.

→ Continue 2 miles S from Tote (above) to find long layby parking/viewpoint on L (set back from road) opp a gated track. Look down to see flat grass plateau with the Leac rock formation. Head to end of layby track, cross gate and bushwhack 300m R steeply down slope. Also try inlet 100m to N which leads to foreshore rock plateau, from the end of which you can swim into several sea caves.

20 mins, 57.5417, -6.1402

355 Camas an Leim, Shieldag

Wester Ross

Crossing Skye Bridge we returned to the mainland but were soon climbing high into the mountains again. We crawled up miles of twisting mountain road to the 2,000-feet Coire na Ba pass where stopped to watch the final rays of the day before descending cautiously to Applecross Bay.

It was dark by the time we arrived. The tide was in as we pitched up on the shadowy shores, bright stars reflecting on a glassy summer sea that was lapping on the beach. I waded out up to my waist and a faint milky glow trailed out in my wake. Time passed as, in raptures, I watched my fingertips make luminous streaks in the water, and when I dived down the swirling patterns were like underwater St Elmo's fire.

I had only experienced phosphorescence once before in the sea at Norfolk one hot summer. It occurs in Britain in warm shallows, especially after days of bright sunlight. The bioluminescence is given off by accumulations of plankton, which are disturbed by motion. Most often seen glowing in the bow waves of boats at night, phosphorescence is a global phenomenon, particularly common in the tropics. For many creatures that inhabit the deep ocean it is the only source of light.

By morning the bay had emptied leaving rivulets of straggling seaweed and stone running down to the shore. We broke camp and headed north up the coast road, the eastern mountain range in shadow but fringed with a halo of celestial rays. We passed the little cove of Sand and a series of stunning waterfall cascades, where we bathed in the deep freshwater

356

354

353

pools that ran to the sea, jumping from the rocks and basking like seals as the sun broke over the hill with a flourish. At Cuaig we found a secret bay and swam with silvery elvers near a ruined fisherman's hut. Long kelp strands waved in the bay, rising up like a forest, and we could almost imagine ourselves swimming with the little eels in their spawning grounds, the great Sargasso Sea.

From here the long road was utterly spectacular as it ran alongside Loch Torridon with its stony bays and tree-cloaked islands. Gairloch and the exquisite Redpoint beaches are a journey of only 5 miles by water but over 40 miles by road. At Gairloch, the giant peach-coloured pebbles are streaked with crimson ripples and the sand glows ochre in the dunes but deep purple on the seabed. There's a meadow-covered islet and a ruined fishing station with rusty anchors lined up along its walls.

If you follow the Gairloch road and head towards Melvaig you'll find an excellent pub and some of the most dramatic cliffs, rock arches and sea caves in Scotland. Pass through Melvaig then walk up the private road towards the lighthouse and outdoor centre at Rudha Reidh, and stop by the first bridge to venture down to the shore. Here you'll find a huge cave, a waterfall and a rock arch where you can swim if the sea is dead calm.

The beaches retain their reddish sand all the way up and around the remaining Wester Ross coast. Firemore near Poolewe has a rocky promontory perfect for snorkelling, while Mellon Udrigle offers sands and ancient hut circles with views over the Summer Isles. But the final set of beaches on Gruinard Bay are the spookiest of all. They overlook the original 'Anthrax Island', chosen by the British government during the bleakest years of the Second World War to test lethal bacterial spores. Gruinard Island was the perfect location: remote, unpopulated yet close to the big allied military base at Loch Ewe. The spores, thankfully, were never used in battle and from 1986 a determined effort was made to decontaminate the land by removing topsoil and then treating the ground with a vast amount of formaldehyde. Finally, a flock of sheep was transported to the island and, when they remained healthy, it was re-opened after 48 years of quarantine. Visit if you dare!

Wester Ross

352 SAND BAY, APPLECROSS
Steep dunes lead down to wide sandy bay
→ 3 miles N of Applecross find aptly
named bay on L.  Applecross (IV54 8ND,
01520 744268) back in the main bay.
3 mins, 57.4680, -5.8670 ▲

353 CUAIG WATERFALL, APPLECROSS
Verdant waterfall ravine with plunge
pools leading to sea.
→ 8 miles N of Applecross (IV54 8XL),
and a mile before Cuaig, park at viewpoint
towards top of hill on R, then walk back
500m to river and follow it downstream
to sea. In deep canyon find pools, or swim
from rocky shore.
10 mins, 57.5396, -5.8537 ▮▮▮▮

354 CUAIG COVE, APPLECROSS
Old quay and beautiful sands in perfectly
sheltered circular hidden bay.
→ Just W of stream bridge in tiny Cuaig
(above) go through field gate and follow
path along stream to shore and cross
stepping stones for beach. Very quiet.
10 mins, 57.560, -5.8376 ▮▮

355 CAMAS AN LÈIM, TORRIDON
Secluded pebble cove on quiet peninsula.
→ Park at N end of Shieldag off A896
(IV54 8XW) and walk up past school and
tennis courts. Bear R off path after ¾ mile.
20 mins, 57.5362, -5.6457 ▮▮

356 REDPOINT BEACHES, BADACHRO
Pink sands and dunes in two wild bays.
Enjoy a waterside sundowner in the
Badachro Inn on the way back.
→ 4 miles S of Gairloch A832 turn off for
Badachro, pass ▮ Badachro Inn (IV21
2AA, 01445 741255) and park at road end
(IV21 2AX, 6 miles). Bear R towards dunes
(500m) for closer beach or turn L through
gate, to and through Redpoint Farm, for
furthest beach (1 mile, 57.6396, -5.7987).
10 mins, 57.652, -5.810 ▮▮

357 BIG SAND, GAIRLOCH
Long sand beach with dune camping.
→ Signed N of Gairloch, 4 miles, B8021.
▲ Sands (IV21 2DL, 01445 712152). Local
seafood, ale and music at ▮ Old Inn in
Gairloch (IV21 2BD, 01445 712006)
5 mins, 57.7334, -5.7641 ▮ ▮

358 RUDHA REIDH, GAIRLOCH
Wild cave and sea arch coastline.
→ Continue past Big Sand (above) to ▮
Melvaig Inn (IV21 2DZ, 01445 771212). 1½
mile further, on lighthouse road, descend
below first river bridge to ledges & arches.
10 mins, 57.8267, -5.8132 ▮▮▮▮▮

359 CAMAS NA MUIC, FIREMORE
Beach with rocky outcrops for snorkelling
→ Leave Gairloch on A832, turn L at
Poolewe (B8057). 4 miles, IV22 2LQ.
2 mins, 57.8331, -5.6779 ▮

360 MELLON UDRIGLE
Remote cove on edge of Gruinard Bay
→ 8 miles N from Poolewe (A832) turn L at
Laide. 3 miles by telephone box (IV22 2NT).
5 mins, 57.9018, -5.5571 ▮

361 GRUINARD BAY, GAIRLOCH
Sheltered sands and coves opposite now
decontaminated Gruinard 'anthrax' Island.
→ 5 miles from Laide (A832) find car park
on R (IV22 2NG). Many coves at LT.
1 min, 57.8565, -5.4558 ▮▮

362 Losgaintir

Outer Hebrides

South Harris and Uist are places of pilgrimage for the beach connoisseur. Ribbons of snow-white sand drift down the islands' Atlantic coasts and collect in sweeping bays. Meadows covered in wildflowers provide the perfect backdrop and offer endless wild-camping potential.

May or June is the best time to visit, before the midges and when the 'machair' (beach meadow) has come to life. The grazing on this western fringe is especially lush owing to dustings of lime-rich sand, and there is a profusion of different grasses intermingled with buttercups, daisies and orchids. So fertile is the land here that its poor communities were among the first to be evicted, around 1824 – a period when landlords across Scotland were destroying crofts and turning instead to large-scale sheep-farming for profit. The highland clearances and village burnings began soon after.

The best way to explore South Harris, which is only 15 miles from end to end, is by bike. Our ride started at Losgaintir and Traigh Rosamol, probably the most famous of the Outer Hebridean beaches, an expanse of estuarine sands and dunes overlooking the Isle of Tarasaigh (Taransay). The intensity of the colours cannot fail to move you. Even on overcast days acres of white sand glow under turquoise shallows, with the mountains of Lewis and a scattering of tiny islets providing an amazing backdrop.

There's also good swimming to be had on the other side of the estuary, two miles along the coast road at Sheileboist and

366

367

366

Niosaboist. From here you can look back in awe at the white estuary and dune expanse that you've just left. Between two coves, a tiny primary school alone on the machair faces sand and sea in every direction, while the Macleod stone stands sentinel on the hillock.

At every switch and turn of the coast road the colours of the ocean, the sense of space and the sheer energy of the place created a real emotional charge; the strong scent of ozone in the air adding to the overall sensation. The island was so small, however, that I feared we would finish the journey all too soon. So we stopped to swim in rolling surf at Traigh Mhor, then lounged for a few hours in an expanse of meadow behind Scarasta before visiting Cleabhaig, the wildest of the beaches, set beneath the hill of Ceapabhal and by a tiny ruined chapel. A storm played out on the horizon as the incoming swell tumbled our bodies. I felt as if I could swim forever, like a selkie – one of the shape-shifting seal fairies of ancient Hebridean folklore.

That evening the ferry manoeuvred through the complex labyrinth of offshore rocks and islets that leads to Uist. We camped down a narrow lane on the machair close to an ancient graveyard at Hornais. The white sandy shallows seemed to turn even more mauve as twilight descended – as if they had stored up the colours of the day – and we were drawn half-mesmerised into the luminescent waters. By morning, a mist had formed, but the mauve-tinted light still permeated everything.

The people of the Uists, islands so remote that even the Reformation did not reach them, remain deeply spiritual. Living on the edge, they experienced great suffering as a result of the clearances and the near-eradication of their Gaelic tongue. The Catholic Church here is one of the most active in Britain and all along the western seaboard tiny white chapels alive with hymns and prayers dot the prairie, mountains towering up behind them on the eastern skyline. Sabbaths on the Uists are still held sacred and the islanders' faith is tangible and strong. This is a place for retreat and purification; a place where you can walk the sands, lie in the meadows, contemplate the beauty of the world and bathe away the day.

Outer Hebrides

362 LOSGAINTIR, HARRIS
Luskentyre, the Outer Hebrides' most famous beach: white sand, turquoise seas, mountain vistas, freezing waters!
→ 10 miles S and W of Tarbert on A859, then R along estuary to car park at end (HS3 3HL). Popular for wild 🏕
5 mins, 57.8891, -6.9600 🏕 🅱

363 TRÀIGH NIOSABOIST, HORGABOST
Camping beach with quiet cove to W.
→ Continue W from Losgaintir (above) on A859. After 3½ mile turn off to R.
2 mins, 57.8651, -6.9805

364 TRÀIGH MHÒR, SGARASTA, HARRIS
Long and empty with good surf.
→ 2 miles beyond Niosaboist (above) park by telephone box/post office and cut across fields. 2 more miles leads to **Tràigh Scarasta** dunes and machair. 🍴 Scarista House (HS3 3HX , 01859 550238).
10 mins, 57.8389, -7.0181 🏕 🚶

365 TRÀIGH NA CLEABHAIG, HARRIS
Four wild coves under Harris' highest hill.

→ 4 miles from Traig Mhor (above) turn R for An Taobh Tuath / MacGillivray Centre (HS3 3JA). Park at road end. Continue on track through gate 1 mile.
15 mins, 57.8070, -7.0849 🏕 🚶 🏕

366 TRÀIGH MHEILEIN, HUISINIS, HARRIS
Shallow azure waters, wild camping.
→ From Tarbet take B887 N to parking at Huisinis. Walk 1½ mile N. Overlooking Scarp island. Wild 🏕
30 mins, 58.0168, -7.0878 🏕 🚣 🚶

367 TRÀIGH NA BEIRIGH, LEWIS
Best beaches in NW Lewis.
→ Near end of the B8011 from Calanias, R over bridge signed to Bhaltos (HS2 9HS.)
5 mins, 58.2163, -6.9301 🏕

368 TRÀIGH GHEARADHA, TOLSTA, LEWIS
Ancient Gneiss stacks and white sand hidden at the N end of Tolsta strand.
→ From Stornoway, f ar end of B895 (HS2 0NN). Road continues to a car park on R.
2 mins, 58.3678, -6.2147

369 CLACHAN SANDA, NORTH UIST
Sand, sea, machair. Old cemetery and standing stone. LT bar to Lingay Island.
→ From Berneray causeway continue 3 miles S and turn R signed for cemetery (HS6 5AY) and continue to beach. Wild 🏕
3 mins, 57.6705, -7.2491 🚣

370 TRÀIGH IAR, GREINETOBHT, N UIST
A peninsula of machair, dunes and beach.
→ Continue from Clachan (above) on B893, then R A865, 5 miles. Bear R at telephone box and continue 2 miles. Wild 🏕
2 mins, 57.6745, -7.3366 🏕 🏕

371 TOBHA MOR, SOUTH UIST
Traditional thatched crofts, hostel, chapel remains, mountain backdrop and ruined castle on nearby loch island.
→ From South Ford causeway continue 7 miles on A865. Tobha Mor is signed to R. Turn up for basic bed 🏕 at Howmore Hostel (white thatched cottage at end of road, gatliff.org.uk trust). Take the preceding R turn for **Loch an Eilein** and Caisteal Bheagram.
5 mins, 57.3073, -7.4007 🏕 🏕

Oldshoremore

Phollain

North West: Assynt and Sutherland

At the extreme north tip, from Ullapool to Cape Wrath and along the Sutherland coast to John o' Groats, the wild coastline harbours some of the most beautiful swimming beaches in Britain.

Sutherland, or southern land, is the most northerly coast of Britain; when you realise it was once part of the great Norse empire the name makes more sense. Neighbouring Assynt, meaning 'rocky when seen from afar', is a reference to the famed mountains of Stach Pollaidh and Suilven that rear up from the flat moor and stand like monuments over the sea. Between the two districts is Achmelvich, literally 'machair meadow and dunes'. It's a stunning beach and one of the most popular in this area, but you can easily escape the handful of summer tourists by walking to the second cove, a wedge of skin-pale sands set between igneous outcrops that form a turquoise swimming pool and suntrap.

From here you can also walk on to the hidden bay of Port Alltan na Bradhan, a deep, sand-lined natural harbour, with very sheltered swimming at the bottom of a vale complete with ruined mill and giant millstones. The stream here has a waterfall and the grassy hummocks between the rocks are an ideal place for camping and picnics. I rejoiced in an entire afternoon of swimming and paddling an inflatable dinghy in baking sunshine and under clear blue skies.

The B869 coast road that passes by Alltan na Bradhan is one of the most scenic in Scotland, winding through a wildlife-rich landscape that is home to red deer, sea otters and even ospreys. Heading north on the A894 I stopped at Badcall Bay and swam out as a golden sun set over the archipelago of

379

377

378

scattered isles. But the usual destination for anyone looking for a wild beach this far north is legendary Sandwood Bay. Owned by the John Muir Trust, this remote beach is 15 miles south of Cape Wrath and accessible only by walking for a distance of 5 miles. This red-sand bay, with dunes and grassy clefts perfect for wild camping, is more than a mile long and framed by cliffs and the ancient alien-looking sandstone stack of Am Buavhaille (the Herdsman). The recently enlarged car park is testament to Sandwood's popularity and the next day I counted 15 groups, all here to make the pilgrimage. The bay is big enough to absorb everyone but you might find fewer people on Oldshoremore and Phollain beaches, which lie just next to the car park. They're safer for swimming and also have beautiful rock formations.

Near Durness, 20 miles north, Balnakeil Bay is a celebrated arc of dune and sand with a wild north shore featuring sea caves and rock arches. Immediately south you'll find the enormous Smoo Cave, which lies at the head of a deep sea-canyon impregnated with caves and swimming ledges. Continue around to the north of the headland beyond Pocan Smoo to Bagh Geal and find my favourite bay, a complex of green and black rock pools with arched entrances, tiny islands and several small caves.

From Durness onwards the remote A838 coast road winds eastwards and every one of the empty beaches and coves that unfolds could win awards. Few are named, let alone visited. I had just one more day to explore before heading to John o' Groats and back south again, so I camped that last night at Chailgeag, a sweeping stretch of perfect sand with rock arches and cove inlets set under the ancient prehistoric remains of a village settlement. Between me and the Arctic Circle far to the north there was no land whatsoever. Early next morning I found a flat rocky ledge by the sea, not far from the beach, and marvelled at the sheer enormity of the landscape around me. After a saltwater shampoo and shave and still covered in soapsuds, I dived into the great blue ocean and swam hard down through the cool waters to the sandy bay floor, washing all the bubbles clean away.

North West: Assynt and Sutherland

372 ACHMELVICH COVE, LOCHINVER

Superb white-sand cove with granite outcrops; a short walk from car park.

→ From Ullapool take A835 then A837 to Lochinver. Or take scenic coastal lanes via Inverkirkaig and 🍴 Achins book and coffee shop (IV27 4LR, 01571 844262). From Lochinver (B869), turn L and L again after a mile (IV27 4JB). Bear R from the car park 500m to find the hidden cove beyond.
10 mins, 58.1727, -5.3043 🏊

373 PORT ALLTAN NA BRADHAN

Very sheltered sandy bay with waterfall and rocks for jumping.

→ Walk 1½ miles N along coast from Achmelvich (above). Or drive 2 miles on up B869 and park at first proper lay-by on R then follow stream path down past ruins.
20 mins, 58.1814, -5.3170 🍴 🏚

374 BADCALL BAY,

Tiny working fishing quay with spectacular sunset swim over archipelago

→ 15 miles N of A387 on A894, signed L turn (IV27 4TH)
3 mins, 58.3237, -5.1377 🏊 🏊

375 OLDSHOREMORE/PHOLLAIN

Two connecting white-sand bays with island, ledges and rock pools between.

→ Continue N on A894, A838, then B801 L to Kinlochbervie and on to Oldshoremore (IV27 4RS). Turn L for Oldshoremore beach car park; quieter Phollain beach, next L.
5 mins, 58.4773, -5.0872 🌊

376 SANDWOOD BAY, BLAIREMORE

Join the pilgrimage to one of Scotland's most iconic wild beaches with sea stacks and lochan, managed by John Muir trust

→ Follow lane 500m from Oldshoremore (above) to Blairemore and John Muir Trust car park and WC. Well-marked track begins over gate opposite. 3 mile walk across moor. Turn L at end of second loch. Beware rip currents in surf conditions. Wild ⛺.
80 mins, 58.5384, -5.0650 🏖 ⛺ ⛺ 🚶

377 BÀGH SHEIGRA, BLAIREMORE

Tiny, remote sand and shingle cove with flat grassland for wild camping.

→ A mile from Blairemore. Turn L on corner and past cemetery to track.
3 mins, 58.4897, -5.1211

378 BALNAKEIL BAY, DURNESS

Spectacular beach dune system set against the backdrop of Cape Wrath.

→ Turn L entering Durness on A383 (IV27 4PT). Explore rock arches of Faraid Head.
15 mins, 58.5794, -4.7693 🚶 🅱

379 POCAN SMOO, DURNESS

Huge cavern at head of sea-filled canyon good for swimming. Wonderful rock pools with arches on headland.

→ Continue through Durness and a mile on to Smoo Cave (signed, IV27 4QA). Descend to cave on path, climb up other side of inlet and go through gate/fence on to headland. See steep path L down to rock ledges for swimming in gorge, but continue 500m on to N foreshore to find rock pools. ⛺ Sango Sands (IV27 4PP, 01971 511726)
20 mins, 58.5678, -4.7123 🏊 🏖 🍴 🏊 🌊

380 TRÀIGH ALLT CHÀILGEAGH

Pink granite, sea caves and ruined village.

→ Continue beyond Smoo (above) 2 miles, to pass Ceannabeinne lost village on roadside L and then beach parking on R.
5 mins, 58.5513, -4.6778 🚶 🌊

Bow Fiddle Arch, Portknockie

North East: Shetland to the Moray Firth

The island of Papa Stour off the west coast of the Shetland Isles is widely regarded as having the most spectacular sea caves, arches and stacks in Britain.

One cave, the Holl a Boardie, stretches for half a mile under the Papa Stour and you can row all the way through it. Another, Kirstan's Hole, was once a loch that collapsed into the sea caves below during a violent stormy night, 30 years ago. Today, the most accessible of these wild-swimming wonders is Brei Holm, which has an impressive set of tunnels, grottoes and catacombs interconnected by multiple arches and sea bridges.

Bearing south again, for the mainland and John O'Groats, the dramatic stacks and cliffs of Duncasby have deep inlets and canyons, and the nearby sands of Sinclair Bay are worth a visit. But if you are looking for more adventure, head for Whaligoe Steps where 365 paved Victorian steps cut out of the sheer cliff-face lead down to a natural inlet and harbour. On a calm day it is possible to swim here.

This impressive stairway was constructed in 1808 to give around 35 local families access to the sea and enable them to earn a livelihood from fishing. Men and women would haul their creel pots 200 feet up to the curing house on the cliff top, and you can still see the waist-high ledges built so they could

381

388

382

rest their loads. Now only rusty winches and chain rings bear witness to a once-thriving industry.

During the nineteenth century the herring fishing boom extended all along the east coast and employed many of those crofters displaced from the west by the clearances. Sixty miles to the south, on the Moray coast, Portknockie is another run-down fishing village with extraordinary coastal features. Here the Bow Fiddle rock sits in a little cove to the rear of the town and the slanted rock strata have created a huge natural arch, heavily stained with guano. The swim out is easy and once underneath you can peer right down into the deep water below. You may even be lucky enough, as we were, to witness a pod of dolphins swimming close by.

Historically, the Moray coast was also a place of resistance. West from Portnockie, Preacher's Cave was one of several used as secret places of prayer when the Free Church was breaking away from the Church of Scotland during the nineteenth century. Much earlier, in the thirteenth century, Findlater Castle, east of Cullen, was an important coastal defence against the Vikings. Today, in this remote yet rural setting, you'll find Sunnyside Cove, one of Moray's best-kept secrets, with a fine sandy cove far below the rolling wheat fields.

A better-known beach is at Pennan, 20 miles east, beyond Banff. The village and its inn - with the famous red phone box outside - were also used as locations for the film, *Local Hero*. The inn is now open again after being closed for many years and is a pleasant place to refuel after visiting Hell's Lum, a cave-and-cove complex on the far side of Pennan Bay. There is a dramatic series of deep plunge pools and inlets, perfect for jumping and snorkelling, and a great cavern on the right leads via a tunnel to tiny Cullykhan Bay. Hell's Lum itself is a gaping scar in the hillside on the left that leads through the hill to a sea cave at the bottom of the cliffs. The jet-black rocks and deep-blue water give this place a sublime feel and the interconnected caverns, beaches and pools – all overlooking beautiful Pennan – make this one of the best wild-swimming locations in north-east Scotland.

388

North East: Shetland to the Moray Firth

381 BREI HOLM, PAPA STOUR, SHETLAND
Spectacular subterranean passages, sea caves and stacks.

→ Ferries leave from tiny West Burrafirth, 25 miles W of Lerwick, N of Westside (day trips Fri/Sat, 01957 722259). From jetty walk ½ mile around Housa Voe bay to S headland. Brei Holm is connected by a tidal causeway with arches on E side. 200m swim in wetsuit but boat support recommended. Also extraordinary **Fogla Skerry** island off W coast (60.33518, -1.74766) has a ½ mile sea-cave tunnel right under island. By boat only
20 mins, 60.3271, -1.6601

382 HALLEY BEACH AND GEO, ORKNEY
Secluded white sands and extraordinary rock arches to explore.

→ 10 miles SE of Kirkwall on A960, cross to Deerness (**Sandi Sands**) then L on B9051 to road end and beach. About ½ mile to NE are the Otter geo stacks and archways and boulder beaches, reached by gulleys or at LT.
5 mins, 58.9508, -2.7834

383 SINCLAIR BAY, WICK
Great 5 mile sand bay. 2 miles E for castle ruins, caves and geos.

→ 3 miles N of Wick on A99. Parking at Ackergill Links club house (KW1 4RG).
5 mins, 58.4840, -3.1247

384 WHALIGOE STEPS, WICK
Old steps cut down cliff-face to reach inlet, once used for herring fishing.

→ 7 miles S of Wick turn L off A99 at telephone box (KW2 6AB), opp SNH sign. Park at end of cul-de-sac and walk down to old house to find steps beyond. Many 'geo' caves and columns too. Calm seas only.
5 mins, 58.3456, -3.16125

385 BOW FIDDLE ARCH, PORTKNOCKIE
Dramatic slanted rock with arch on edge of small town. Caves in nearby bay.

→ E of Elgin, A98. Follow road through town down to the seafront, turn R and park by church hall (AB56 4NN, bottom of Admiralty St). Follow track down past sheds to shore 300m, to arch. Preacher cave 200m to L, below Patrol Rd.
5 mins, 57.7072, -2.8489

386 SUNNYSIDE, SANDEND
Beautiful walk to hidden beach by ruins

→ Take A98 E through Cullen and after 2 miles turn L at cross roads (signed Findlater Castle). Turn L up to farm and parking after ½ mile. Castle is ½ mile through fields on cliff edge. Bear L (W) for Sunnyside Cove, ½ mile further.
20 mins, 57.6932, -2.7787

387 PORTSOY TIDAL POOL
→ Sited 500m W of harbour (AB45 2QA).
10 mins, 57.6861, -2.6990

388 HELL'S LUM / CULLYKHAN, PENNAN
Sandy cove plus dramatic network of snorkelling inlets, caverns and tunnels.

→ From Banff (A98) then B9031. A mile before Pennan turn L down track signed for Cullykhan Bay. Descend to the beach on R, or drop down L to follow stream steeply to rocky inlets and caves at bottom (300m) with tunnel though to beach at R. The scar to the L is Hell's Lum, with cave tunnel to emerge at sea under cliffs. ◻ Pennan Inn (AB43 6JB, 01346 561201)
5 mins, 57.6857, -2.2755

Aberdeen and Dundee

Peering down into the deep abyss early that evening we wondered if we could ever find a way down to the beautiful lagoon. The cliffs were sheer but the still, sapphire and cobalt waters gleamed temptingly when the low sun shone in through the cave mouth.

The Bullers of Buchan is a massive collapsed cave with a 150-foot-high arched entrance and a deep internal pool. It's clearly impossible to get down to without serious climbing equipment, but it's not impossible to swim into, if the sea is calm. So we returned early the next morning and followed the overgrown path down into the adjacent cove, working our way along the right-hand side as far as we could go. We changed and swam across the small bay, then scrambled around the headland before diving in beneath the cave. Lifted up by gentle swell, we peered fleetingly into the depths with our goggles as the 'cathedral doors' of the huge chamber opened above us. The acoustics inside the cave were fantastic and we hummed and sang after landing on one of the tiny rocky islands that must have once formed part of the cave roof.

Coming into such close contact with these geological wonders is awe-inspiring, so we were excited when a sea-kayaking guide told us of another set of arches just down the coast from Stonehaven. The Garran is rarely visited and there is no easy path but a route along the cliff brings you down to a rock platform the size of a football pitch.

It harbours three massive rock pools with ledges that form

393

392

389

perfect diving boards. To the right is another bay with a deep pool connected to the sea via a natural arch, and to the left two giant caves gape in the nearby cliffs – their openings large enough to sail a yacht into.

This coastline must have a thousand stories to tell: certainly the superb ruins of Dunnottar Castle have seen much bloodshed. Dating from the ninth century, the castle sits on a narrow outcrop and is protected by the sea on three sides. During the Wars of Scottish Independence its entire English garrison was burned alive by William Wallace, but today the location is comparatively peaceful. Two shingle coves on either side are good for swimming at high tide and the daring might try to circumnavigate the castle via the various stacks; one of them is said to have a cave that reaches right up through the centre like a chimney.

Cliffs, caves and conflict aren't the only characteristics of this coast. It has softer features, not least some of the largest expanses of sand dunes in the country. North of Aberdeen, near Peterhead, ruined Kirkton church and graveyard stand behind sand hills that glow peach in the evening light. In the south, near Montrose, the Red Castle at beautiful Lunan Bay takes its name from the red sands set in a wide crescent before it. A few miles to the north you'll find the ruins of a fort-like limekiln beneath Boddin Farm, and the Elephant rock arch a little further on. To the south is the tiny cliff-top village of Auchmithie, true home of the famous Arbroath 'smokie' – haddock smoked over hardwood until it takes on a burnished gold colour – and also But and Ben, one of the best family-run restaurants in Scotland.

The prize for the best sands in Scotland must, however, go to Forvie, a national nature reserve with extensive dunes and four miles of foreshore with marram grass, pennywort, crowberry and creeping willow. A village and its church once stood amid these dunes but the entire community was overwhelmed by a sandstorm in 1413, allegedly the result of a curse uttered by three sisters who were put out to sea in a leaky boat. The church ruins have been excavated but the rest of the village lies silently under the sand, still waiting to be found.

390

Aberdeen and Dundee

389 KIRKTON CHURCH AND DUNES
Remote dunes and beach accessed via
ruined church.

→ 4 miles N of Peterhead on A90, between
Hallmoss and St Fergus, turn R (AB42 3EN),
signed cemetery. Park by cemetery and
pass round to R, over rabbit warren and
fence to dunes. Or continue a mile to St
Fergus to find main beach car park on R.

10 mins, 57.5467, -1.8026

390 BULLERS OF BUCHAN
Spectacular collapsed cave among
dramatic cliffs and stacks. Deep lagoon
accessed via swim through rock arch.

→ L off A90 4 miles S of Peterhead, dir
Cruden Bay then park in large signed layby
on L after a mile (AB42 0NS). View arch
and lagoon then descend to cove on S side
and scramble along cove edge 100m as far
as possible (swimming gully if necessary).
Swim across cove N, scramble around
headland, then swim in through arch. Calm
seas only. Good walk N to North Haven bay.
Bay of Cruden (just over 1 mile S) has a
beautiful undeveloped beach.

20 mins, 57.43317, -1.81868

391 SANDS OF FORVIE, NEWBURGH
Huge dune system with secret bay.
Ruined church and lost village in sands.

→ From Bullers (above) 10 miles S on A975
past Collieston, to car park on L (AB41
6AA) opp river, before causeway. Take
path a mile, then bear L along coast up to
beautiful **Hackley Bay**.

30 mins, 57.3336, -1.9552

392 CASTLE HAVEN, STONEHAVEN
Swim from rocky bays on either side of
Dunnottar Castle, located on its rocky
headland, or swim right around.

→ Signed 2 miles S of Stonehaven on A90
(AB39 2TL). Castle Haven (shingle) on N
side is good at HT in calm seas.

10 mins, 56.9483, -2.1998

393 THE GARRAN, CATTERLINE
Sea arch and lagoon, huge rock pools and
giant sea caverns made for adventurous
coasteering and swimming. Little-known
coast. Excellent seafood pub.

→ Follow A92 from Stonehaven past
Dunnottar Castle and turn L signed
for Catterline and seafood gastro-pub

Creel Inn (AB39 2UL, 01569 750254).
Find primary school and cross into field
behind playground and walk to far end of
second field, towards and beyond farm,
about ½ a mile. Note lagoon beach behind
first rock arch, then huge LT rock pools
on rock platform and sea caves in cliffs
beyond (N). Drop down to rock platform at
far end via difficult scramble to explore
and swim.

15 mins, 56.9013, -2.2037

394 LUNAN BAY, MONTROSE
Great sweep of sheltered sandy beach.
Ruined castle and harbour.

→ Signed Lunan, 6 miles S of Montrose
L off A92. Continue R then L for car park
(DD11 5ST). Some space for ▲ wild
camping. Limekiln and arch at ruined
Boddin Harbour are 2 miles N with adjacent
coves. Turn off A92 signed Usan and turn
R (dead end) after Dunninald Castle (DD10
9TD). Heading 6 miles S, visit Auchmithie
for famous smokies, and ⊞ But and Ben
for great for family fare (DD11 5SQ, 01241
877223).

2 mins, 56.6535, -2.5029 B

Fife and East Lothian

When the bell rang out in the village of Elie, its inhabitants knew that Lady Jane Anstruther was bathing naked off the headland. You can still see the remains of her eighteenth-century bathing tower complete with changing hut built into the rocks below, from where she could plunge into the deep inlets.

Climb up above the Ship Inn and pass Ruby Bay, where they say garnets lie in the sand, to reach the tower. Below, at low tide, there is a variety of gulleys and pools. There are fantastic views, too, and you can imagine sitting in here by a warming fire on a summer evening – a fine place to dry off and watch the colours of dusk fade across the sea.

At about the same time Lady Jane was building her tower at Elie, Alexander Selkirk, the inspiration for Daniel Defoe's Robinson Crusoe was setting sail from neighbouring Lower Largo in the galleon Cinque Ports and heading for the southern oceans. After many months at sea the vessel dropped anchor at the uninhabited archipelago of Juan Fernández, off Argentina, to collect fresh water but Selkirk was so worried about the state of the ship he decided to stay on the island in the hope of being picked up. The Cinque Ports did indeed sink so Selkirk lived alone on the island for the next four years and four months and wasn't visited by a single ship. All he had brought with him was a musket, gunpowder, carpenter's tools, a knife, a Bible and some clothing. For the first year Selkirk stayed on the beach and camped in a cave, fearing the sounds of wild animals in the interior of the island. Eventually hordes of raucous mating sea lions forced him to go inland where he

237

397

402

401

survived by eating feral goats. Selkirk was finally rescued by a British boat and returned home to Lower Largo where he lived out his days alone with his cats.

If you'd like your own small adventure then try the Elie's chain walk, just three miles east of Lower Largo. The UK's only via ferrata, this series of chains and footholds takes you on a difficult scramble over a black volcanic landscape of pools, inlets and caves at Kincraig Point, a brilliant place to swim in calm seas at any tide. Apparently it was built to help the lighthouse keeper reach the cliff-top. To the north, the famous East Neuk coastline extends through several pretty villages; artists' colony Pittenweem with its cottage-lined foreshore and archaic tidal swimming pool was my favourite. Past Crail you'll come to sweet Cambo Sands, the beautiful beaches of St Andrews and the wild dunes of Tentsmuir Forest.

To the south, on the opposite side of Edinburgh and the Forth, the East Lothian coast is superb. The best beach in the area is at Seacliff with inspiring views to Tantallon Castle to the left and to great guano-iced Bass Rock straight ahead. You'll also find a tiny harbour inlet here, hewn from the stone – a wonderful place to swim and jump with the castle in view. A few miles before Tantallon we also found Canty Bay, a secret cove just visible beneath the coast road.

Other good beaches along this stretch include those around the John Muir Country Park, near Dunbar. The park commemorates Scotland's pioneering wilderness-lover, who established the Yosemite National Park in America. Peffer and Ravensheugh Sands to the north, though, are less crowded. Further south the aptly named Cove has an old track leading to an abandoned harbour quay with a long tunnel built through the cliffs. Here you can snorkel and jump off the quay on a calm day; there's also a rock arch on the far side of the bay. But the greatest attraction on this coast is St Abb's Head with its deeply folded red, green and yellow-coloured cliffs. If the sea is flat the most beautiful place to swim is from the rock pools and coloured slabs in Horsecastle Bay. Otherwise make for Pettico Wick shingle cove and marvel at the extraordinary power deep within the earth that must have created such elaborate formations.

Fife and East Lothian

395 TENTSMUIR SANDS, LEUCHARS
Dunes and huge beach backed up forests.
→ Heading S on A919 from Dundee
to St Andrew's, turn L into Leuchars at
roundabout and bear L up School Hill, L
onto Pitlethie Rd and out of town (KY16
0EJ). Turn R after 2 miles then 2 miles to
beach parking.
3 mins, 56.4074, -2.8088 🏖️ B

396 CAMBO SANDS, KINGSBARNS
**Quiet family beach below naturalistic
coastal gardens with tea rooms.**
→ 6 miles E of St Andrews A917, turn L at
Kingsbarns and continue through to beach
car park. Walk a mile N for most secluded
sands at Airbow Point. 🏠 Cambo Gardens
are next L (KY16 8QD, 01333 450 054).
15 mins, 56.3010, -2.6399 🏖️ B

397 RUBY COVE, ELIE
**Visit Lady's Tower Victorian bathing
house. Bathe in narrow inlet below.**
→ From the convivial bay-side 🏠 Ship Inn
(KY9 1DT, 01333 330246), turn R and R
again up hill to headland.
10 mins, 56.1850, -2.8083 🏖️

398 ELIE CHAIN WALK, KINCRAIG POINT
**Unusual mile long *via ferrata* scrambling
route with chains around dramatic
headland. Inlets, caves and ledges for
swimming in calm seas.**
→ Leaving Elie N on A917, turn L after
a mile signed camping, coastal path
and beach, and park at Shell Bay (KY9
1HB). Head S on coast path to find first
chain after ½ mile. Best on a falling tide.
Swimming from the plateau.
10 mins, 56.1870, -2.8632 🏖️🏊‍♂️🏖️🏞️

399 SEACLIFF BEACH / TANTALLON
**Woodland beach overlooking Bass Rock.
Intriguing tiny harbour inlet for jumps.
Views of Tantallon Castle.**
→ 3 miles E of North Berwick (A198), ½
mile after castle turing, turn L straight
down private track at Auldhame Farm
(EH39 5PP). Pass sign board 'Private Rd to
Seacliff, £2' and continue to woods.
5 mins, 56.0535, -2.6326 🏖️🏊‍♂️🏞️

400 RAVENSHEUGH / PEFFER SANDS
Huge sand beach with woods.
→ Continue 3 miles S from Seacliff (above)
on A198, take second L after Whitekirk for
Ravensheugh to L, or Tyne Sands to R
10 mins, 56.0275, -2.5983 🏖️

401 COVE HARBOUR, COCKBURNSPATH
**Quaint harbour with quay and steps for
swimming. Tunnel leads through to E side
of cove and to the rock arch.**
→ From Dunbar S on A1, exit for Cove at
roundabout a mile before Cockburnspath.
Down Pease Bay road, turn L after 200m
into Cove (TD13 5XD). Park & follow track.
5 mins, 55.9380, -2.3461 🏖️🏞️🏖️

402 ST ABB'S HEAD, COLDINGHAM
**Dramatic cliff formations, rock colours
and marine wildlife at St Abb's Head.**
→ Take A1107 8 miles S and turn off in
Coldingham for St Abbs. Park at 🏠 NTS
visitor centre/café. Follow coast path
N past Starney Bay to Horsecastle Bay
(1 mile) where wall starts, below loch.
Swim from the stony beach but better to
scramble on to the coloured slabs on L (N)
side of bay where you will find some giant
pock pool 'tubs' at LT.
20 mins, 55.9100, -2.1325 🏖️

Badcall Bay

Inspiration, Safety and Navigation

From seashore foraging to swimming with dolphins, camping on the beach to exploring sea grottoes, exploring our secret coast opens up new worlds of adventure and discovery. Here we share some of our favourite ideas and a set of more detailed maps to help you find your way.

Beach Games

If you're spending a day at the beach with family take some ideas for games and activities, especially those for warming everyone up before or after a swim.

Wet sand makes a great Olympic arena so why not prepare a 100-metre sprint, a long jump and a hurdling course? Older kids might try javelin throwing with sticks, or the shot put with stones – ideally at a distance from everyone else! Beach 'musical chairs' is also fun: everyone lies down on the sand outside a large perimeter circle and when the sign is given they must race in to grab a stone or stick – except there's always one fewer than the number of people taking part.

Scavenger hunt competitions are a great way to explore a new beach – and do some litter picking at the same time. Send pairs out to collect by colour, or even by letter of the alphabet. Arrange the returns in a rainbow or use them to make a crazy golf or croquet course. Or why not build an obstacle course, with things to climb under and through at speed?

Boules with pebbles is a classic beach game: the aim is to see who can get their stone closest to the marker. Beach tennis is also fun. Start by marking out a large rectangle for the court and dividing it into three so the middle becomes the 'net' into which the ball must not fall. Use a beach ball and bat it with your hands, or use a picnic rug – get each team to hold it by the corners and use it to catch and bounce the ball.

Make an open fire and cook supper as night draws in; what could be more delicious? Then bed down under the stars to be lulled to sleep by the gentle sound of the waves. Only make fires below the high-tide line. Where fires are prohibited, create a warm glow with candle lanterns: put tea lights in white paper bakery bags weighed down with sand. If you're sleeping out, even on a dry summer night, you'll need an insulated ground mat and a good sleeping bag to keep you warm. You could use a tarpaulin, made from lightweight tent material; prop it up with sticks and anchor it with guy ropes to large stones or driftwood stakes.

Beach arts and crafts

- Build a fairy house and garden from seaweed and driftwood.
- Make a mosaic from collections of shells, sea-glass, stones and fossils.
- Have a sand-building competition – make castles, animals or cars. Or dribble wet sand to make Gaudi-esque spires and towers.
- Build a network of ponds and moats and race miniature boats made from discarded cuttle-fish shells.
- Use a driftwood rake to make a Zen garden with sand patterns – or make a huge sand maze.
- Balance stones on top of each other to make a stone cairn or a statue. Take care!
- Make a heart splash in the water: two people face each other and flick back their hair.
- Go rock-pooling with a bucket, net and identification guidebook.
- Make a kite and see whose can fly the highest.
- Teach your dog some new tricks.

Seashore Foraging and Food

The seashore offers a surprising variety and abundance of delightful wild foods and many can be sustainably harvested. Get yourself a good guide book – John Wright's *Edible Seashore* is recommended – light your fire, and get cooking!

Seashore green plants include sea-beet, sea holly, sea kale and sea-pea. One of my all-time favourites is marsh samphire (glasswort) found near sand dunes, sand flats and marshes above the high-tide mark. It has succulent, cactus-like stems that point upwards in clumps, about 20cm tall. Nip off stems at the base, boil for five minutes then eat with butter, using your teeth to strip the salty flesh from the stem.

Seaweeds are packed full of vitamins and minerals. No seaweeds are poisonous but some taste better than others. All can be eaten raw, after washing and dicing, and work well as an addition to salads, dressed with soy sauce. They're also good dried and used as a snack or condiment, particularly in a seafood soup. Harvest the tender young shoots by hand at low tide or at higher tides while snorkelling. Bladderwrack, one of our most common seaweeds, grows on rocks and has long fronds with a mid-rib and little flotation bladders along each side. It's best eaten dried.

Laver is boiled for four hours to yield a purée known as laverbread that is traditionally served with fried bread and bacon in Wales. When young the plant is green, but later turns deep purple. Its thin membrane-like leaves are often bunched and layered on rocks, like wet hankies, and it can be found quite high up the tide line. Tasty sea lettuce is similar but is a much more intense emerald-green colour. Dulse is another classic edible seaweed. It is purplish-red and its branched leaves have lots of tough flat fronds with blunt ends. Cook it with hash browns and other potato dishes. On the west coast of Ireland dulse is known as 'dillisk' and is usually sold dried as a snack food – often alongside winkles – on stalls in seaside towns.

Kelps are the traditional flat seaweeds you may have seen dried in Japanese supermarkets or served with sushi. Forests of plants

Cooking on the beach

- Make your fire below the high-tide line.
- Dig a small fire trench and lay a grill on top.
- Let wood burn to glowing embers before grilling.

sway about in deep water off rocky coasts. Furbelows has lots of parallel strap-like, brownish and leathery fronds held to the rock floor by one strong central stem. Sugar kelp (also known as sea belt or oarweed) has only one frond but has fancy crinkled edges.

Blue Mussels are the classic foragers' food and are delicious boiled or barbecued with butter. The largest are found in deep water offshore – a great excuse for a long snorkel around sea stacks and rocky islets at low spring tides. Mussels are filter feeders and can concentrate toxins, so if you are suspicious about water quality leave your mussels to soak for 24 hours in fresh water to clean them, rejecting any that are open. Boil for 20 minutes to cook and then discard any that remain closed. Never collect mussels where there might be sewage outflows or red algal blooms. As an extra precaution in built-up areas, avoid summer months when bacterial levels can be higher.

Cockles have a distinctive scallop-shaped shell. You can find them buried in wet sand on low-tide flats and marshes, sometimes up to 1,000 per square metre! They tend to hide about 15cm below the sand. Professionals use rakes to unearth them, but bare feet and toes also work. Be quick because these shellfish burrow very fast once they are disturbed. Soak cockles in fresh water overnight then boil or barbecue. Clams, dog whelks, oysters, razor clams, winkles and sea urchins can also be collected; large limpets can be eaten in survival situations, though they are tough and rubbery. Knock them sharply and swiftly to surprise them before they clamp on hard. Cut off the black sack then cook shell-side down on embers, or kebab them on a stick.

Crabs have delicious meat and four main species are found in the UK: the spider crab (with long legs); the edible crab (brick-red in colour); the common crab (also known as green crab); and the velvet swimming crab (with back legs like flippers). All are good to eat and the spider crab has the sweetest meat. They can be baited with some raw meat on the end of a two-metre line or string. Wait until they bite then pull them up slowly, net them and store them in a bucket. Alternatively, take a net with you when snorkelling as you may find one hiding under a rock ledge or in the seaweed. It is possible to pick a crab out of the water with your hands, but not recommended. Hold them at the back between thumb and finger. Crabs take 5–15 minutes to cook in boiling water, depending on size.

Swim with Dolphins and Other Beasties

One of the delights of swimming off the wilder areas of our coastline is the chance to see and experience amazing animals at close quarters.

Dolphins and porpoises are cetaceans – small, toothed whales – and highly intelligent and inquisitive mammals. Travelling in pods of up to 10, they breathe through lungs – relying on air from the surface – and communicate via a large vocabulary of sounds and echo-location. Dolphins and porpoises have outstanding vision both in and out of the water. They sleep by taking catnaps at the surface for a few minutes. The main British species of dolphin is the bottlenose, so-called because of its pointy nose. Sometimes dolphins are confused with their more reserved relative, the porpoise, which has a flatter nose, a shorter dorsal fin and never jumps above the water. Porpoises keep a low profile, making them difficult to spot unless the sea is dead flat.

Seals and walruses are also mammals with four flipper 'legs' but no real tail. The common seal tends to be found along southern and eastern British coastlines and loves to bask on sand banks (particularly in Norfolk and Lincolnshire). The grey seal (part of its taxonomic name, Halichoerus grypus, means 'sea pig') frequents the rocky western shores of Britain. Tamer and more curious than common seals, grey seals tend to practise 'bottling' – the endearing habit of standing upright in the sea to have a good look around. Their pups are white and furry and remain on land for several weeks. Common seal pups swim with their parents right from birth.

Seals are very fast swimmers and are confident in the water. They may well approach you and are known to nip snorkellers' flippers in play. However, never approach seals when they are on land and never approach seals with pups (early summer for common seals, winter for grey seals). Also be wary when exploring very remote coves, inlets and sea caves in case you surprise them.

Places to see dolphins

- The Moray Firth coastline, Scotland
- North Wales, particularly Harlech and Criccieth
- Pembrokeshire and Cardiganshire: Mwnt and Strumble Head
- Durlston Head, Purbecks, Dorset
- Prawle Point, Devon
- Penwith coastline, Cornwall
- Gairloch, Wester Ross, Scotland

Basking sharks are the most heart-stopping and other-worldly of the large British sea creatures. This shark may be just a fish, but it can grow as big as a bus and has a gaping, terrifying mouth. Despite its fearsome appearance, it's actually a harmless filter feeder that sifts plankton from the water. There are more basking sharks in Britain than in any other country; global numbers are threatened by the high value placed on their fins and livers in Asian countries. These sharks can be found close to the shore along remote Cornish coasts during the summer, though most are now heading north because climate change is causing our seas to warm.

Seaweeds and fishes inhabit the silent, underwater world and snorkelling is a great way to see them. Porthkerris on the Lizard, in Cornwall, and Kimmeridge Ledges in Dorset have well-known skin-diving centres, but almost anywhere in this book offers opportunities, especially in calm seas when visibility is higher. The most beautiful seaweeds include carpets of pink coral weed, vibrant blue rainbow wrack and impressive stands of golden thongweed and japweed. Rocky reefs provide cover for all manner of crustaceans, including the red-eyed velvet swimming crabs and even the occasional lobster.

Favourite fish to look out for include shimmering shoals of silver sand eels, mackerel – often striped and colourful – and the most vivid, almost tropical-looking fish of all: the ballan and corkwing wrasse, which builds seaweed nests in late spring. In summer, shallow-water bays such as Kimmeridge are usually a degree or two warmer than the open sea and make ideal nursery areas for juvenile fish such as pollack, bib and mullet. Why not buy yourself a pocket photographic guide to the seashore – Chris Gibson is my recommendation.

Phosphorescence is quite magical. The tiniest creatures – plankton – are also spectacular and can produce amazing displays of summer phosphorescence, or more accurately bioluminescence: a chemical reaction that causes them to emit light when they are disturbed. Norfolk is one of the better-known coasts for experiencing what local people call the 'burning', when the night sea becomes milky and glows in the bow waves of a boat or around the moving legs of a swimmer. But these conditions can occur throughout Britain in shallow, warm seas after prolonged sunlight – go night-swimming and you may just get lucky!

Boats and Boards

Body or boogie boards offer an excellent introduction to surfing and are easy to carry with you to coves and secret beaches. The cheapest are about £5–15 from a beach-side shop. They're made from polystyrene so are light and quite rigid, but can break easily when used by adults. For £20–50 you'll get a rubber-plastic composite that is stronger but bendy, making it difficult to control. Ideally there should be a thick layer of plastic on the bottom, known as a 'slick', to make the board more rigid. You can also hire full-size boards and wetsuits in most resorts. For beginner's tips on surfing visit *www.britsurf.co.uk*.

Adults may prefer to wear fins (short flippers) to help pick up speed when catching waves and make the most of short boards. They cost about £20–40 but use them over neoprene 'socks' to minimise the cold and blisters. Aim for shorter, stiffer fins for efficiency and cross-cut fins if you're keen to ride 'drop-knee' rather than on your belly. Of course, it's also possible to **body surf** in big waves, especially if you pick up a bit of speed before the wave arrives. **Skim-boarding** is fun when the surf is down completely. The boards are flat and thin like a tray and are used to skate over very shallow water on the shoreline.

Some places now offer the opportunity to try **sea kayaking**. These long, thin craft have good handling as well as speed, and can cover long distances, but they require skill and a good knowledge of currents and rescue techniques. For calm seas and local trips **'sit-on-top' kayaks** are great fun for the beginner and prices start at about £300. They are stable, unsinkable and you can get in and out of them at sea so they're perfect for swimmers, snorkellers or scuba divers.

Inflatable kayaks also have potential though they can be slow. They may also be blown off course by wind and currents, and can split on sharp rocks. Make sure your kayak is double-skinned with multiple chambers, and don't plan long, complex expeditions. Finally, some people have a lot of fun visiting remote beaches in small **sailing dinghies**. Toppers are about the cheapest type (£500 second-hand).

Coasteering

Coasteering is a mixture of swimming and exploring along the edge of the water, including climbing into caves, playing in the swell and jumping into pools. Many companies now offer coasteering and this is an excellent way to gain some experience. If you want to try some simple coasteering yourself then this book will give you plenty of inspiration, but don't attempt it at rocky and very exposed locations unless the sea is really calm. You need to be a strong swimmer, confident when clambering about over rocks and understand the basics of tidal flows, particularly if you are outside the protection of a cove or bay. You'll need adequate footwear, such as trainers, and a wetsuit if you plan to be in for more than 15–20 minutes. Make sure you know how to get off the foreshore and on to the land if you get into difficulty.

Learn to deal with swell and rocks by building up your skills and confidence first in calm seas and sheltered areas. Once in the water, assume a squat or armchair position with your feet out in front as the main form of defence, and your hands ready to push off the rocks. As you approach your exit rock, work with the moving swell, riding it up and down, letting it launch you up to your chosen rock-hold but letting go and dropping back down again if you fail to get a strong enough hand-hold. Never haul yourself out on to rocks on your stomach – you'll only be dragged back down and suffer grazes. Remember that swell is intermittent so wait for a lull and beware of large ferries and tankers, which can create a large wake even at a mile's distance.

Exploring sea caves and swimming through them is a magical experience but even a light swell can suddenly strengthen as a cave narrows. Sudden high swell can also dump you on the rocks below, or knock your head against the ceiling. Take particular care if waves start breaking on the rocks.

'Deep Water Soloing' will definitely appeal to climbers. It's a new sport that specialises in locations above deep water, which means no ropes are required. For more information visit *www.dwsworld.com.*

Currents, Tides and Safety

RIP CURRENTS
Break the Grip of the Rip!

Rip currents are offshore surface currents that re-circulate water out to the back of the surf breaks during high surf. They increase in strength as the surf increases and do not occur in calm seas. Rips tend to form in natural channels: between sand bars; in a river mouth or estuary; or along a pier, jetty, groyne or rock stack. In coves, rips tend to form along the edges. Look for a calmer, possibly rippled, channel between the incoming surf breaks. Sometimes the channel is deep green in colour, or may be carrying foam or debris, or stirring up sediment. The waterline at the shore will also be a little lower where the rip begins. Surfers often use rips to take them out beyond the breaks, so ask them for advice.

Escaping a rip is straightforward if you are a strong swimmer and remain calm. People drown from panic, followed by exhaustion, so never fight against the current. Keep an eye on a shore landmark to establish whether you are in a rip. If so, stand or wade if possible. If not, swim out of it at 90 degrees parallel to the beach for about 20m. Once out of the rip, head back towards the beach, using the waves to body-surf you back in. If you are too exhausted to swim, raise your arm to attract attention and lie on your back – or on a board of you have one – to conserve energy. Remember, rips only extend to the back of the surf, rarely more than 100m, often less. They also slow down as they get further from shore.

Cross-shore rips occur when surf is coming in at an angle to the coast and creating a current across the beach. They will not take you out to sea, but may take you out of your depth.

'Dumping' surf forms on steeply shelving beaches (particularly on the shingle beaches of the south and east coasts, such as Chesil or Dungeness). This type of surf breaks quickly and heavily, dumping you hard on the ground. An immediate and highly localised undertow then sucks the water back out again, making it difficult to stand up and negotiate the steep shelf, especially if you are tired. Aim to land behind the breaking wave or try to find a more gently sloping part of the beach.

Jumping is great fun, but the danger of death, paralysis or severe injury is obvious. Check depths thoroughly before every jump and never trust your eyes – water always looks deeper than it actually is. A high tide one week may be many metres shallower than it was the previous week. Winter storms can also move underwater boulders around. On entry, keep your legs together, your head up and your arms tight in, either straight down or crossed on your chest. Jumping from a height of more than five metres can be painful and dangerous. For more safety information visit **www.wildswimming.co.uk**

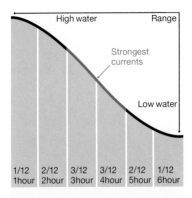

High water — Range
Strongest currents
Low water

1/12	2/12	3/12	3/12	2/12	1/12
1hour	2hour	3hour	4hour	5hour	6hour

Rule of twelfths

If in doubt avoid the fastest flow in the middle hours of the tide. In the first hour of the tide, approximately one-twelfth of the water moves; in the second hour two-twelfths moves, during the third hour three-twelfths moves, and so on as the flow-rate decreases again.

What time is the tide?
Tide cycles repeat every 12 hours, occurring half an hour later each time. They occur about an hour later each day.

Spring tides

Contrary to popular belief spring (strong) tides occur every fortnight at new and full moons and are only partly affected by the season.

Find tides for the whole country at bbc.co.uk/weather/coast/tides

Tides are created by the moon. The sea floods as the tide comes in and levels rise. It **ebbs** as the tide goes out and levels drop. The power of the tide varies from day to day and affects the tidal range (height) and the flow rate (current). Tides are predictable but are highly variable and localised. Determinants of the tide's strength include whether the water is slack, or in full flow (see rule of twelfths, left), and how close it is to a spring or neap tide.

Spring and neap tides are respectively, strong and weak. At full or new moons the sun and moon are, astronomically speaking, in line. This creates the strongest gravitational pull on the sea and therefore strong tides, known as 'spring' tides occur, roughly every fortnight. At half-moons, sun and moon oppose each other, resulting in weak gravitational pull on the sea and creating weak tides, known as 'neap' tides. Spring tides might typically have a range of 5–6m, and 3–4 knots peak current. Neap tides are about a half to a third of that range. 'Springs' and 'neaps' always occur at the same time of day for a particular part of the coast. For Atlantic-facing coasts such as Cornwall, Devon and west Scotland, the peak spring

high tides are always around 6am and 6pm – very handy for enjoying really low-tide beaches in the heat of the day!

The direction of flow is of vital importance for swimmers. Britain's south and west shores fill from the Atlantic up into the English Channel and Irish Sea, so tidal currents flow east in the flood and are progressively later as you go east to Dover or north to Liverpool. Britain's east and north coasts fill from the North Sea, with waters moving south in the flood and becoming progressively later as you go south down the east coast. The east Dorset coast has very small tides where the two flows cancel each other out.

Coves and bays are protected from tidal flows (though of course the sea levels will still change) but open coast is exposed to tidal currents. Currents strengthen around restrictions, such as headlands or islands (Portland Bill or Ramsay Sound) or at estuary or harbour mouths (Chichester Harbour or Blackwater Estuary). Remember that at an estuary or river mouth the current will be carrying you inshore as the tide comes in (relatively safe) but offshore when the tide goes out (potentially very dangerous).

Map Annex: 1 Grid Square = 1 km (see notes on final page)

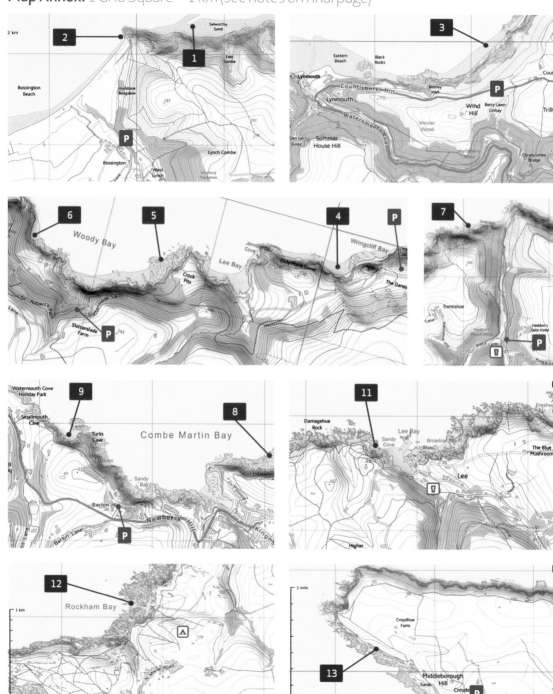

254

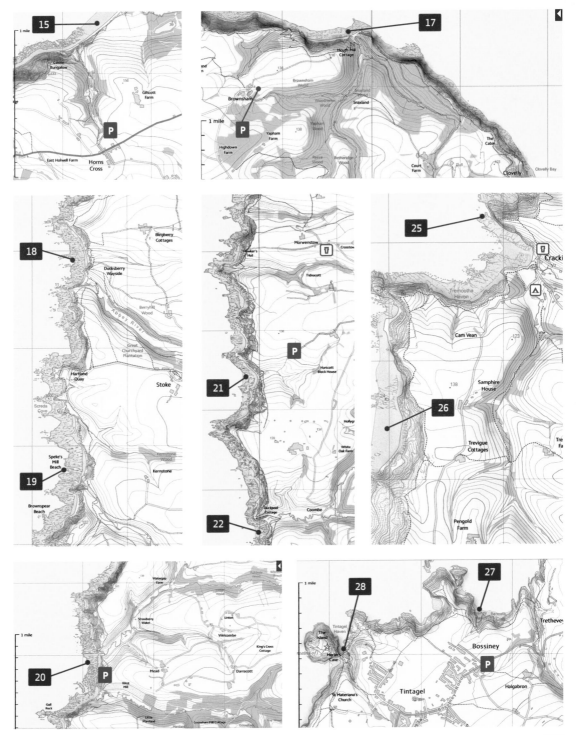

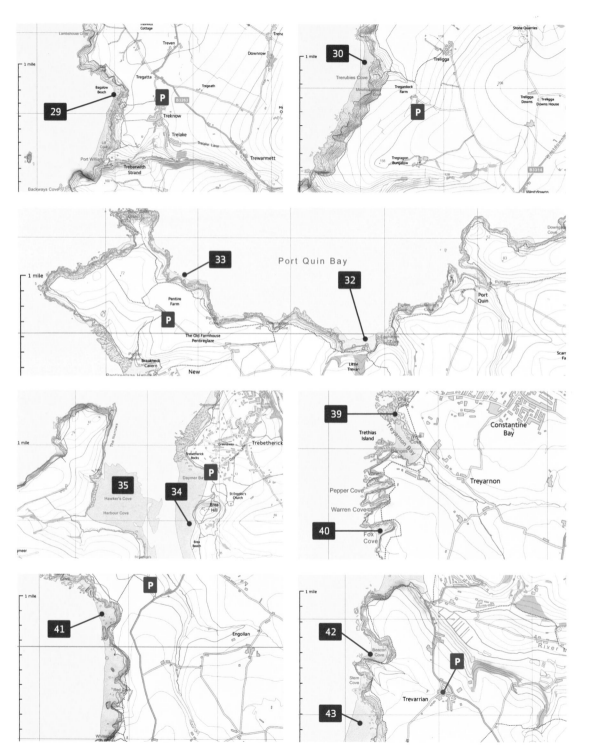

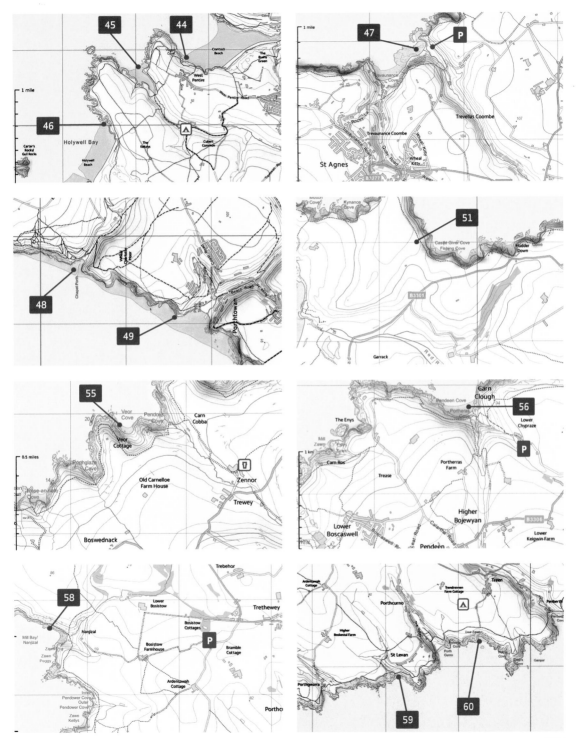

257

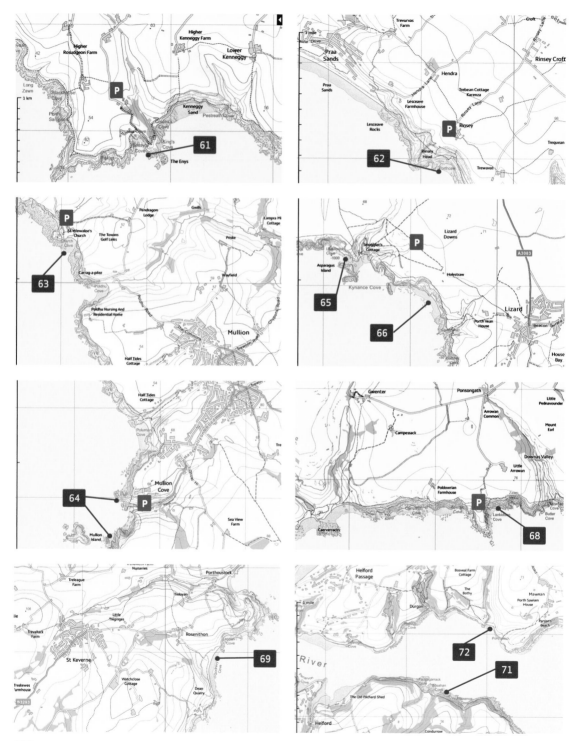

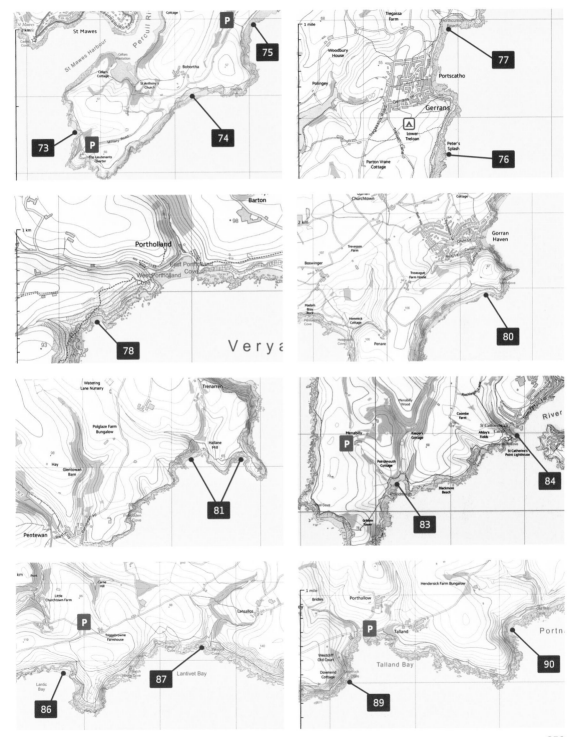

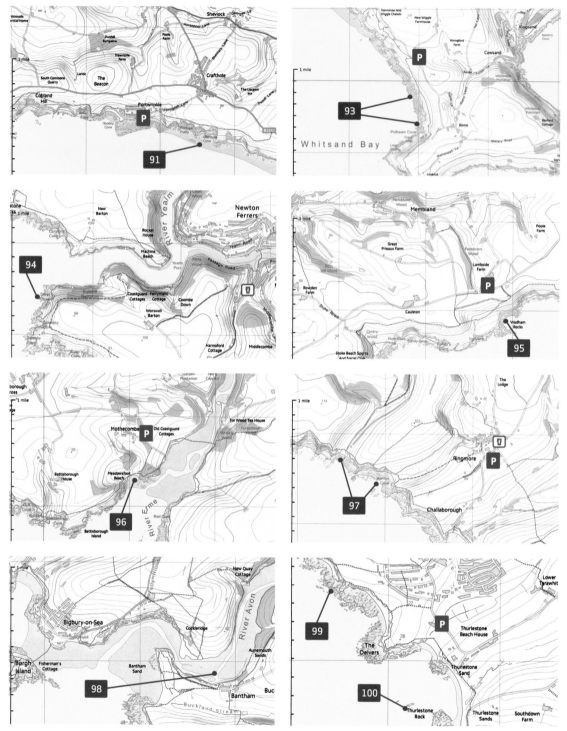

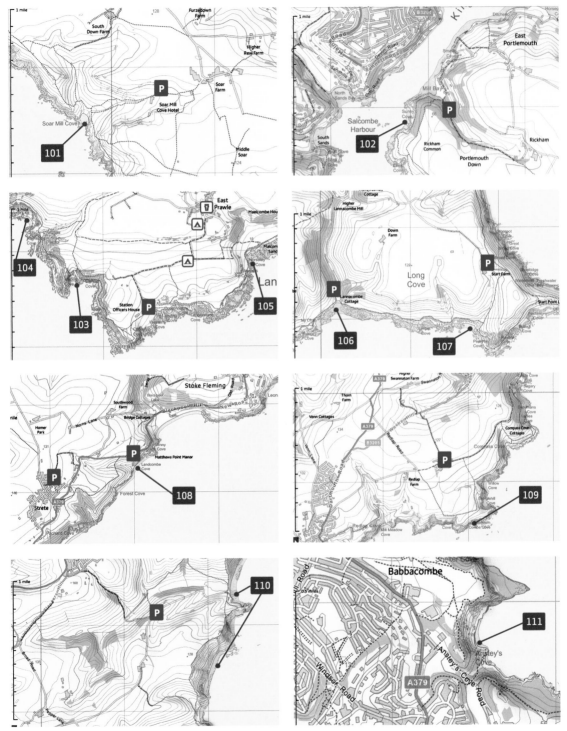

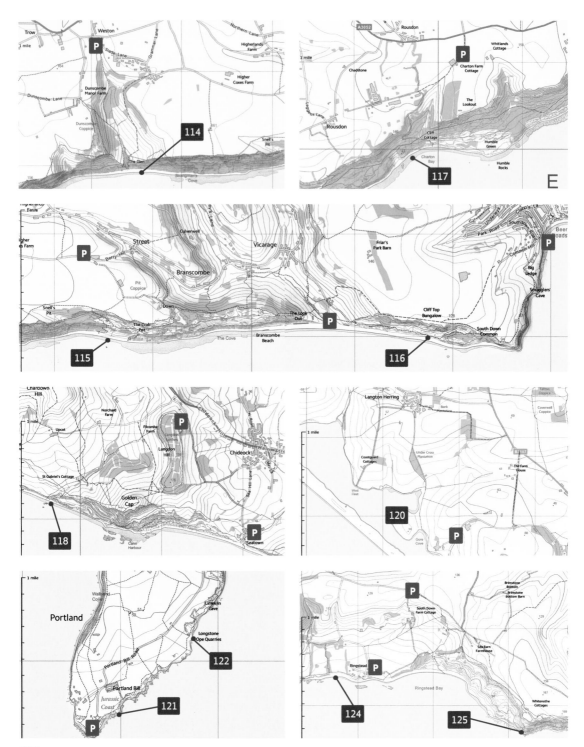

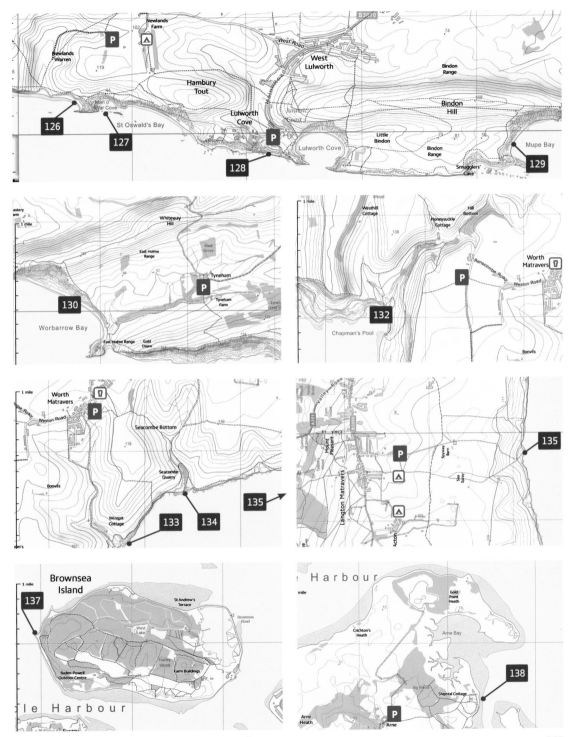

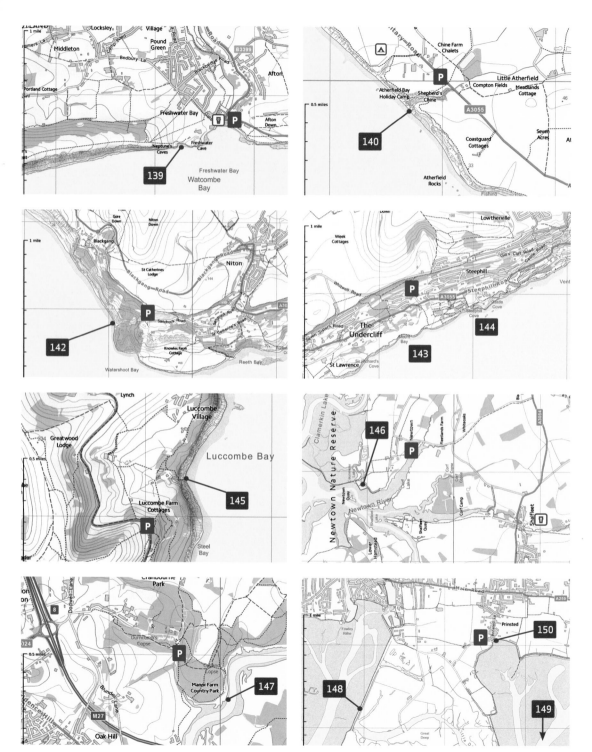

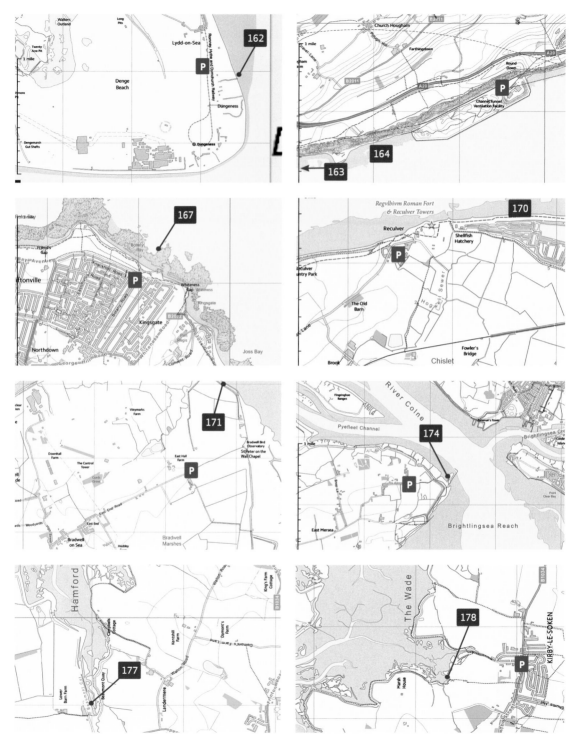

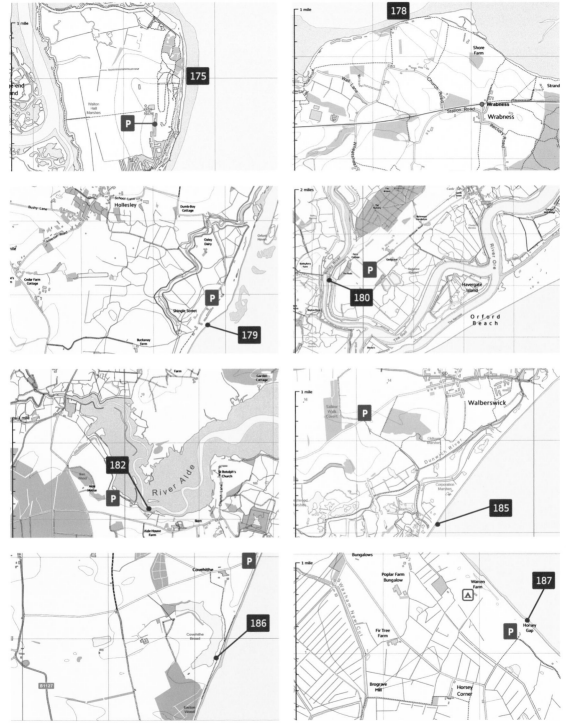

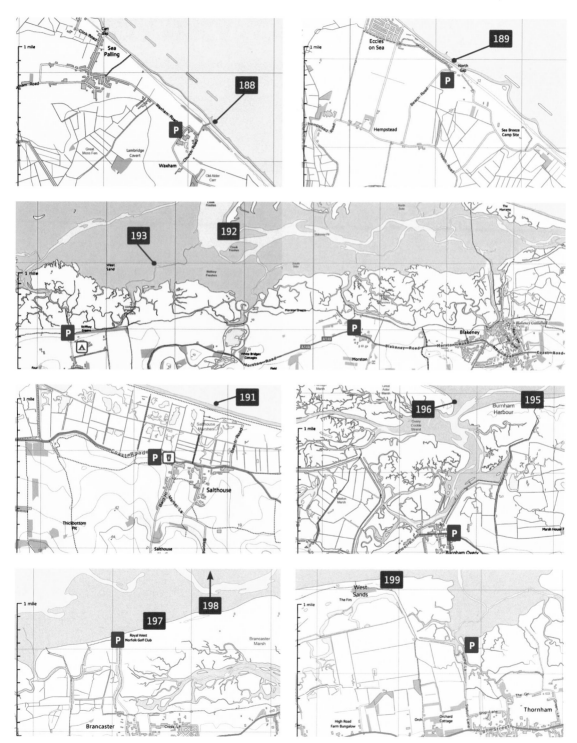

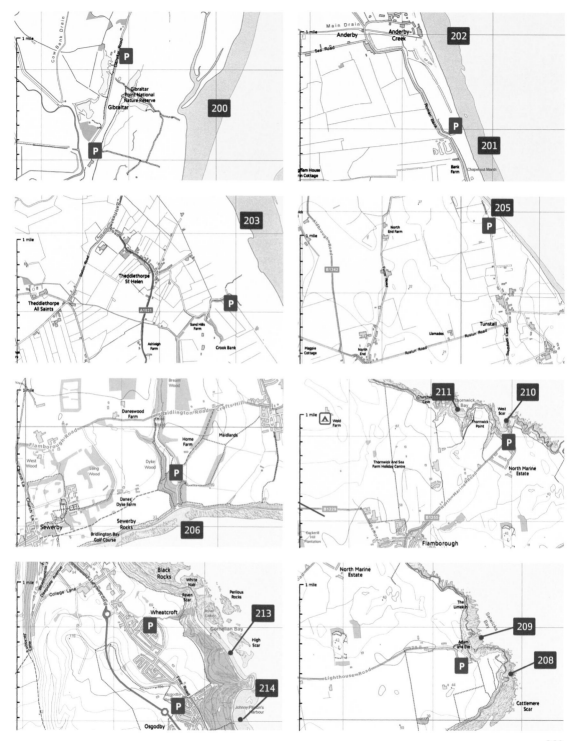

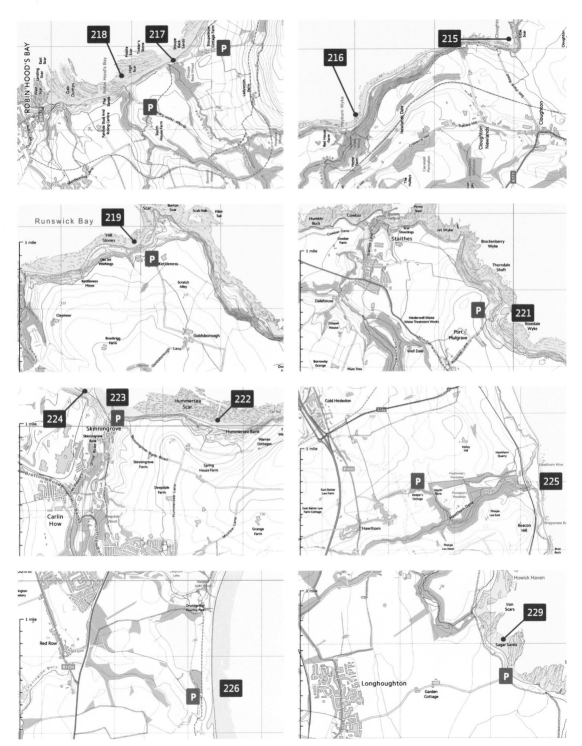

ROBIN HOOD'S BAY

218 217

East Scar
Shooting Scar
Oab Dumps
Middle Scar
High Scar
Robin Hood's Bay
The Robin Hood's Sands
Tinker's Stone
Stoupe Beck Sands
Stoupe Beck Wood
Stoupebrow Cottage Farm

P

Fairlide Stud And Riding Centre
South House Farm
Stoupe Brow Lane
Laybridge Farm

P

216 215

Hayburn Wyke
Newlands Dale
Tralifes Hill
Crown's Hill
Caymord Plantation
The Hullers

Cloughto
Clobe Scar
Cloughton
Cloughton Newlands

Runswick Bay 219

Scar
Barton Scar
Scab Nab
Filfer Tail

1 mile

Hill Stones
Old Jet Workings
Kettleness
Kettleness Mines
Scratch Alley

P

Claymoor
Brockrigg Farm
Goldsborough
Goldsborough Lane

Humble Buck
Cowbar
Cowbar Lane
Cowbar Farm
Harbour
Penny Steel
Scar Shootings
Staithes
Jet Wyke
Brackenberry Wyke
Thorndale Shaft

1 mile

Dalehouse
Cooper House
Hinderwell Waste Water Treatment Works
Port Mulgrave

P

221

Rosedale Wyke

Borrowby Grange
Plum Tree
Well Dale

224 223

Skinningrove

P

Hummersea Scar 222

Hummersea Bank

1 mile

Skinningrove Bank
Skinningrove Bank Road
Skinningrove Farm
Deepdale Farm
Warren Cottages
Spring House Farm

Brotton Road
Carlin How
Deepdale Wood
Moxlow Lane
Grange Farm

Cold Hesledon

1 mile

Kieley Hill
Hawthorn Quarry
Hawthorn Hive

P

Haythorn's Plantation
East Batter Law Farm
East Batter Law Farm Cottage
Keeper's Cottage
Worth Dene
Thompson's Plantation
Hawthorn Dene
Hawthorn
Thorpe Lea East
Beacon Hill
Thorpe Lea West
Shippersea Ba
Shot Rock

225

Links Wood
Druridge Bay Country Park

1 mile

Red Row

1 mile

B1333

P

226

Howick Haven

1 mile

Iron Scars
Sugar Sands

229

Longhoughton
Garden Cottage

P

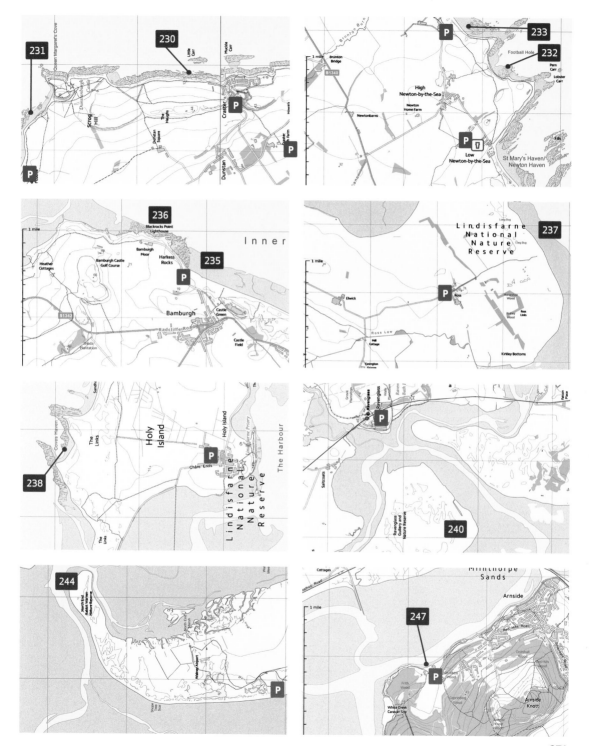

231 230 233 232

Queen Margaret's Cove
Bruton Burn
Little Carr
Muckle Carr
P
Brunton Bridge
B1340
Football Hole
Dunstanburgh Castle
Hawk's
Pern Carr
Lobster Carr
Scrog Hill
The Heughs
High Newton-by-the-Sea
Craster
Dunstan Square
Newtonbarns
Newton Home Farm
P
Dunstan Farm
P
P
Dunstan
Fills
P
Low Newton-by-the-Sea
St Mary's Haven/ Newton Haven

236 235 237

1 mile
Blackrocks Point Lighthouse
Inner
Lindisfarne National Nature Reserve
Long Dog
237
Heather Cottages
Bamburgh Moor
Harkess Rocks
235
Long Dog
Bamburgh Castle Golf Course
P
1 mile
Horseshoe Wood
B1342
Bamburgh
Elwick
Ross
Ross Links
Radcliffe Road
Castle Green
Kedley Wood
Ross Wood
Shada Plantation
Castle Field
Ross Low
Mill Cottage
Kirkley Bottoms
Easington Grange

238 240

Seahou
The Links
Holy Island
Holy Island
Grove Wauklands
Ravenglass
Ravenglass
Rannin
Bath Ha
Felton Place
Coves Haven
P
Lindisfarne Priory
P
238
Chare Ends
The Harbour
Lindisfarne National Nature Reserve
Saltcoats
Ravenglass Gullery and Nature Reserve
240
The Links

244 247

North End Rabbit Warren Nature Reserve
Cottages
Arthmon Road
Milnthorpe Sands
Arnside
244
North End Haws
Red Hills Road
247
Red Hills Road
Walney Airport
Dobshall Wood
P
P
Redhills Wood
Frith Wood
Snow Close Scar
White Creek Caravan Site
Copriding Wood
Arnside Knott

271

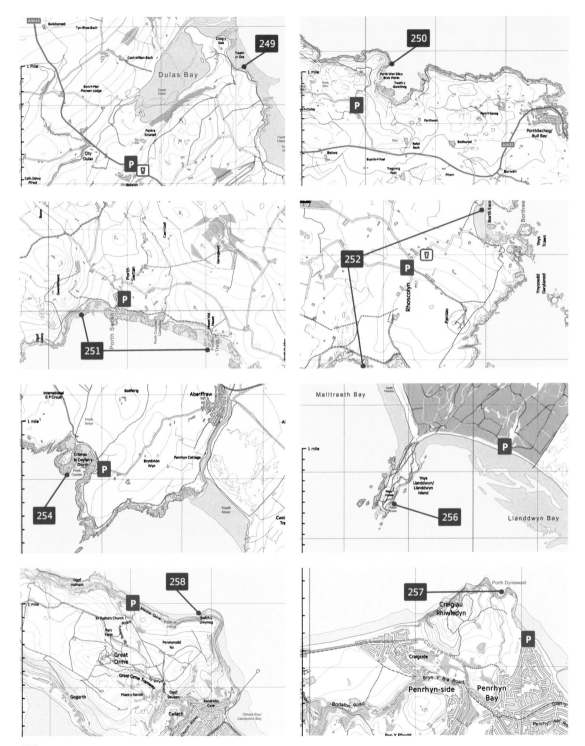

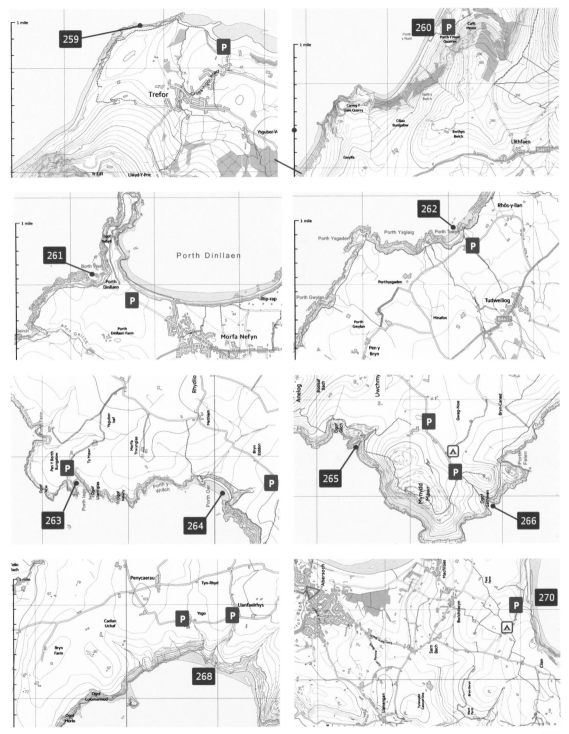

259

260

P

Caffi Meinir

Porth y Nant

Porth Y Nant Quarries

P

Carreg y Llam Quarry

Gallt y Bwlch

Cilan Bungalow

Bwthyn Bwlch

Trefor

Crossing Road

Gwylfa

Llithfaen

B4417

Ysgubor-W

1 mile

Yr Eifl

Llwyd-Y-Pric

Ygubor-W

261

Ogof
Nefyn

Borth Wen

Porth
Dinllaen

P

Porth Dinllaen

Deirch

Afon Geirza

Porth
Dinllaen Farm

Morfa Nefyn

Porth Dinllaen

Rip-rap

262

Rhôs-y-llan

Porth Ysglaig

Porth Towyn

P

Porth Ysgaden

Porthysgaden

Tudweiliog

B4417

Porth Gwylan

Porth
Gwylan

Minafon

Pen y
Bryn

1 mile

1 mile

Rhydllo

Ysgubor
Isaf

Morfa
Trwynglas

Ty Mawr

Bryn
Eidon

Methlem

263

P

Pen Y Berth
Bungalow

Porth Iago

Ogof
Llanllawen

Ogof
Nefyn

Porth y
Wrâch

Porth Oer

264

P

Ogof
Cáe

Anelog

Bodisaf
Bach

Uwchmy

Gwag-Noe

Bryn-Caned

P

265

Ogof
Gôch

Mynydd
Mawr

P

Porth
Felen

Ogof
Llanllawen

266

Felin
Bach

Penycaerau

Tyn-Rhyd

Llanfaelrhys

P

Ysgo

P

Cadlan
Uchaf

Bryn
Farm

268

Ogof
Colomennod

Ogof
Morlo

Abersoch

Hachlros

Pant
Farm

P

270

Bwlchtocyn

Sarn
Bach

Llangian

Trwyn
Cilan

Cilan

273

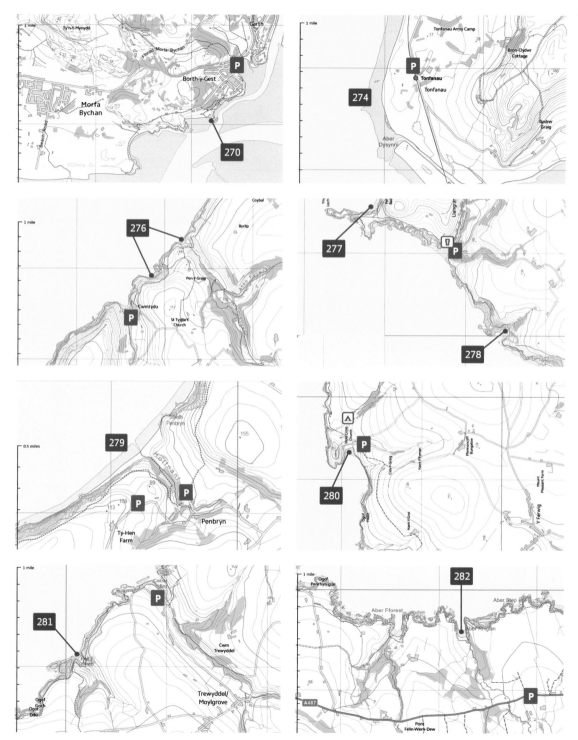

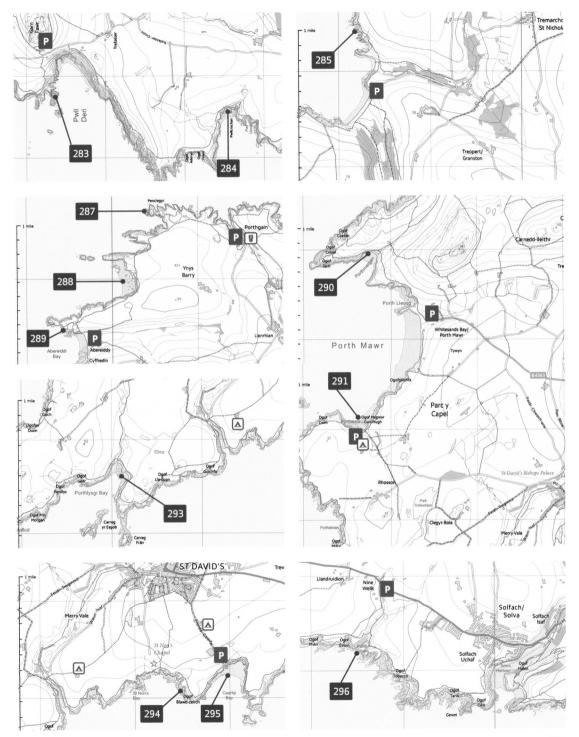

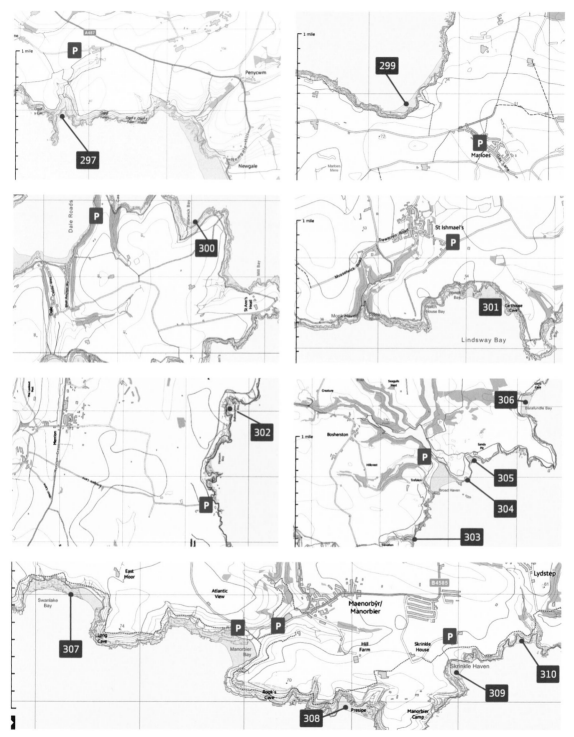

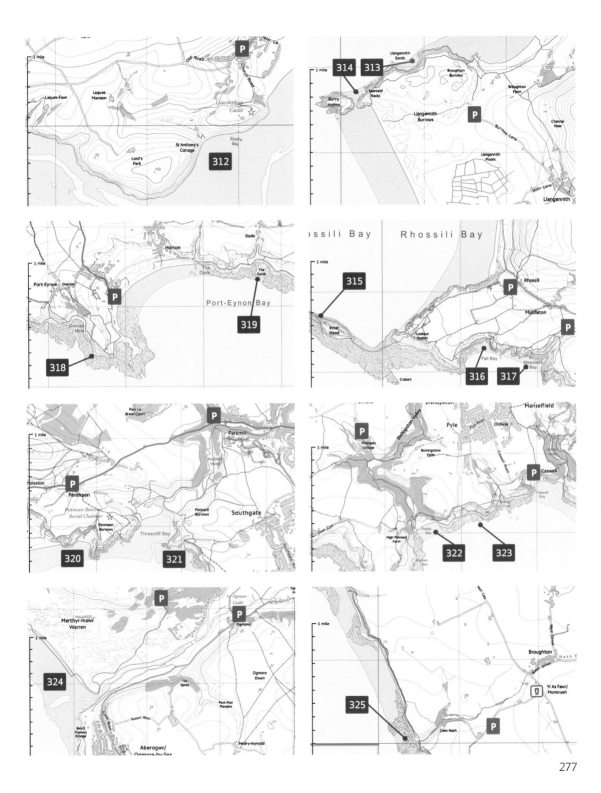

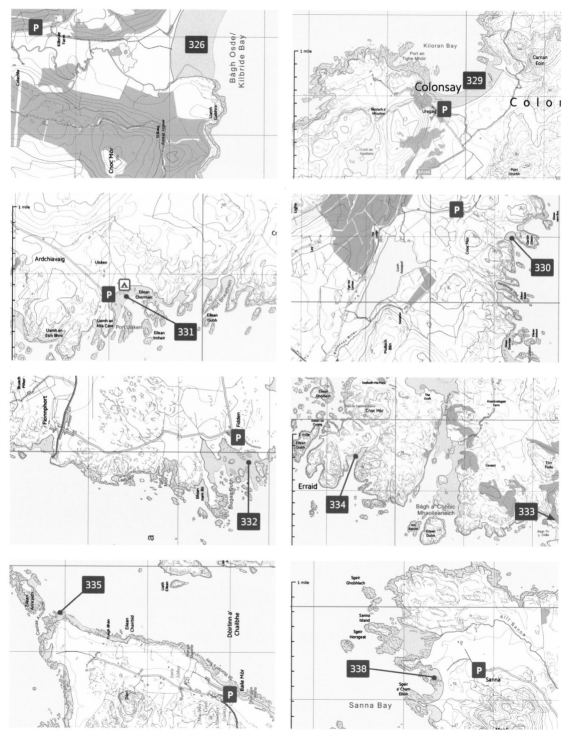

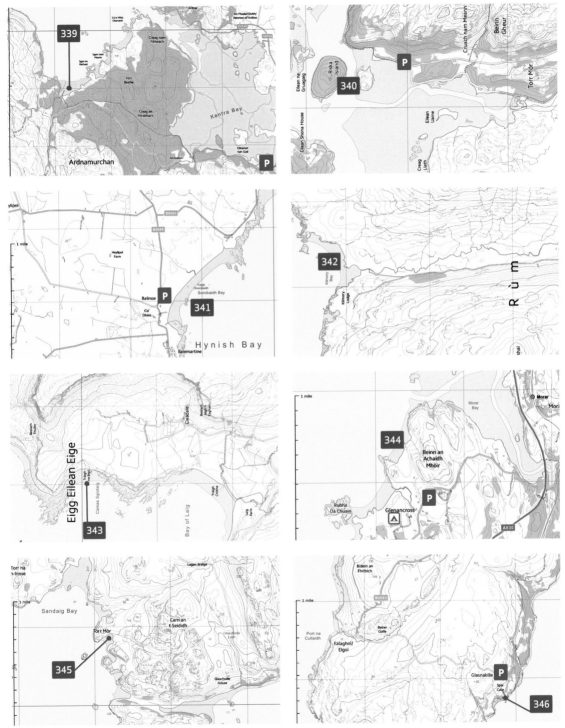

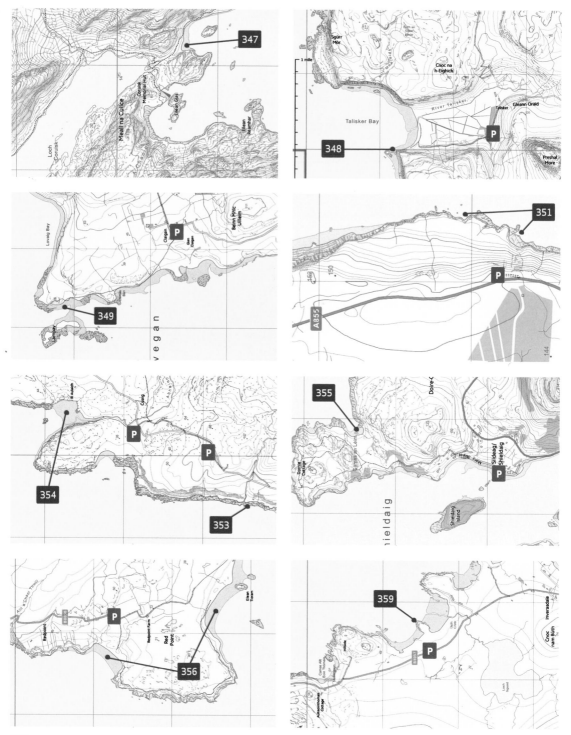

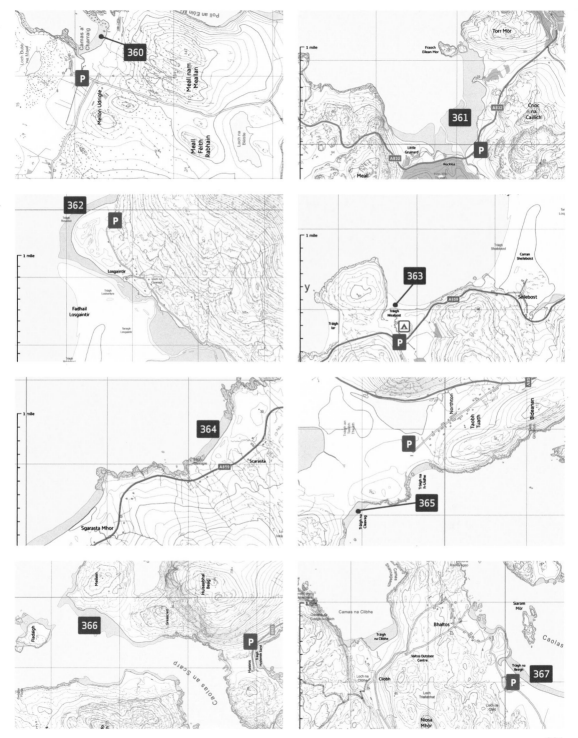

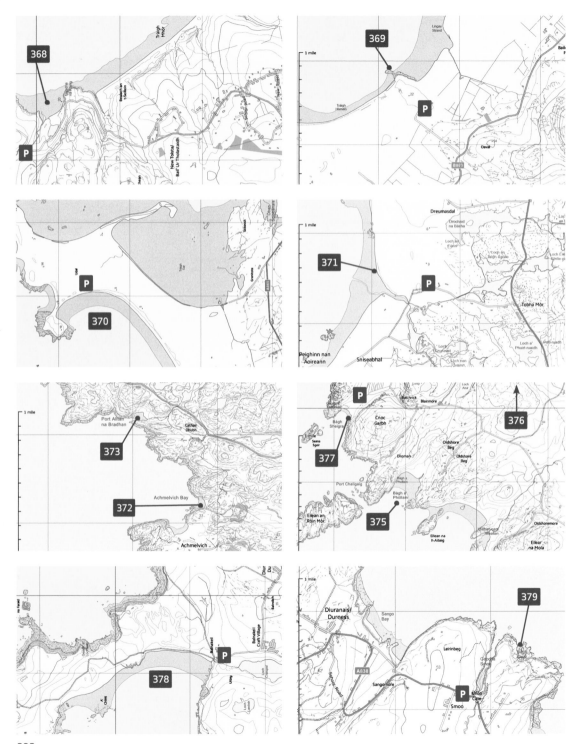

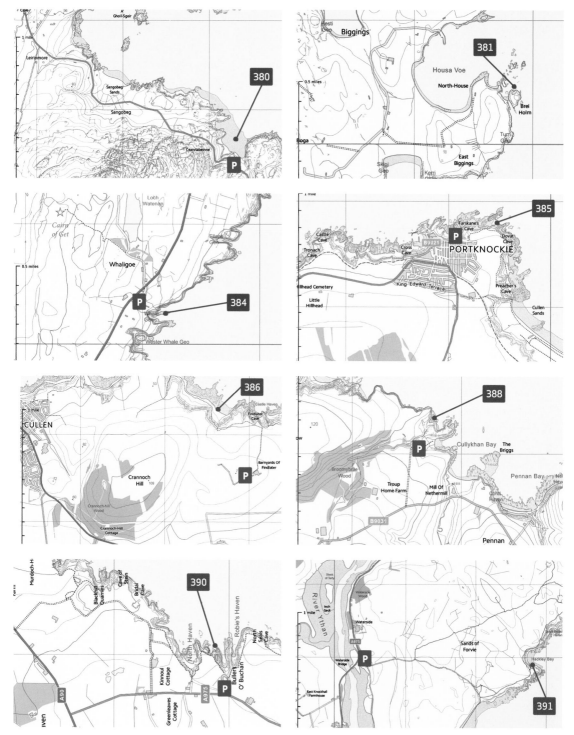

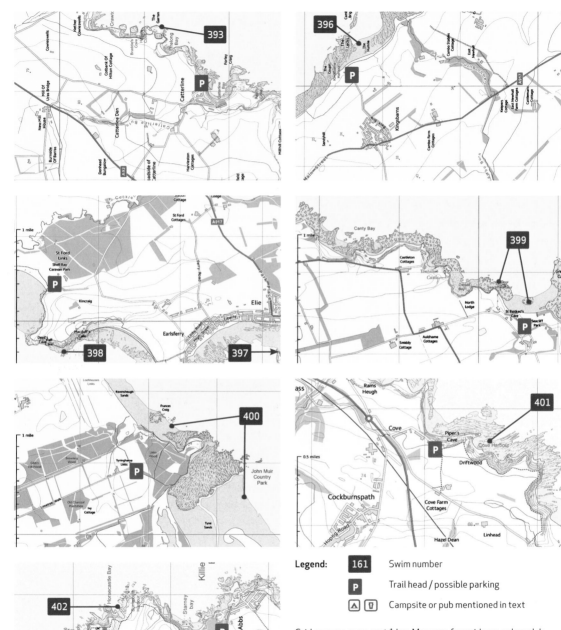

Legend:

161 — Swim number

P — Trail head / possible parking

▲ ⊤ — Campsite or pub mentioned in text

Grid squares represent 1 km. Maps are for guidance only and do not contain all footpaths or names. To help improve these maps for a future edition please contribute to Open Street Map. For more accurate mapping insert the Lat Long into *bing.com/maps* and choose the Ordnance Survey layer.

Ordnance Survey maps © Crown copyright and database right 2014. Superimposed paths © OpenStreetMap.org contributors. With thanks to 'UK Map App' for iPhone (Philip Endecott)

OS National Grid conversion table (from Lat Longs given in swim boxes)

No	National Grid ref										
1	SS9071349346	71	SW7735626302	142	SZ4904975824	213	TA0601086056	284	SM8855936466	355	NG8188155424
2	SS8981349087	72	SW7817926958	143	SZ5426076553	214	TA0641485208	285	SM8825035343	356	NG7337467427
3	SS7397249775	73	SW8468231568	144	SZ5506476851	215	TA0212195062	286	SM8514033894	357	NG7601877745
4	SS7022549646	74	SW8635231991	145	SZ5834379299	216	TA0112297045	287	SM8056132745	358	NG7368288286
5	SS6859249187	75	SW8707532908	146	SZ4186891130	217	NZ9596903445	288	SM8021432059	359	NG8174988553
6	SS6777748996	76	SW8786534781	147	SU5008810687	218	NZ9557704193	289	SM7952631443	360	NG8931995811
7	SS6548949679	77	SW8794036114	148	SU7520804828	219	NZ8290515789	290	SM7278327913	361	NG9506190461
8	SS5810747741	78	SW9528340792	149	SU7715000652	220	NZ8110415890	291	SM7266426058	362	NG0616399639
9	SS5628647892	79	SW9936940446	150	SU7660605070	221	NZ7970917523	292	SM7696624934	363	NG0475397061
10	SS5140547798	80	SX0135040906	151	SU8032303781	222	NZ7270120022	293	SM7312123664	364	NG0230994314
11	SS4768246727	81	SX0378548063	152	SZ7668999410	223	NZ7126120299	294	SM7548124148	365	NF9808291065
12	SS4588146113	82	SX0891452461	153	SZ8743095030	224	NZ7075720703	295	SM7608624266	366	NA9966914396
13	SS4549544455	83	SX1035050406	154	TQ0072700776	225	NZ4434045932	296	SM7861924309	367	NB1059535880
14	SS4234340211	84	SX1187651031	155	TV5163997701	226	NZ2730598513	297	SM8268522995	368	NB5362449874
15	SS3818124268	85	SX1156056953	156	TV5538295975	227	NU2581106472	298	SM8607717157	369	NF8716376641
16	SS3541123744	86	SX1478450839	157	TV5925995524	228	NU2518510676	299	SM7849808908	370	NF8198877493
17	SS2984526673	87	SX1658451177	158	TQ6787405199	229	NU2606516045	300	SM8171704022	371	NF7491836994
18	SS2248425975	88	SX2104450746	159	TQ8528910599	230	NU2589320540	301	SM8429906595	372	NC0576825190
19	SS2253723647	89	SX2221751096	160	TQ9053214785	231	NU2472522670	302	SR9409394335	373	NC0506926195
20	SS2131018012	90	SX2418851453	161	TQ5698618540	232	NU2427225662	303	SR9744993131	374	NC1634541523
21	SS1996713383	91	SX3705553445	162	TR0964917905	233	NU2354126604	304	SR9830094003	375	NC2008658477
22	SS2016011629	92	SX3921052188	163	TR2725738496	234	NU2105032812	305	SR9833894209	376	NC2169165217
23	SS2014509982	93	SX4205849331	164	TR2828538708	235	NU1462937739	306	SR9929794783	377	NC1817559949
24	SS1842200168	94	SX5310147578	165	TR3681144407	236	NU1817135526	307	SS0456597984	378	NC3908569032
25	SX1425296864	95	SX5790146958	166	TR3715055853	237	NU1736235979	308	SS0705996897	379	NC4234667605
26	SX1293195475	96	SX6140847554	167	TR3909671185	238	NU1271743832	309	SS0810997369	380	NC4427865689
27	SX0663089415	97	SX6403445495	168	TR3692171495	239	SD0556297073	310	SS0862797517	381	HU1887260385
28	SX0512289003	98	SX6560543919	169	TR1116267245	240	SD0809994873	311	SN3276107836	382	HY5502707329
29	SX0502287281	99	SX6697142405	170	TR2427969431	241	SD1205481005	312	SN3432309298	383	ND3451955636
30	SX0401384135	100	SX6743241426	171	TM0263509139	242	SD1554577890	313	SS4094893089	384	ND3212240264
31	SX0016181007	101	SX6973137475	172	TL9302305800	243	SD1990875798	314	SS4018092690	385	NJ4951268917
32	SW9577879840	102	SX7379637944	173	TL9675210543	244	SD1740373405	315	SS3882487758	386	NJ5367767308
33	SW9369780623	103	SX7667135730	174	TM0740515515	245	SD1835566265	316	SS4131487279	387	NJ5842066466
34	SW9268576900	104	SX7617936364	175	TM2665523755	246	SD2330963532	317	SS4189087082	388	NJ8367266424
35	SW9124777124	105	SX7868436051	176	TM2218123399	247	SD4426077898	318	SS4653884547	389	NK1191550748
36	SW8902076266	106	SX8020237218	177	TM1896824003	248	SD4566175478	319	SS4876685492	390	NK1098638107
37	SW8889975893	107	SX8170936917	178	TM1765832390	249	SH4899988609	320	SS5279287689	391	NK0279627008
38	SW8509176136	108	SX8504547278	179	TM3684842812	250	SH4022094664	321	SS5398487643	392	NO8794484134
39	SW8566974297	109	SX8814248568	180	TM3926348198	251	SH3004689350	322	SS5755287007	393	NO8769178902
40	SW8550773291	110	SX9225053422	181	TM4528249093	252	SH2591476170	323	SS5857487357	394	NO6926551413
41	SW8486770466	111	SX9358464863	182	TM4028756126	253	SH3326770070	324	SS8563276282	395	NO5018724240
42	SW8448566707	112	SX9268467351	183	TM4671057500	254	SH3378968361	325	SS9045870011	396	NO6049912247
43	SW8432466068	113	SY0978585204	184	TM4780267586	255	SH3660965535	326	NR9592166957	397	NT4992799446
44	SW7760460980	114	SY1640387919	185	TM5001974452	256	SH3891362829	327	NR6546626008	398	NT4652299710
45	SW7766460042	115	SY1827788023	186	TM5231280777	257	SH8179582685	328	NR2068062857	399	NT6069884694
46	SW7652260134	116	SY2180987947	187	TG4660424229	258	SH7784883849	329	NR4008598075	400	NT6280981783
47	SW7263352126	117	SY2983590002	188	TG4425326425	259	SH3656547343	330	NM4105518740	401	NT7847871715
48	SW6967049570	118	SY3957292226	189	TG4131128908	260	SH3471345034	331	NM3931118847	402	NT9181568552
49	SW6906248394	119	SY4903288789	190	TG2458641175	261	SH2748441580	332	NM2999221471		
50	SW6419544648	120	SY6153280820	191	TG0779444433	262	SH2303137543	333	NM3399117245		
51	SW5960542989	121	SY6797168457	192	TF9875145455	263	SH1683031705	334	NM2941819465		
52	SV9241716509	122	SY6867069073	193	TF9732244706	264	SH1659229854	335	NM2939826063		
53	SV9003614261	123	SY6975170969	194	TF8831145726	265	SH1460726644	336	NM3244435035		
54	SV8761814122	124	SY7511681338	195	TF8582145975	266	SH1398425187	337	NM3722951243		
55	SW4448238905	125	SY7717180661	196	TF8474445822	267	SH1858725513	338	NM4418169632		
56	SW3892035744	126	SY8052280258	197	TF7710245268	268	SN2072726414	339	NM6140469149		
57	SW3555930097	127	SY8088380201	198	TF7827746391	269	SH2819726410	340	NM6624972490		
58	SW3575623599	128	SY8224079841	199	TF7178245164	270	SH3110224794	341	NL9882542234		
59	SW3816721865	129	SY8435579912	200	TF5667758444	271	SH5832236912	342	NG3632104147		
60	SW3931822325	130	SY8705079715	201	TF5567074953	272	SH5832236912	343	NM4712889944		
61	SW5569927918	131	SY9089878862	202	TF5529675991	273	SH5685131545	344	NM6622092306		
62	SW5929326919	132	SY9560977088	203	TF4909688463	274	SH5598203797	345	NG7219800871		
63	SW6615920422	133	SY9774676063	204	TA4143712332	275	SN6085694339	346	NG5395412813		
64	SW6668601787	134	SY9842676630	205	TA3029733263	276	SN3623058296	347	NG4931919306		
65	SW6846013261	135	SY9977164286	206	TA2162769198	277	SN3153955135	348	NG3116429982		
66	SW6926612781	136	SZ0344083581	207	TA2318969262	278	SN3005853471	349	NG2230855022		
67	SW7210814622	137	SZ0091688106	208	TA2579970479	279	SN2922452520	350	NG5203960454		
68	SW7566916640	138	SY9836688440	209	TA2547470859	280	SN1938551922	351	NG5234157734		
69	SW8074121162	139	SZ3428785504	210	TA2389172119	281	SN1014845085	352	NG6821148372		
70	SW7381027309	140	SZ4465479821	211	TA2337672295	282	SN0265539556	353	NG6946156490		
		141	SZ4684078250	212	TA1260681760	283	SM8885038626	354	NG7055258704		

Converting decimal degrees to minutes and seconds. The whole units of degrees will remain the same (i.e. 50.1355° starts with 50°). Then multiply the whole decimal by 60 (i.e. 0.1355 x 60 = 8.13). The whole first number becomes the minutes (8'). Take the remaining decimal digits and multiply by 60 again. (i.e. .13 x 60 = 7.8). The resulting number becomes the seconds (7.8").

Health, Safety and Responsibility.

Like any water-based activity, sea swimming and coastal exploration has risks and can be dangerous and these are described more fully inside. Few of the locations featured in this book have lifeguards and all are prone to tidal immersion, currents and sea-state changes. While the author and publisher have gone to great lengths to ensure the accuracy of the information herein they will not be held legally or financially responsible for any accident, injury, loss or inconvenience sustained as a result of the information or advice contained in this book. Swimming, jumping, diving, scrambling or any other activities at any of these locations is entirely at your own risk.

Wild Swimming Hidden Beaches
Explore the secret coast of Britain

Words and Photos:
Daniel Start

Additional Photos:
Chris Parker, Petra Kjell
and those credited

Editing:
Anna Kruger, Michael Lee,
Sarah Jones, Candida Frith-Macdonald,

Design and layout:
Oliver Mann, Marcus Freeman,
Tania Pascoe

Distribution:
Central Books Ltd
99 Wallis Road, London, E9 5LN
Tel +44 (0)845 458 9911
orders@centralbooks.com

Published by:
Wild Things Publishing Ltd.
Freshford, Bath,
BA2 7WG, United Kingdom

hello@wildthingspublishing.com

Photographs © Daniel Start except the following (all reproduced with permission or with CC-BY-SA): p1 Chris Parker, p10, Thomas Magnussan, p20-21 Chris Parker, p28 Dave Carter, p56 Philip Halling, p82 John Palmer, p92 Michael Robinson, p104 Robin Webster, p106 Michael Rogers, p136 Paul Allison, p138 Scott Rimmer, p154 Tony Sinton, p164 Eric Jones, p169 Martin Turtle, p194 John Powell, p195 Graham Taylor, p195 Tim Edwards, p199 Chris Parker, p203 Chris Parker, p204 Judith Cutler, p205 Chris Parker, p206 Niall Corbet, p208 Wendy Kirkwood, p208 Iamthehughes, p209 Chris Parker, p212 Douglas Wilcox, p218 Chris Parker, p220 Scott Eden, John Fergusson, E Taylor, p221 Chris Parker, p230 Jim Taylor, p244 Sion Roberts, p 245 Seb de Grange, p246 Rene, p247 Seb de Grange, Richard Ling, Cover back flap Michael Walsh.

Author acknowledgements: Special thanks to the friends and colleagues who helped find, test and photograph all these swimming holes, come rain or shine, particularly to: Tania and Rose Pascoe; Marijka, Ivan and Tony Pascoe; Yvette, Kaspar and Minna Alt-Reuss; Paul, Jessica and Myla Rothwell; Emily Walmsley; Ciaran Mundy & Liquorice; Petra Kjell; Carl Reynolds, Chris Parker; Seb de Grange; Charlotte Macpherson, Nick Cobbing, Briony Greenhill, Jack Thurston, Charlie Cory-Wright, Anthea Lawson, Catherine Howarth, Chloe Kinsman and the Flickr, Geograph and Panoramio community of photographers. The dedication and commitment of the Punk editorial and production teams has, as ever, been truly inspiring: Jonathan Knight, Anna Kruger, Paul Hamilton, Nikki Simms, Sophie Dawson, Carol Farley, Catherine Greenwood, Marcus Freeman and Leanne Bryan. Also thanks to (South West) Christopher Somerville, Douglas King-Smith, Emma Bradshaw, Alfie and Bella, John Such, Seb de Grange, James Heath, Luke and Amanda Hudson, Chloe and Ben Fletcher, Polly Braden, Catherine Howarth, Sam Williams of Cornish Coast Adventures, Diana Evans and Caroline Andrews, Sophie Howarth, Fiona Gerrans and Angus, Amy and Sabrina Lee, Naomi and Suna Nightingale, Joanna Johnston, John Start. (South and East) Lucy and Jon Rouse, Tom Currie and Tor Udall, Charlotte Macpherson and Pete, Rae and Flora Durgerian, Redge, Sophie and Anna Hurpy, Natalie Start, Ralph, Caroline and Mishka Taylor, Alison de Braux, Maria Glauser and Seth Reynolds, Mit Fitzgerald and family, Ben Fletcher and family, Marcus Freeman, Jessica Lack & Zac, Sarah and David Boyle, Jessica Williams, Cosmo and Toby, Charlotte and Philip Hampson and family, Donna Fry and family, Sara Reeves and family, Harry Cory Wright and family, Joshua, Romeo Phillips and Stiffkey friends, Joanna Adams and family, Kate Grange, Ed Gillespie, Chris Knight, Rachel and Piers Mahon, Sarah McGeehan. (Wales) John and Caroline Walmsley, Mungo and Ishbel Amyatt-Leir, Fiona Smith, Leanda Thomas, Rosie Jones and Toby, Janine Bonnet, Martin Turtle, Tom Bullough. (North and Scotland) Jack Thurston, Roma Backhouse, girls at Boggle Hole, Tom Walmsley, Nell Boase, Sue and Gavin King-Smith, Kat Jones, Jake and Isabel Willis, Katy Marks, Tom Alcott, Tom Crompton. With final thanks to all the local wild-swimmers and secret cove-hunters we met who shared their knowledge so generously. Please explore sensitively and respect the local countryside.